THE LETTERS OF MARGARET FULLER

Margaret Fuller. Engraving by Henry Bryan Hall, Jr. Courtesy of the National Portrait Gallery, Smithsonian Institution, Washington, D.C.

THE LETTERS OF
Margaret Fuller

Edited by

ROBERT N. HUDSPETH

VOLUME II · 1839–41

Cornell University Press

ITHACA AND LONDON

PUBLICATION OF THIS BOOK WAS ASSISTED BY A GRANT
FROM THE PUBLICATIONS PROGRAM OF THE NATIONAL ENDOWMENT
FOR THE HUMANITIES, AN INDEPENDENT FEDERAL AGENCY.

First published 1983 by Cornell University Press.
Published in the United Kingdom by Cornell University Press Ltd.,
Ely House, 37 Dover Street, London W1X 4HQ.

International Standard Book Number 0-8014-1575-6
Library of Congress Catalog Card Number 82-22098

Printed in the United States of America

Librarians: Library of Congress cataloging information appears on the last page of the book.

The paper in this book is acid-free, and meets the guidelines for permanence and durability of the Committee on Production Guidelines for Book Longevity of the Council on Library Resources.

PREFACE

This second volume of Margaret Fuller's letters covers the thirty-six months during which she became prominent as a writer, conversationalist, and editor. After leaving Providence, where she had taught school for eighteen months, Fuller spent the spring of 1839 translating Johann Peter Eckermann's *Gespräche mit Goethe*. In May, George Ripley published her work as Volume 4 of his *Specimens of Foreign Standard Literature*. In early summer 1839 she wrote a long essay on contemporary French literature, which she circulated among her friends but never published. When she returned to Boston in August from a vacation in Bristol, Rhode Island, Fuller was satisfied that she had written well on topics that interested her.

Early in the autumn of 1839 two events gave her an even wider audience. First, she began a series of "conversations" for women. These thirteen weekly meetings at Elizabeth Peabody's bookshop in Boston drew twenty-five of the most prominent women in the area. Fuller opened each two-hour meeting with a general statement on mythology, and then drew the others into the discussion. These highly successful conversations became a custom, repeated each fall and spring from 1839 to 1844.

At the same time, the Transcendental Club, a group of liberal clergymen and writers who had formed at Frederic Henry Hedge's invitation to discuss theology, literature, and philosophy, decided to start a new magazine. Fuller agreed to edit the journal, Emerson was to be the associate editor, and George Ripley became the business manager. By November 1839 they had firm plans to publish in April 1840, but delays postponed the first issue of the *Dial* till July. In less than a year, Fuller left schoolteaching for good, became a public figure, and assumed the responsibility for editing a literary journal that competed with the *North American Review* and the *Christian Examiner*. After her apprenticeship, Fuller had the forum she wanted, where she could say what she wanted about literature and art.

While Fuller created this public life, she was thrust into the most emotionally tumultuous time of her private life. In the course of little more than a year, from September 1839 to October 1840, she was rejected by Samuel G. Ward; she had a deeply moving religious experience; she was rebuffed again, this time by Emerson; and she watched Ward marry Anna Barker, a close friend. Fuller had met Ward, the son of a Boston banker, in the mid-1830s. They had planned to go to Europe together as the companions of John and Eliza Farrar. Just then, however, Fuller's father died, and she could not go. From 1836 to 1839 the friendship between Fuller and Ward deepened into love. They shared several interests—poetry, painting, and German literature—and Fuller encouraged him to develop his talent as an artist. Then, in the summer of 1839, Ward broke off the romance, decided to become a banker in his father's office, and fell in love with Barker, a rich, beautiful New Orleans woman. In late autumn, Ward and Barker announced their plan to marry in 1840.

As her letters show, Fuller was badly hurt by Ward's rejection. Partly as a result, she turned to Emerson, challenging him to become a better friend. From August to October 1840 she demanded with increasing fervor that he be less aloof and more warmly responsive to her. For several weeks Emerson defended himself and analyzed the nature of friendship. But after she delivered an emotional ultimatum, he cut the discussion short. "There is a difference in our constitution," he wrote. "We use a different rhetoric. It seems as if we had been born & bred in different nations. You say you understand me wholly. You cannot communicate yourself to me. I hear the words sometimes but remain a stranger to your state of mind." Wearily he refused to write more: "Perhaps all my words are wrong. Do not expect it of me again for a very long time."[1]

Only a month before, Fuller had had a deeply moving religious experience that Emerson described as "a sort of ecstatic solitude."[2] She thought herself quite changed and tried to describe her altered state at her first meeting of the conversation group.

All of these emotions came to a focus on 3 October 1840, when, on

1. Ralph Waldo Emerson, *The Letters of Ralph Waldo Emerson*, ed. Ralph L. Rusk, 6 vols. (New York: Columbia University Press, 1939), 2:353.

2. *Memoirs of Margaret Fuller Ossoli*, ed. R. W. Emerson, W. H. Channing, and J. F. Clarke (Boston: Phillips, Sampson, 1852), 1:308.

Ward's birthday, he and Anna Barker married. Fuller bore the time with outward calm but kept coming back to the event. The next year she wrote in her journal: "Only a year today since the event that I felt so sure was an era on the earth of the same kind as the union of the Red Cross Knight & his spotless maid. All has vanished." As late as 1844 she considered 3 October the "anniversary of the most moving event in my life, when the Ideal seemed nearest an earthly realization. alas!"[3]

Contrasted to this time of unrelieved tension, 1841 seems at first to have been uneventful. But this was the time when Fuller was most involved with her work as the *Dial*'s editor. Some of her best writing dates from this period: she wrote on Beethoven, Goethe, and modern poetry; she reviewed exhibitions in Boston and a stream of new books. The one dark cloud toward the end of the year was the engagement, then the marriage of her sister Ellen and Ellery Channing, Sam Ward's close friend. Though Channing was a handsome and amusing member of a prominent Boston family, he was an improvident young poet, and Fuller knew the future would treat the young couple harshly.

Throughout this time Fuller's letters give us a consistent record of the emotional ebb and flow of her loves and of the growth of her intellectual accomplishments. In them we come to know what was important to her and why she valued the world of ideas as she did.

ROBERT N. HUSDPETH

State College, Pennsylvania

3. Ralph Waldo Emerson, *The Journals and Miscellaneous Notebooks of Ralph Waldo Emerson*, vol. 11, *1848–1851*, ed. A. W. Plumstead, W. H. Gilman, and Ruth H. Bennett (Cambridge: Belknap Press of Harvard University Press, 1975), p. 460.

Contents

Preface   5

Acknowledgments   17

Editorial Method   21
     Format, 22; Text, 22; Annotation and Index, 22

Editorial Apparatus   25
     Editorial Devices, 25; Descriptive Symbols, 25; Location
     Symbols, 26; Short Titles and Abbreviations, 26

1839

196. ca. 1839?, to William H. Channing   31

197. 7 January, to Ralph Waldo Emerson   32

198. 8 January, to James F. Clarke   33

199. 10 January, to Caroline Sturgis   34

200. 23 January, to Caroline Sturgis   36

201. 24 January, to Arthur B. Fuller   38

202. 27 January, to Caroline Sturgis   39

203. 2 February, to Caroline Sturgis   45

204. 7 February, to Caroline Sturgis   46

205. 21? February, to Caroline Sturgis   49

206. 21 February, to George Ripley   51

207. 4 March, to Ralph Waldo Emerson   53

208. 4 March, to Charles K. Newcomb   55

209. 4 March, to Caroline Sturgis   57

210. 10 March, to Arthur B. Fuller   61

211. 31 March, to Eugene Fuller   62
212. 18 April, to Charles K. Newcomb   64
213. 13 May, to ?   66
214. 15 May, to Elizabeth Hoar   66
215. 29 May, to Hiram Fuller   67
216. 29 May, to Charles K. Newcomb   67
217. 3 June, to Ralph Waldo Emerson   68
218. 8 June, to Eugene Fuller   70
219. 10 June, to Sarah Helen Whitman   74
220. ca. 21? June, to Jane F. Tuckerman   76
221. 25 June, to Caroline Sturgis   79
222. 28? June, to Caroline Sturgis   79
223. July, to Caroline Sturgis?   80
224. July, to Samuel G. Ward   80
225. 11 July, to Caroline Sturgis   81
226. August, to Jane F. Tuckerman   82
227. 17 August, to Elizabeth Hoar   83
228. 27 August, to Sophia Ripley?   86
229. September, to Samuel G. Ward   90
230. 24 September, to Elizabeth P. Peabody   91
231. 7 October, to Caroline Sturgis   92
232. 10 October, to A. Bronson Alcott   94
233. 15 October, to Samuel G. Ward   95
234. ca. Autumn?, to ?   97
235. November, to Ralph Waldo Emerson   97
236. November, to Ralph Waldo Emerson   97
237. 24 November, to Ralph Waldo Emerson   98
238. 25 November, to Charles K. Newcomb   100
239. 25 November, to ?   101
240. 24 December, to Caroline Sturgis   102
241. 26 December, to Ralph Waldo Emerson   104

1840

242. 1840?, to Caroline Sturgis   105
243. 1840?, to Caroline Sturgis   106
244. 1840, to William H. Channing   108
245. 1840, to Ralph Waldo Emerson   110
246. 1 January, to William H. Channing   111
247. 1 January, to Frederic H. Hedge   113
248. 14 January, to Richard F. Fuller   115

Contents

249. 20 January, to Ralph Waldo Emerson   115
250. 21 January, to Sarah Helen Whitman   118
251. 10 February, to Caroline Sturgis   120
252. 23 February, to Ralph Waldo Emerson   121
253. 24 February, to Charles K. Newcomb   122
254. ca. March, to Caroline Sturgis   124
255. 10 March, to Frederic H. Hedge   124
256. 22 March, to William H. Channing   125
257. April, to Ralph Waldo Emerson   127
258. 12 April, to Ralph Waldo Emerson   128
259. 19 April, to William H. Channing   130
260. 25 April, to Ralph Waldo Emerson   132
261. 31 May, to Ralph Waldo Emerson   134
262. June, to A. Bronson Alcott   143
263. 3 June, to Richard F. Fuller   143
264. ca. July, to James F. Clarke   144
265. July, to Almira P. Barlow?   145
266. 5 July, to Ralph Waldo Emerson   145
267. 12 July, to Caroline Sturgis   149
268. 19 July, to Ralph Waldo Emerson   151
269. 24 July, to Caroline Sturgis   153
270. 28 July, to John Neal   155
271. 16 August, to Caroline Sturgis   157
272. 8 September, to Caroline Sturgis   157
273. 26 September, to Caroline Sturgis   158
274. 29 September, to Ralph Waldo Emerson   159
275. 2 October, to Albert G. Greene   161
276. 10 October, to William H. Channing?   162
277. 18 October, to Caroline Sturgis   163
278. 19 October, to William H. Channing?   164
279. 22 October, to Caroline Sturgis   166
280. ca. 25 October, to Caroline Sturgis   169
281. 25 and 28 October, to William H. Channing   170
282. ca. 31 October, to William H. Channing?   178
283. November, to Ralph Waldo Emerson   181
284. 7 November, to Ralph Waldo Emerson   181
285. 8 November, to William H. Channing   183
286. 1 December, to Henry D. Thoreau   185
287. 3 December, to William H. Channing?   187
288. ca. 4 December, to Ralph Waldo Emerson   187
289. 6 December, to Ralph Waldo Emerson   188
290. 8? December, to William H. Channing   190

Contents

291. 10 December, to William H. Channing   191
292. 13 December, to William H. Channing   192
293. 20 December, to Arthur B. Fuller   195
294. 26 December, to Maria Weston Chapman   197

1841

295. 24 January, to Caroline Sturgis   198
296. 2 February, to William H. Channing   201
297. 19 February, to William H. Channing   202
298. 20 February, to Elizabeth Hoar   203
299. 21 February, to William H. Channing   204
300. 25 February?, to Charles K. Newcomb   204
301. 29 March, to William H. Channing?   205
302. 5 April, to William H. Channing   205
303. 6 April, to Richard F. Fuller   206
304. ca. 25 April, to Ralph Waldo Emerson   208
305. 10 May, to Ralph Waldo Emerson   209
306. 25 May, to Richard F. Fuller   209
307. June?, to Caroline Sturgis   211
308. June, to Charles K. Newcomb   212
309. 21 June, to Ralph Waldo Emerson   212
310. July?, to William H. Channing   213
311. 18 July, to Charles K. Newcomb   216
312. 20 July, to Margarett C. Fuller   216
313. 22 July, to Caroline Sturgis   218
314. 29 July, to Margarett C. Fuller   219
315. 31 July, to William H. Channing   220
316. 5 August, to Margarett C. Fuller   221
317. 6 August, to William H. Channing   223
318. 22 August, to Margarett C. Fuller   225
319. 29 August, to William H. Channing   227
320. 31 August, to Margarett C. Fuller   228
321. 8 September, to Ralph Waldo Emerson   230
322. 16 September, to Ralph Waldo Emerson   231
323. October, to Ralph Waldo Emerson   233
324. October, to Ralph Waldo Emerson   234
325. 2 October, to Charles K. Newcomb   237
326. 3 October, to Ellery Channing   239
327. 5 October, to Margarett C. Fuller   240
328. 10 October, to Caroline Sturgis   241

Contents

329. 18 October, to Henry D. Thoreau   242
330. ca. 20? October, to Elizabeth Hoar   246
331. 25 October, to Richard F. Fuller   247
332. November, to Ralph Waldo Emerson   248
333. 5 November, to Richard F. Fuller   249
334. 9? November, to Ralph Waldo Emerson   250
335. 9 November, to Ralph Waldo Emerson   250
336. 17 November, to Richard F. Fuller   251
337. 25 November, to Samuel. G. Ward   253
338. 1 December, to Richard F. Fuller   253
339. 2 December, to Richard F. Fuller   255
340. 6 December, to Samuel G. Ward   256
341. 13 December, to Margarett C. Fuller   257
342. 17? December, to Margarett C. Fuller   259
343. 24 December, to Margarett C. Fuller   261
344. 30? December, to Richard F. Fuller   263

Index   265

ILLUSTRATIONS

MARGARET FULLER 2

SARAH HELEN WHITMAN 78

BOSTON FROM DORCHESTER HEIGHTS 85

WILLIAM HENRY CHANNING 112

RICHARD FREDERICK FULLER 117

FULLER'S LETTER TO WILLIAM H. CHANNING, 19 APRIL 1840 139

STATE STREET, BOSTON 156

ALBERT GORTON GREENE 177

HENRY D. THOREAU 186

MARIA WESTON CHAPMAN 200

ELLEN KILSHAW FULLER 244

ELLERY CHANNING 245

Acknowledgments

I am grateful to John C. Fuller, Willard P. Fuller, Elizabeth Channing Fuller, and Richard E. Fuller for permission to publish Margaret Fuller's letters. I also thank the following institutions and individuals for permission to publish the Fuller letters in their possession which appear in this volume: the Trustees of the Boston Public Library; the Brown University Library; the Trustees of the Ralph Waldo Emerson Memorial Association, the Harvard College Library, and the Houghton Library, Harvard University; the Massachusetts Historical Society; the Middlebury College Library; the Pierpont Morgan Library; the Rhode Island Historical Society; the Humanities Research Center, University of Texas; and the University of Virginia Library.

The following librarians have been generous with their time and attention: John Alden of the Boston Public Library; Edmund Berkeley, Jr., and Barbara C. Bettcher of the University of Virginia Library; W. H. Bond, director of the Houghton Library, Harvard University, and of the Ralph Waldo Emerson Memorial Association; Robert Buckeye of the Middlebury College Library; Herbert Cahoon of the Pierpont Morgan Library; Rodney Dennis of the Houghton Library, Harvard University; Ellen S. Dunlap of the Humanities Research Center, University of Texas; Christine D. Hathaway of the Brown University Library; Carolyn Jackeman of the Houghton Library, Harvard University; Clifton Jones of the Brown University Library; James Lawton of the Boston Public Library; David Martz of the Brown University Library; June Moll of the Humanities Research Center, University of Texas; Martha Ramsey of the Houghton Library, Harvard University; C. A. Ryskamp of the Pierpont Morgan Library; Marte Shaw of the Houghton Library, Harvard University; Nathaniel

Shipton of the Rhode Island Historical Society; and Louis L. Tucker of the Massachusetts Historical Society. The staff of the reading room at the library of the New England Historic Genealogical Society greatly assisted my use of that splendid collection.

Among the scholars who have helped me locate letters, solve textual puzzles, and identify mysterious references are Patricia Barber, Charles Blackburn, Paula Blanchard, Arthur W. Brown, Lynn Cadwallader, Larry Carlson, Joseph Jay Deiss, Russell E. Durning, Alfred R. Ferguson, Elizabeth Maxfield-Miller, Howard N. Meyer, Alice deV. Perry, Bruce A. Ronda, Fred Shapiro, Madeleine B. Stern, Carl F. Strauch, Eleanor M. Tilton, Barbara M. Ward, and Richard P. Wunder. Kathy Fuller of the Division of Research Programs at the National Endowment for the Humanities was generous with her help; Karen Szymanski alerted me to the existence of several Fuller letters; Stephen Riley of the Massachusetts Historical Society very kindly helped me gain access to several uncatalogued collections in that library. My departmental chairmen have been patient, full of support, and generous to me in my research: Robert B. Heilman and Robert D. Stevick of the University of Washington, and David Stewart, Arthur O. Lewis, Robert Worth Frank, Jr., and Wendell V. Harris of the Pennsylvania State University. I am particularly pleased to be able to acknowledge the assistance given me by my colleagues Andrew Hilen, Roger B. Stein, Robert Shulman, and most especially Richard E. Baldwin in Seattle, and Robert D. Hume, Robert Lougy, John Moore, James Rambeau, and Ernst Schürer of the Pennsylvania State University. Wilma R. Ebbitt has given her time and wisdom far beyond the call of friendship, and Charles Mann, Rare Books and Manuscripts Librarian of the Pennsylvania State University, has acquired Fuller material for this edition and given me very helpful advice. For years Joel Myerson of the University of South Carolina has generously shared his knowledge about Fuller; his work has been invaluable to me.

I have been fortunate to have many able research assistants: Iris Malveau helped me prepare the original calendar of Fuller letters; Carolyn Kephart read manuscripts and tracked down many literary references; Charles Hackenberry read manuscript letters to me to check the accuracy of the transcriptions; Larry Carlson worked long on the annotations; Anne Hostetler searched for the sources of obscure allusions; Robert D. Habich checked and rechecked my facts, read my prose with skill and patience, and lent a hand in times of pressure. Barbara Salazar, Senior Manuscript Editor of Cornell University Press, has made this a better edition by her meticulous attention to the manuscript and by her judicious suggestions for revisions. Once more, Kay Hudspeth took time from her own work to be an assistant, an adviser, and a support through long hours of work on this edition.

This volume of Fuller letters received the financial support of the University of Washington Graduate School Research Fund; the Pennsylvania State University College of Liberal Arts Research Fund, administered by Thomas Magner; and the Pennsylvania State University Institute for the Arts and Humanistic Studies, administered by Stanley Weintraub. I am grateful for this support. The preparation of this volume was made possible in part by grants from the Program for Editions of the National Endowment for the Humanities, an independent federal agency.

R. N. H.

EDITORIAL METHOD

This edition brings together for the first time all the known extant letters written by Margaret Fuller. The texts are presented in their entirety in chronological order. Only conservative emendations, as outlined below under "Text," have been incorporated in the text; all others are recorded in textual notes. The text has been prepared from holographs whenever possible. When a holograph is lacking, the text is based on a manuscript copy of the lost holograph. When two manuscript copies of the same letter survive in the absence of a holograph, the more nearly complete version has been chosen. If both are of the same length, I have chosen the copy prepared by the Fuller family, because a spot comparison of other family copies with their surviving holographs shows them to be more nearly accurate than copies by other hands, if not exact. Only those letters with no manuscript authority have been taken from printed sources. Those letters dated by year only appear at the head of the year; those dated only by month, at the head of the month; undated letters come at the end of the edition, arranged alphabetically by recipient when known.

To establish the text, I first gathered microfilm or Xerox copies of all the manuscript letters and then made typed copies of these photoreproductions. I also typed versions of all the letters that now exist only in printed versions. I then corrected the typescript twice: first an assistant read aloud to me all the photoreproductions and the printed versions of the letters; later, two other assistants (working with me at different times) accompanied me to the libraries that hold the original manuscripts and read those manuscripts aloud to me as I again corrected the typescript. The final text derives from the corrected typescript, and proof was read aloud at two stages.

Format

The letters are numbered chronologically and the recipients identified in uniform headings. All dates, locations, salutations, and signatures are regularized in the following manner: dates and locations are
set flush against the right margin, salutations flush against the left
margin; signatures are set in large and small capitals and indented
from the right margin at the bottom of the letter; when two or more
initials are used in a signature, they are regularized with a space
between each pair.

Text

The text is presented as faithfully as possible with conservative
emendations. Fuller's spelling, capitalization, and punctuation are retained, as are her occasional slips of the pen (e.g., *and and*). Her end
punctuation is often ambiguous, for her period resembles a comma.
In all instances this mark is preserved as a period. Punctuation is
supplied in brackets only when its absence leads to confusion. A paragraph is often indicated in the holographs only by a space at the
end of the preceding line. In all such instances the following paragraph is silently indented. Fuller used the dash as an all-purpose
mark of punctuation; her dashes are consistently retained. Abbrevia-
tions are not expanded save in those instances where ambiguities
might otherwise result. In such cases the additions are enclosed in
square brackets. Cancellations are omitted from the text, and super-
scriptions and interlined additions are lowered; all such emendations
are reported in the textual notes. Cross-hatching (Fuller occasionally
turned the sheet and wrote at a right angle across her letter) and all
symbols, notes, and marks added by later hands are emended and
unreported. The German ß is set as "ss"; "&" becomes "and." Unless
otherwise noted, the matter canceled by a later hand in the collection at the Boston Public Library has been recovered. All the letters
and fragments taken from Emerson's "Ossoli" journal (MH: bMS Am
1280 [111]) are in his hand.

Annotation and Index

The text of each letter is followed by a provenance note that indi-
cates the source of the text, any surviving manuscript copies, any
previous publishing history, the name and address of the recipient
as written by Fuller, the postmark, and the recipient's endorsement,

if any. A brief biography of the recipient follows the provenance note to the first surviving letter to him or her, unless the recipient has already been identified. Then come textual notes listing editorial emendations and variants among manuscript copies, Fuller's cancellations, and her interlined insertions. Fuller's words here are set in roman type; editorial interpolations are set in italics.

The numbered annotations that follow the textual notes identify all people mentioned in the letter except those well known to readers (for example, Dante, Shakespeare, Milton) and those previously identified, and all books, literary and historical allusions, and quotations that can be established. Brief biographies of well-known individuals who are not identified in the notes can be found in *Webster's Biographical Dictionary*.

Citations to the Massachusetts vital records office take two forms. Citations to nineteenth-century records refer only to volume and page numbers. Thus "MVR 331:102" cites page 102 of volume 331 of the death record. Beginning in this century, the reference has a preceding date. Thus "MVR 1906, 36:120" cites the death record for 1906, volume 36, page 120. Unless otherwise noted, all citations are to death records.

Publication data come from the *National Union Catalogue* of the Library of Congress or, when otherwise necessary, from the *British Museum General Catalogue of Printed Books*. Occasional notes explain ambiguities in the text, summarize events in Fuller's life, or refer the reader to other letters. The surviving letters written to Fuller have provided explanatory material for many of the annotations. Unidentified items are usually silently passed over.

An appendix in the final volume lists chronologically the letters Fuller is known to have written but which have not survived.

Each volume of the letters has a separate index. A comprehensive index appears in the final volume.

EDITORIAL APPARATUS

Editorial Devices

The following devices are used in the text:

[Square brackets] enclose editorial additions.
[I] [II] [III] indicate sections of a letter recovered from various sources.
[   ] marks matter missing from the text.
Superscript^n refers the reader to a textual note.
Superscript^1 refers the reader to an explanatory note.

The following devices are used in the textual notes:

⟨Angle brackets⟩ identify recovered cancellations.
⟨?⟩ identifies unrecovered cancellations.
↑ Opposed arrows ↓ indicate interlined insertions.
Italics indicate editorial comments.

Descriptive Symbols

AL   Autograph letter, unsigned
ALfr   Autograph letter fragment, unsigned
ALfrS   Autograph letter fragment, signed with name or initial(s)
ALS   Autograph letter, signed with name or initial(s)
AMsfr   Autograph manuscript fragment; may not be a letter for the reason stated
EL   Edited letter, as previously published; holograph now lost
ELfr   Edited letter fragment, as previously published; holograph now lost
L   Letter dictated by Fuller
MsC   Manuscript copy of a Fuller letter in a hand other than Fuller's; unless otherwise indicated, the holograph has not been recovered

MsCfr   Manuscript copy of a fragment of a Fuller letter in a hand other than Fuller's; unless otherwise indicated, the holograph has not been recovered

Location Symbols

DLC   Library of Congress
MB   Boston Public Library, Department of Rare Books and Manuscripts
MH   Harvard University, Houghton Library
MHi   Massachusetts Historical Society
NNPM   Pierpont Morgan Library, New York
OCHP   Cincinnati Historical Society
RHi   Rhode Island Historical Society
RPB   Brown University Library
TxU   University of Texas, Humanities Research Center
ViU   University of Virginia Library
VtMiM Middlebury College Library

Short Titles and Abbreviations

Baker's Biographical Dictionary: Theodore Baker, *Baker's Biographical Dictionary of Musicians,* rev. Nicolas Slonimsky, 6th ed. (New York: Schirmer Books, 1978).

Barker Genealogy: Elizabeth F. Barker, *Barker Genealogy* (New York: Frye, 1927).

Briggs, *Cabot Family*: L. Vernon Briggs, *History and Genealogy of the Cabot Family,* 2 vols. (Boston: C. E. Goodspeed, 1927).

Bullard, *Rotches*: John M. Bullard, *The Rotches* (New Bedford, Mass.: Privately published, 1947).

CC: *Columbian Centinel* (Boston).

Chevigny: Bell Gale Chevigny, *The Woman and the Myth: Margaret Fuller's Life and Writings* (Old Westbury, N.Y.: Feminist Press, 1976).

Cleveland and Cleaveland: Edmund J. Cleveland and Horace G. Cleveland, *The Genealogy of the Cleveland and Cleaveland Families,* 3 vols. (Hartford, Conn.: Case, Lockwood & Brainard, 1899).

Collected Poems of Thoreau: *Collected Poems of Henry Thoreau,* enl. ed., ed. Carl Bode (Baltimore: Johns Hopkins Press, 1964).

Complete Works of Emerson: *The Complete Works of Ralph Waldo Emerson,* Centenary ed., ed. Edward W. Emerson, 12 vols. (Boston: Houghton Mifflin, 1903–4).

CVR: *Vital Records of Cambridge, Massachusetts, to the Year 1850,* 2 vols. (Boston: Wright & Potter, 1914–15).

DAB: *Dictionary of American Biography,* ed. Allen Johnson and Dumas Malone, 20 vols. (New York: Scribner's, 1928–36).

Dana Family: Elizabeth Ellery Dana, *The Dana Family in America* (Cambridge, Mass.: Privately published, 1956).

Davis, *Ancient Landmarks*: William T. Davis, *Ancient Landmarks of Plymouth*, 2d ed. (Boston: Damrell & Upham, 1899).

Dwight, "History of Music": John Sullivan Dwight, "The History of Music in Boston," in *Memorial History of Boston*, ed. Justin Winsor, 4 vols. (Boston: Ticknor, 1881), 4:415–64.

Emerson–Carlyle Correspondence: *The Correspondence of Emerson and Carlyle*, ed. Joseph Slater (New York: Columbia University Press, 1964).

Emerson Lectures: *The Early Lectures of Ralph Waldo Emerson*, ed. Stephen E. Whicher, Robert E. Spiller, and Wallace E. Williams, 3 vols. (Cambridge: Belknap Press of Harvard University Press, 1961–72).

GVR: *Vital Records of Groton, Massachusetts, to the End of the Year 1849*, 2 vols. (Salem, Mass.: Essex Institute, 1926).

Hanscom, *Friendly Craft*: Elizabeth Derring Hanscom, *The Friendly Craft* (New York: Macmillan, 1908).

Heralds: Samuel A. Eliot, *Heralds of a Liberal Faith*, 3 vols. (Boston: American Unitarian Association, 1910).

Higginson, *MFO*: Thomas Wentworth Higginson, *Margaret Fuller Ossoli* (Boston: Houghton Mifflin, 1884).

Higginson, *Reverend Francis Higginson*: Thomas Wentworth Higginson, *Descendants of the Reverend Francis Higginson* ([Cambridge?, Mass.]: Privately published, 1910).

Hodgman, "Elias Parkman": Arthur W. Hodgman, "Elias Parkman of Dorchester and His Descendants," NEHGS.

Hudspeth, *Ellery Channing*: Robert N. Hudspeth, *Ellery Channing* (New York: Twayne, 1973).

Ipswich Emersons: Benjamin Kendall Emerson, *The Ipswich Emersons* (Boston: D. Clapp, 1900).

JMN: *The Journals and Miscellaneous Notebooks of Ralph Waldo Emerson*, ed. William H. Gilman et al. (Cambridge: Belknap Press of Harvard University Press, 1960–).

Kinkeldey, "Beginnings of Beethoven": Otto Kinkeldey, "Beginnings of Beethoven in America," *Musical Quarterly* 13 (1927):217–48.

Letters of JFC: *The Letters of James Freeman Clarke to Margaret Fuller*, ed. John Wesley Thomas (Hamburg: Cram, de Gruyter, 1957).

Lowells of America: Delmar R. Lowell, *The Historic Genealogy of the Lowells of America from 1639 to 1899* (Rutland, Vt.: Tuttle, 1899).

Memoirs: *Memoirs of Margaret Fuller Ossoli*, ed. R. W. Emerson, W. H. Channing, and J. F. Clarke, 2 vols. (Boston: Phillips, Sampson, 1852).

Memorial Biographies: *Memorial Biographies of the New England Historic Genealogical Society*, 9 vols. (Boston, 1880–1908).

Miller: *Margaret Fuller: American Romantic*, ed. Perry Miller (Garden City, N.Y.: Doubleday, 1963).

Mt. Auburn: Burial records, Mount Auburn Cemetery, Cambridge, Mass.

MVR: Massachusetts vital records, Boston.

Myerson, "Calendar": Joel Myerson, "A Calendar of Transcendental Club Meetings," *American Literature* 44 (May 1972):197–207.

Myerson, *New England Transcendentalists*: Joel Myerson, *The New England Transcendentalists and the "Dial"* (Rutherford, N.J.: Fairleigh Dickinson University Press, 1980).

NAW: *Notable American Women, 1607–1950*, ed. Edmund T. James, 3 vols. (Cambridge: Belknap Press of Harvard University Press, 1971).

NEHGR: *The New England Historical and Genealogical Register.*

NEHGS: The New England Historic Genealogical Society, Boston.

OCGL: Henry and Mary Garland, *The Oxford Companion to German Literature* (Oxford: Clarendon Press, 1976).

Peabody Genealogy: Selim H. Peabody, comp., *Peabody (Paybody, Pabody, Pabodie) Genealogy* (Boston: Charles H. Pope, 1909).

Plymouth Church Records: *Plymouth Church Records, 1620–1859*, 2 vols. (New York: New England Society, 1920).

Rusk, *Letters of RWE*: *The Letters of Ralph Waldo Emerson*, ed. Ralph L. Rusk, 6 vols. (New York: Columbia University Press, 1939).

Sanborn, *Thoreau*: F. B. Sanborn, *Henry D. Thoreau* (Boston: Houghton Mifflin, 1882).

Sturgis of Yarmouth: Roger Faxton Sturgis, ed., *Edward Sturgis of Yarmouth, Massachusetts* (Boston: Stanhope Press, 1914).

Swan, *Athenaeum Gallery*: Mabel M. Swan, *The Athenaeum Gallery, 1827–1873* (Boston: Boston Athenaeum, 1940).

Thayer, *Ripley*: James B. Thayer, *Rev. Samuel Ripley of Waltham* (Cambridge, Mass.: Privately published, 1897).

Thoreau Correspondence: *The Correspondence of Henry David Thoreau*, ed. Walter Harding and Carl Bode (New York: New York University Press, 1958).

Thoreau, *Week*: Henry D. Thoreau, *A Week on the Concord and Merrimac Rivers*, ed. Carl F. Hovde, William L. Howarth, and Elizabeth Hall Witherell (Princeton, N.J.: Princeton University Press, 1980).

VR: vital records.

Wade: *The Writings of Margaret Fuller*, ed. Mason Wade (New York: Viking Press, 1941).

Wilhelm Meister's Apprenticeship and Travels: Johann Wolfgang von Goethe, *Wilhelm Meister's Apprenticeship and Travels*, trans. Thomas Carlyle, in *Centenary Edition of the Works of Thomas Carlyle*, ed. H. D. Traill (London: Chapman & Hall, 1907), vols. 23 and 24.

WNC: Margaret Fuller, *Woman in the Nineteenth Century, and Kindred Papers*, ed. Arthur B. Fuller (Boston: John P. Jewett, 1855).

Works: Manuscript copybooks, Fuller family papers, Houghton Library, Harvard University.

THE LETTERS OF MARGARET FULLER

196. To William H. Channing

[ca. 1839?]

I wish I could hear you speak at the same time with Waldo, for it would be beautiful to me to see my two friends thus brought near to one another upon a common platform; but for this, I should have no wish to be at Concord now. For as the full soul loathes the honeycomb,[1] so is it with me as to popular excitements, even on great and vital subjects, when my longing is for the deep places of silent thought, where alone I am perfected. I felt content to see you go after our meeting the other day, while I remain without one of my kind to whom I can speak a free word. Sometimes such loneliness seems desolate, but I rejoice to feel that you are now upon your chosen path; and so farewell, and may the good Spirit guide you. Of your own future it seems I might yet have some clear word to say [   ] You know my confidence in your powers; daily you have my prayers for your success. Persevere, my dear brother, and be forever happy.

ELfr, from Octavius Brooks Frothingham, *Memoir of William Henry Channing* (Boston, 1886), p. 181.

William Henry Channing was the nephew of Dr. William Ellery Channing, the most influential American Unitarian of this time. The younger Channing became the minister of the Unitarian church in Cincinnati in 1838. He and Fuller were acquainted in the late 1820s, but their friendship grew increasingly strong after 1838.

Frothingham gives the approximate date.

1. Prov. 27:7. "The full soul loatheth an honeycomb; but to the hungry soul every bitter thing is sweet."

197. To Ralph Waldo Emerson

Groton 7th Jan 1839.

How could you omit your lecture?[1] I stayed in town only to hear it, and shall have no chance at another this winter. Could you not have taken some other time for your "slight indisposition." I fancied L. was worse and had passed from diet on ricewater to nothing at all. I sent a maiden to inquire at Mrs. A.'s and she returned all smiles to tell me that Mrs. E. was quite well, that Mr. E. had lost a night's rest!! but had since rode to Waltham, walked five miles, sawed wood, and by use of these mild remedies was now perfectly restored. Imagine my indignation: lost a night's rest! as if an intellectual person ever had a night's rest; one too of that sect who are supposed to be always

> "Lying broad awake and yet
> Remaining from the body, and apart
> In intellect, and power, and will, To hear
> Time flowing in the middle of the night
> And all things creeping to the day of doom."

—that such an one should adjourn a lecture on Genius because he has lost a night's sleep.

I would tell you of my visit in town, but that I have uttered the record in so circulating a medium, that I cannot but fancy it may have vibrated as far as Concord. Lest it should not, I will say that three things were specially noteworthy. First, a talk with Mr. Alcott, in which he appeared to me so great, that I am inclined to think he deserves your praise, and that he deceived neither you nor himself in saying that I had not yet seen him.[2] Beside his usual attitude and closeness to the ideal, he showed range, grasp, power of illustration, and precision of statement such as I never saw in him before. I will begin him again and read by faith awhile.

There was a book of studies from Salvator Rosa, from the Brimmer Donation, at the Athenaeum, which I looked over with great delight and got many thoughts of my journal.[3] There was at last an interview with Mr. Allston.[4] He is as beautiful as the towncriers have said, and deserves to be Mr. Dana's Olympus, Lares, and Penates, as he is. He got engaged upon his art, and flamed up into a galaxy of Platonism. Yet what he said was not as beautiful as his smile of genius in saying it. Unfortunately, I was so fascinated, that I forgot to make myself interesting, and shall not dare to go and see him.

MsCfr (MH: Os 735 Laa 1839.1.7); MsCfr (MB: Ms. Am. 1450 [67]). Published in part in Higginson, *MFO*, p. 95; Rusk, *Letters of RWE*, 2:178; and Chevigny, pp. 122–23.

1. Emerson began a series of lectures, "Human Life," in Boston on 5 December 1838. "Genius," the fifth lecture, had been scheduled for 2 January but was postponed until the ninth. In his letter to Fuller of 18 January, Emerson apologized: "I was quite sorry to deprive you of the hearing of so many definitions & flourishes." He went on to satirize himself: "Human Life in Ten Lectures or the Soul of man neatly done up in ten pin-boxes exactly ten" (*Emerson Lectures*, 3:1–171; Rusk, *Letters of RWE*, 2:178–79).

2. Bronson Alcott, a self-taught philosopher, had conducted an experimental school in Boston where Fuller had served as an assistant. In his journal for 1838, Alcott records the meeting with Fuller, who was on her way home to Groton from Hiram Fuller's Greene-Street School in Providence, where she had been teaching. Alcott admits his disappointment that the Greene-Street School was not living up to his high educational ideals (MH: 59m-308 [11], p. 500).

3. In 1838 George Watson Brimmer (d. 1838), who graduated from Harvard in 1803, donated more than one hundred books on art and architecture to the Boston Athenaeum (*Boston Daily Advertiser*, 18 September 1838). Among them was probably *Six Etchings from Salvator-Rosa* (London, 1788) by Sarah Green. Salvator Rosa (1615–73), known also as Salvatorelli, was an Italian poet-painter famous for his landscapes.

4. Washington Allston (1779–1843) was at this time America's best-known living painter. A native of South Carolina, he studied with Benjamin West in London. He later settled in New England. Allston married twice: his first wife was Ann Channing (1779–1815), Dr. Channing's sister; his second was Martha R. Dana (1784–1862), daughter of Francis and Elizabeth Ellery Dana (*DAB*; *CC*, 19 July 1809; James N. Arnold, ed., *Vital Record of Rhode Island, 1636–1850* [Providence, 1891], 8:442; Jared B. Flagg, *The Life and Letters of Washington Allston* [New York, 1892], p. 114; *Dana Family*, p. 488). Allston was a brother-in-law of Richard Henry Dana, Sr. (1787–1879), the Cambridge poet. The two men were close friends, so that Fuller's allusion to the Roman household spirits and gods defines what Allston meant to the poet (*DAB*).

198. To James F. Clarke

Groton, 8 January 1839

And I wish now, as far as I can, to give my reasons for what you consider absurd squeamishness in me. You may not acquiesce in my view, but I think you will respect it *as* mine and be willing to act upon it so far as I am concerned.

Genius seems to me excusable in taking the public for a confidant. Genius is universal, and can appeal to the common heart of man. But even here I would not have it too direct. I prefer to see the thought or feeling made universal. How different the confidence of Goethe, for instance, from that of Byron!

But for us lesser people, who write verses merely as vents for the overflowings of a personal experience, which in every life of any value craves occasionally the accompaniment of the lyre, it seems to me that all the value of this utterance is destroyed by a hasty or indiscriminate publicity. The moment I lay open my heart, and tell the fresh feeling to any one who chooses to hear, I feel profaned.

When it has passed into experience, when the flower has gone to seed, I don't care who knows it, or whither they wander. I am no longer it,—I stand on it. I do not know whether this is peculiar to me, or not, but I am sure the moment I cease to have any reserve or delicacy about a feeling, it is on the wane.

About putting beautiful verses in your Magazine, I have no feeling except what I should have about furnishing a room.[1] I should not put a dressing-case into a parlor, or a book-case into a dressing-room, because, however good things in their place, they were not in place there. And this, not in consideration of the public, but of my own sense of fitness and harmony.

ELfr, from *Memoirs*, 1:73–74. Published in part in Miller, pp. 47–48.

James Freeman Clarke, another New England friend who had moved west, was the minister of the Unitarian church in Louisville. He and Fuller exchanged lengthy letters in which they discussed German literature. Clarke helped to found and was an editor of the *Western Messenger*, a literary and religious magazine published in Cincinnati.

1. The *Western Messenger*. Fuller did contribute two poems to the magazine: "Thoughts on Sunday Morning" in the first volume (1836) and "Jesus the Comforter" in the fourth (1837).

199. To Caroline Sturgis

Groton 10th Jany 1839—

My dear Cary,

The mountain and the valley express it exactly— We do not soar up direct like the lark! but our advance is always in the undulating line. You are *down* now but think how long you were *up* at Naushon. You must expect a season of dimness and grey discontent.

As to the premonitions of action and passion, I know the Titanic era must come ere long, but, oh Cary, do nothing to hasten it. Ward it off as long as possible by occupation. Give yourself time to ripen and strengthen for that tremendous strife. They never entered Olympus, those Titans, rather chained to earth, they vented their smouldering rage in volcanoes, "at which Jove laughs"— Do thou build high and strong the ladder before thou dost try to climb—

The modelling seemed to me the very thing for you at this juncture. You can pursue that without hurting yourself, and it seems to suit the cast of your mind. Let books alone—you have other and better hieroglyphics before you.

Tell me about all the pictures you see; that bit of Poussin was admirable.—[1]

No doubt I was somewhat pained by your want of affection towards me while in Boston, but I did not dislike you, on the contrary I loved you as much as was consistent with the crowded, wearied state of my mind at that time. And, not being upborne by excitement, I had time to feel bodily pain and fatigue. But I could not seriously think there was any danger of your ceasing to love me. There is so much in me which you do not yet know and have faculties to apprehend that you will not be able I believe, to get free of me for some years.

I send you many of Jas Clarke's letters On reading them over they seemed to me among the most valuable I possessed. There are allusions to the 3 love affairs which formed him into manhood which I wish were not there.[2] But all that is dead and gone, the pain and passion have passed into Experience and I know he would entirely confide in my judgment as to the propriety of showing them. Perhaps some things may slightly disgust you in detail but I think when you have got through and look at it as a whole you will think it a fine picture of an intellectual friendship, and an interesting history of the growth of a practical character. I think many critiques on books and pictures will interest you. And it will let you see how a large class of men feel towards women, more clearly than you could in books. I have left in many notes which may seem trifling, because I wished you to see the two sides of the thing— I have kept out, however, many which I thought it best not to show and am not sure that a chain is left when so many links are taken away.

I send also letters of S. Clarke's[3] which I think will charm you by their dignity of tone and elegance of expression— They are slight affairs for S. has small need of utterance.

I also send two or three other letters which I think of an interesting character— There is not one of S. W's that I could lend they are so tinged with personalities—

Are not dear Jane's the finest Platonism—[4] One is but a fragment. She requested I would burn the original, and I did but kept the best part under feigned names.

I send those of Mr E's which you have not seen and which I think very beautiful— I send some of the best and worst of my scholars' letters— I suppose they will seem terribly crude and tame, but they will give you an insight of the common estate of the universal mind, which may not be useless— You may show these, if you wish, but I suppose scarce any one would be philosophic enough to take an interest in them—

You are at liberty to show Mr E's letters to Jane and Marianne,ⁿ requesting them not to mention them to any one, as I do not wish to have it told about that I show Mr E's letters—[5] From the others you may read to them and if you wish, to your sister Ellen alsoⁿ any critiques on lit[eratur]e art, or character carefully omitting everything personal.[6]

You can keep them a month or return [   ]

ALfr (MH: bMS Am 1221 [214]). Published in part in Chevigny, pp. 114–15.

Caroline Sturgis, daughter of a wealthy Boston merchant, was Fuller's closest friend.

Jane and Marianne] Jane and ⟨Mary Ann⟩ Marianne

to them and if you wish, to your sister Ellen also] ↑ to them and if you wish, to your sister Ellen also ↓

1. Either Nicolas Poussin or his brother-in-law, Gaspard Dughet (1613–75), known as Gaspard-Poussin.

2. Fuller refers here to Clarke's romances with Louisa Hickman, Elizabeth Randall, and an unidentified Eleanor.

3. Sarah Clarke, James Clarke's sister, was an artist who studied under Washington Allston. She and Fuller had a long, warm friendship.

4. S. W. is Samuel G. Ward, son of a wealthy Boston banker. Ward and Fuller met in the early 1830s, when he was a Harvard student. He had planned a career as an artist, but decided instead to become a banker. In 1839 Fuller was in love with Ward. Jane is Jane Tuckerman, daughter of Gustavus Tuckerman of Boston. At one time she was Fuller's private pupil.

5. Marianne Jackson was another young Boston woman who was Fuller's pupil and friend.

6. Ellen Sturgis, who married Dr. Robert Hooper of Boston, contributed poetry to the *Dial*.

200.   To Caroline Sturgis

Jany 23dⁿ 1839
[Groton]

I thought I should feel very much like writing to my dear Cary to day, but find I do not; the extreme cold seems to benumb all my faculties. This winter air is too bracing for me, I have had another attack of spasmodic headach and lost almost three days. Mother is now ill. I will write to you in a better hour.—

I will also keep your drawing books which have suggested some thoughts to me, that these may be fres[h] in my mind when I next send to Boston which will be about a fortnight hence. Perhaps you would give me the boy with the grey hound, and one other leaf which I fancy?

Meanwhile have you no letter to send me by Eugene when he comes up on Sunday?—[1]

I want to hear very much about Vautin, Poussin, and not only about the ins but the is s particularly C. S^n is[2]

Tell, too, about Mr E's Protest.[3] I was very sorry not to hear that

I enjoy my solitude and [s]ilence as much as I expected If only I were stronger,—but I cannot bear any thing like application. I have got a vol of Plato and other good books, but can read little. All the time I am well enough I spend on my translation.[4] Have read J. Dwight's notes (which are *excellent*;) and G. Simmons's article and one by T. Parker on Ackermann's Platonism of Christianity in the last Christian Examiner both of which I think would interest you.[5]

More thoughts next time— Adieu, my love—

M. F.

Send Ellen's pocket hdf by Eugene. I think it must be tired of so much quiet, and want to be "faithful to some tears"— Mother wants to know how Mrs Goodwin is.[6]

ALS (MH: bMS Am 1221 [215]). *Addressed:* Miss Caroline Sturgis / ⟨50⟩ 52 Summer St. *Endorsed:* Jany 23d 1839.

Jany 23] Jany 2⟨2⟩3
particularly C. S] particularly ⟨S⟩ C. S

1. Eugene Fuller, oldest of Margaret Fuller's brothers, graduated from Harvard in 1834 and became a lawyer. He later was a businessman in New Orleans.

2. Mr. N. Vautin, an eccentric Englishman, taught watercolor and drawing in Boston. Reputed to be "truly cultivated," Vautin was also morbidly sensitive about the deficiencies of American manners, having once been driven into a rage by neighbors who were rehearsing a brass band on the other side of a thin wall (Samuel L. Gerry, "The Old Masters of Boston Schools," *New England Magazine,* 2d ser. 3 [February 1891]:687).

3. Emerson's "Protest" was the sixth lecture in the "Human Life" series.

4. Fuller was translating Johann Peter Eckermann's *Gespräche mit Goethe* for George Ripley's series, *Specimens of Foreign Standard Literature.* The volume was published in the spring as *Conversations with Goethe.*

5. John Sullivan Dwight reviewed Schiller's *William Tell,* translated by C. T. Brooks, in the *Christian Examiner* 25 (January 1839):385–91. George Simmons reviewed Hannah Lee's *Historical Sketches of the Old Painters* and the *Catalogue of the Twelfth Exhibition of Paintings at the Athenaeum Gallery* in the same issue, pp. 304–20. Theodore Parker's piece, pp. 367–84, was a review-essay of Georg Christian Benedict Ackermann's *Christliche im Plato und in der Platonischen Philosophie entwickelt und hervorgehoben* (Hamburg, 1835). George Frederick Simmons (1814–55), son of the Honorable William Simmons of Boston, graduated from Harvard in 1832 and from the Divinity School in 1838. He became minister at Mobile, Alabama, and preached strong antislavery sermons there.

In 1845 he married the Reverend Samuel Ripley's daughter Mary (1820–1907) (Harvard archives; *Heralds*, 2:173–74; MVR 1907 26:290; Thayer, *Ripley*, p. 32).

6. Ellen is Ellen Sturgis, Caroline Sturgis' sister; Mrs. Goodwin is their aunt Ellen Watson Davis Goodwin (1787–1856), daughter of John and Ellen Watson Davis of Plymouth and wife of the Reverend Ezra Shaw Goodwin (1787–1833) of Sandwich, whom she married in 1814 (Davis, *Ancient Landmarks*, p. 120; *CC*, 9 February 1833; *Plymouth Church Records*, p. 694; Dr. Channing's record book, Arlington Street Church, Boston).

201.   To Arthur B. Fuller

Groton 24th Jany 1839.

My dear Arthur,

I was much pleased with your letter. If you *act* upon such feelings, you cannot fail to become an honored man and worthy friend.

I write at your request, though I am but a poor scribe about such things as you wish most to know. The bargain for the sale of this place is not yet concluded. Eugene is going to Boston about it tomorrow, and, if he should be detained over Sunday, you will probably see him and he will tell you all you wish to know. Richard will write you the particulars of Mr Kelly's tragical fate.[1] He killed himself, too selfish to stay and sustain his wife and children through anticipated want, which they need not have met if he would but have kept sober. Mother caught a bald cold at the time, as she made every exertion during the aftn and night to restore him to a life, of which he was unworthy.

I enjoy being at home as much as I expected, except that I am by no means well. Mother and Eugene are, as usual, all kindness to me, and Richard, who is surely one of the best boys the sun ever shone upon, does every thing for my comfort Richard improves in his studies; he works very hard at "larning" and has a strong, manly way of thinking. He and Lloyd get along very well with Lily, but do not seem to become fond of her.[2] I see them but little except when they are reciting to me, as I pass great part of my time in my own room. Ellen is Miss F. down stairs now![3] High life below stairs— She plays her part very well!

I wish you to send me by next oppory the catalogue of the Leicester school if you have it with you, if not, say where it is to be found at home I want to look at it on R's account— Write a long letter and tell what you learn of men and books to your affectionate sister

S. M. F.

I suppose you have heard of John Moore's illness. Mr Butler is dismissed from the P. office. Mr Henry Woods has got it.[4]

ALS (MH: fMS Am 1086 [9:55]); MsCfr (MH: fMS Am 1086 [Works, 1:637–39]). *Addressed:* Arthur B. Fuller / Waltham / Mass.

Her brother Arthur Buckminster Fuller was studying with Samuel and Sarah Bradford Ripley in Waltham, Massachusetts, in preparation for Harvard. After teaching school in Illinois, Arthur became a minister. He volunteered as a private in the Civil War and died at Fredericksburg.

1. Richard Frederick Fuller, then fifteen years old, was Margaret's favorite brother. Like Eugene and Arthur, he graduated from Harvard. Noah Kelly, a laborer, died on 18 January 1839 in Groton (*GVR*).

2. Lloyd Fuller, who was emotionally disturbed, was the youngest of the Fuller children. Lily is probably a servant.

3. Ellen Kilshaw Fuller was Margaret's only surviving sister. She married Ellery Channing, a poet and a nephew of Dr. William Ellery Channing.

4. Who Fuller means by John Moore is not clear, but possibly she refers to John Moors (1819–95), son of Benjamin and Abigail Moors of Groton, who later became a minister (*GVR*; Harvard archives; *Boston Evening Transcript*, 28 January 1895). Caleb Butler, a Groton lawyer, had been appointed postmaster on 1 July 1826; Henry Woods replaced him on 15 January 1839, but Butler returned to the post in 1841 and served until 1846. A man of many interests, Butler taught school for a number of years, was a surveyor, a lawyer, an amateur astronomer, and a businessman (Samuel Abbott Green, *An Historical Sketch of Groton, Massachusetts* [Groton, 1894], pp. 173, 177; Frances Brooks, "Caleb Butler," *Memorial Biographies*, 2:266–79). Henry Woods (1802–41), son of Sampson and Alice Woods of Groton, was a merchant (*GVR*).

202. To Caroline Sturgis

Groton Sunday evening
Jany 27th 1839—

My dear Cary,

I have now three good letters from you and think I will write you one. I pay you a compliment in so doing for I have just been reading Plato's Phaedrus, and last night I banqueted with him,—so I think I must be tuned up to concert pitch.[1]

To prefer at such a time your accompaniment to the flageolet, the bugle, the harp any of which are at my command; to say nothing of my kettle drums, fifes and absurd acchordion is complimentary. Pray apply the tuning key to yourself at once.

I have many feelings in reading Plato, perhaps not orthodox. So many words often weary me. I am often so impertinent as to think I know it all, and it is not Greek enough to keep me so long on my way, when suddenly some sublime thought abashes and reproves me.

Plato's thoughts have, indeed, so passed into our intellectual life that I feel as if only returning to my native mountain air while with these philosophers and cannot be quite enough of a disciple. It is true it is like the banquets of the Gods after our common life, but I never, never, never have lived in the actual and find here my own aspirations in golden letters.

I am delighted as ever in any thing really Greek with the exquisite decorum of every word. Socrates does not soar, he does not look up, he sees all around him, the light wells out from him, every object round assumes its proper hue. He is a man, not an angel For my part I should be ashamed to be an angel before I have been truly man. But these Greeks no more merged the human in the divine, than the divine in the human, the wise charioteer managed both his steeds; he needed not to unyoke either but chose rather to remember their several natures The mere Idealist vexes me more than the mere Realist, because he seems to me never to have lived. He might as well[n] have been a butterfly; he does not know the human element.

I love the stern Titanic part, I love the crag, even the Drachenfels of life—[2] I love its roaring sea that dashes against the crag— I love its sounding cataract, its lava rush, its whirlwind, its rivers generating the lotus and the crocodile, its hot sands with their white bones, patient camels, and majestic columns toppling to the sky in all the might of-dust. I love its dens and silvery gleaming caverns, its gnomes, its serpents, and the tigers sudden spring. Nay! I would not be without what I know better, its ghostly northern firs, haggard with ice, its solitary tarns, tearful eyes of the lone forest, its trembling lizards and its wounded snakes dragging to se[c]retest recesses their slow length along.

Who can know these and, other myriad other children of Chaos and old night, who[n] can know the awe the horror and the majesty of earth, yet be content with the blue sky alone. Not I for one. I love the love lit dome above I cannot live without mine own particular star; but my foot is on the earth and I wish to walk over it until my wings be grown. I will use my microscope as well as my telescope. and oh ye flowers, ye fruits, and, nearer kindred yet, stones with your veins so worn by fire and water, and here and there disclosing streaks of golden ore, let us know one another before we part. Tell me your secret, tell me mine. To be human is also something?

But to quit a rhapsody which would by the always wise majority be technically denominated "stuff". Surely it is not beyond us, this idealizing common life. Head heart, eye, hand be steady, and it shall be done. The way is not, however, to live in a trance; nor yet in a whirl.

For my part I shall never be happy, unless I could live like Pericles and Aspasia.[3] I want the long arcade, the storied street, the lyre and garland. I want the Attic honey on the lip, the Greek fire in the eye. This cannot be, and we cannot be happy, but we need not, we will not be vulgar— We will live better than we do now. We will be as good as the feudal ages.

And that we may do so— Caroline—do not write to me about Wm S. and Maria W.—[4] I think they are both base persons with all their elements of beauty. This may not be Delphic but it has struck me so from the very first.— Now you have got out of your sublime fit, and want to try experiments dont, Dear, walk in the mud. You have always been right till now, always liked right things, and right people. Even where you were selfish, obstinate, or angular, no wise person would take a hammer, to strike[n] off a splinter from such a marble, secure that the waters would take the trouble to wear it into proportion.— But now—these two people are mere studies, mere objects of taste and you let them get near you— I am repelled by your party with M. White. Marianne always seems to me noble, almost beautiful, by her side you looked yourself. But it is beneath you to amuse yourself with active satire, with what is vulgarly called quizzing. It is beneath you to laugh at such people as you did. When such a person as Mr Morrison is *thrown in your way* and chooses to rub himself against you, I sympathize entirely with your keen perception of his ridiculous points but[n] to laugh a whole evening at vulgar nondescripts is that an employment for C. who I thought had the heroic element in her.[5] Who was born passionately to love, to admire, and sustain Truth.— This would be much more excusable in a chameleon like me, yet (whatever may be the vulgar view of *my* character) I can truly say I know not the hour in which I ever *looked for the ridiculous*. It has always been forced upon me and is the accident of my existence. I would not *want* the sense of it when it comes for that would show an obtuseness of mental organization, but on peril of my soul I would not move an eyelash to look for it.

Then for W. S. I do not view him with illiberal eyes. I too[n] can see why he did as he did. Few male natures can long endure a nature as pure, as open, as trusting, above all, as *overflowing* as J's.[6] They want folds to penetrate, dragons to slay, pepper to the cream tart. But he O, profane wretch, not only cast aside "that most precious possession a heart capable of love and passion," but did it with smiles and lies.— Of course I would not have you Miss Prim it, or look severe in youthful beauty on the curl-paper Dark Eyed One. But he must know that you know the past, know that he like the base[n] Ethiop threw a pearl away Richer than *all* his tribe[7] and will you let him think more such can be got without *diving*, even where his past prodigality is known. No! let him live on *husks* at least till he says I have sinned against heaven and against Thee &c—

You know how unfit I consider it either for you or me that I should advise you. But these passages in your life and letters displease me— As a friend I tell it you—am I right?—

And since I have taken you for the topic of my letter I will speak farther as to your drawings— You say Mr Vautin finds fault with your want of shading &c but I suppose this refers only to the execution. I should make the same criticism in a deeper sense. In all these drawings I see a nobleness but also a poverty. Trees and lakes say We are sacred, we are lonely, here you can be at home. Lovely eyes look out for love, untouched bosoms swell above a virgin zone. Earnest male heads seem worthy of the infinite, the boys' eyes are deep, dark, pregnant with a noble purpose. But every where character is in propre, we perceive only what may be. All the minute traits, the fleshly undulations, the myriad touches, work of Time's gentle ripples are wanting—Your ugliness is all carricature; i[   ] you are not comic in your satire, you are only[n] burlesque. Your characters sink as soon as they go out into life, your Thalaba cannot *act* with the fine scorn and eager flush of the warrior; if your noble boy were to grow up and leave the forest for the tented field he would not be worthy of his greyhound. Why is this, C. Is it that your powers of execution fall so short of your thought, or that you do not study human nature with the loving eye of a Scott, a Shakspeare, a Cervantes, a Moliere, a Goethe, a Raphael, a Mozart, yet perhaps these two last needed little study; they loved so fervently they must have seen a great deal in each moment. Little Mozart would say almost every moment— Do you love me and if any one said No the tears would roll down his cheeks. Raphael was not contented with the glowing sky and swelling grapes of Italy, but took the Fornarina for his mistress u s. w.[8]

In Salvator I saw this sublime poverty in its finest state.[9] But you have not his sinewy arm C[   ] What you say of your reasons for going to the assembly is really fine. This is the only good thing I ever heard from you on the subject of society and leads me to hope you are coming to a just view of your own position. Many fine remarks occurred to me on that subject apropos to Salvator but I think I will suppress them for the present.

I want very much to come to town for a week or fortnight in the spring to look at the Atheneum engravings at my leisure. Do you be strong so as to pass whole mornings with me, if I can. I feel so beautiful just now in my soul. I hope I shall not be plagued out of it—

I am displeased that you are disappointed in S. Clarke's letters. There is not so very much of [   ] And are not in the letters elegance, self-possession, accurate perceptions, a love of beauty delicate even to coldness, and a subdued harmony over the whole like a soft grey brooding afternoon in "green and bowery summer"

J. had three loves 1st Louisa. A girl with creamy skin, bright, not loving blue eye and long curling locks of gold. She had some talent and a good deal of natural melody of character. She was one of those who act a part[n] all the time in real life, not for the sake of being seen by others but to gratify natural dramatic propensities. James was the hero of one of her little melodramas. There was no real love in it, but it was pretty, and did pen a picture on the wall of life's vestibule This was the love of fancy!

Next came Eleanor. This was one of what Mr Emerson calls "urns of expression." She had one of the untouched bosoms like those in your book. She had (what you [   ] secret eye, the mantling cheek, the timid consciousness of possible womanhood. Her long chestnut locks fell around her like a veil, and she seemed happy to walk in a veil, so that young men were naturally tempted to try to make her come out. No one can predict what will be the fate of these Undine's when they get their souls by wedlock.[10] They may become heroines, syrens, or angels, or as likely domestic cats or spaniels. Eleanor became the latter. This too was not love, but only fancy, now tinged with passion.[n] Both these maidens loved J. as much as he loved them. He got as good as he gave. Then came Elizabeth, a premature woman, a morbid, sickly but fascinating child. Half passion half devotion, by turns sinner and saint. She was worthy to be loved. J. loved her at first little[n] more than the previous eidolon but, as she did not return it, it became a deep passion and gave the needed crisis to his character.

I enclose two pieces, though I am not sure but I have read them to you without telling the circumstances. One is addressed to her, the other to me after the close of the first act in the tragedy of life. To me they have always been deeply affecting. You can keep but not show them unless to Jane.

I will send Tasso, please be very careful of it, as I have no other copy.[11]

Adieu—live worthy of thee and me— Love to "my *own dear* child"
to Jane. Will she not write? Tenderly hers and yours

M. F.

After all I forgot to write about Individuals— Another time I will.

ALS (MH: bMS Am 1221 [216]). *Endorsed:* January 27th 1839.
He might as well] He might ⟨has⟩ ⟨w⟩ as well
and old night, who] and old night, ⟨and be⟩ who
a hammer, to strike] a hammer, ↑ to ↓ strike
ridiculous points but] ridiculous points ⟨w⟩ but
I too] I ↑ too ↓
he like the base] he like the ⟨pu⟩ base
you are only] you are ⟨a⟩ only
those who act a part] those who act ↑ a part ↓
tinged with passion.] tinged with passion⟨s⟩.
at first little] at first ↑ little ↓

1. "Phaedrus" explores love, rhetoric, and philosophy. Having read a French translation of Plato, Fuller uses "Banquet" in place of the English title for the "Symposium."

2. The Drachenfels is a peak of the Siebengebirge on the Rhine. On its summit stands a ruined castle, a relic of the Thirty Years' War. In 1836 Fuller wrote a poem titled "Drachenfels" (manuscript book of Fuller poems, MB: MS. Am. 1450 [145]).

3. Pericles, the Athenian statesman and orator, was responsible for Athens' dominance. Aspasia, his mistress from about 445 B.C. until his death in 429, was an intellectual who had talked with Socrates and taught rhetoric.

4. Probably William Wetmore Story (1819–95), son of Judge Joseph Story of Cambridge, and Maria White (1821–53), daughter of Abijah White of Watertown and later the wife of James Russell Lowell (1819–91). Both Story (who was to become one of Fuller's closest friends in Italy) and White were members of the social set called the "Brother and Sister Club" (also called the "Band"), which formed during the early 1840s in Cambridge and Boston. If Story and White are the objects of scorn here, then Lowell's later bitterness toward Fuller in his *Fable for Critics* was more than literary (Story: *DAB*; Perley Derby, *Elisha Story of Boston and Some of His Descendants* [Salem, 1915], p. 25; Lowell: *Lowells of America*, p. 121; *DAB*; Martin Duberman, *James Russell Lowell* [Boston, 1966]).

5. Mr. Morrison may be Nathaniel Holmes Morison (1815–90), a Harvard senior (Harvard archives).

6. As a member of the "Band," Fuller's friend Jane Tuckerman is probably the person meant.

7. *Othello*, V.ii.347–48.

8. Marie Henri Beyle [Stendhal], *The Lives of Hayden and Mozart*, 2d ed. (London, 1818), p. 338. Fuller repeated the anecdote in her review of the book in *Dial* 2 (October 1841):168. A *fornarina* is a baker's daughter; Raphael supposedly took one as his model for his *Donna Velata* and the Sistine Madonna, though the story is no longer accepted. Usw: *und so weiter*, German for "and so forth."

9. Salvator Rosa.

10. *Undine*, the first book of *Die Jahreszeiten*, by Friedrich Heinrich Karl, Freiherr de La Motte-Fouqué, was first published in Berlin in 1811. Undine is a water sprite who gets her soul by marrying Huldbrand, a knight. He rejects her, but she returns to kill him with a kiss (*OCGL*).

11. Fuller had translated Goethe's verse drama *Tasso*. Never published in her lifetime, it was part of the material her brother Arthur published in his edited volume *Art, Literature, and the Drama* (Boston, 1860), pp. 355–449.

203. To Caroline Sturgis

Groton 2d Feby 1839—

I must write a few lines, my dear Cary, though really I have not time. I fear you will jar Jane's feelings very much if you show her that I called William *base*.[1] I ought not to have used a word which might give her pain, but if you show her the letter say it is only in my own sense of *self-seeking*— I think all persons of energetic passions, and varied characters who have not noble views or for whom the love of some noble person is not "building the stair to heaven," must be so.

Let not the sweet Jean think that it is[n] any recent disclosures which made me use this epithet. I have thought it all along from the strong tinge of selfishness I observed in every one of his actions. I thought her love might regenerate him, but all she told me, brought to mind this saying of Sir J. Mackintosh's about somebody. "He has cultivated the delicacy of his sentiments at the expense of the health of his virtues."[2]

You say Jane's other friends have been "really unkind." I think active severity of manner is vulgar in such cases, but I think too[n] when we know such a large fact against a person, it ought to affect our manner, and that[n] coldness is but his due. But if you do as you feel permanently is right you cannot[n] err.

I have no idea he has formed any *deliberate*[n] *plan* to win your heart, yet I think he might try for it. But I have not time to state what I have observed about this.

I have no good reason for what I think of M. White; it is a demoniacal intimation like what you have had on one or two topics, I know.— Your first letter about her gave me an impression unfavorable to her; every-thing you have told me since has the same. Every thing I heard of her at Waltham gave me the same feeling, though every body praised her. About this party the night I was at Waltham, M. and G.[?] Ripley went to a party where she was[3] When they came home, they talked about her with delight and by the nature of their encomiums, and their account of what she said gave me the same feeling that your description of your party did. I have not expressed it before, for I thought it would be wrong as I have no reason to give. This is the only instance in which I have not had faith, if you liked a person. Perhaps I am wrong now; perhaps if I saw her, a look would give me a needed clue to her character and I should change my feeling. I do not judge her till I have seen her for myself, yet I have *never* been mistaken in these intimations that I recollect. I hope I am now.— You know all my natural predilections are for

45

people like her and W., with individuality, passion, beautiful eyes, and love of the beautiful, "those episodical characters" as Raphael 2d[n] calls them.[4] So do not you[n] or Jane suppose I am willing to be harsh, with my schoolmistress *goodness*.

I am very glad I exaggerated about the party and intimacy with M. but you gave a charcoal sketch and it was not *shaded* into truth. As to the fault, however, I saw too much bitterness and coldness in your letters and conversation. You say I was right, so it was well to speak though I took too strong an[n] impression. Adieu, dearest, you can show the letter to Jane, if you think it will not wound her.

M. F.

Thanks for the pretty leaves and pretty wafers.

ALS (MH: bMS Am 1221 [218]); MsCfr (MH: bMS Am 1280 [111, p. 220]). Published in part in *JMN*, 11:493. *Addressed:* Miss Caroline Sturgis / Boston, / Mass. *Postmark:* Groton Mass Feby 3. *Endorsed:* Feby 2d 1839.

the sweet Jean] the sweet ⟨Ja⟩ Jean
that it is] that it ⟨w⟩ is
I think too] I think ↑ too ↓
and that] and ⟨I think⟩ ↑ that ↓
is right you cannot] is right ↑ you cannot ↓
formed any *deliberate*] formed any ↑ *deliberate* ↓
as Raphael 2d] as Raphael ↑ 2d ↓
do not you] do not you⟨r⟩
too strong an] too strong ⟨a side.⟩ an

1. Jane Tuckerman; she is also frequently called Jean.
2. Fuller reviewed Robert James Mackintosh, *Memoirs of the Life of the Right Honourable Sir James Mackintosh* (London, 1835), in the *American Monthly Magazine*, n.s. 1 (June 1836):570–80. The quotation is unidentified.
3. Fuller mentions two children of the Reverend Samuel and Sarah Bradford Ripley. M is Mary Emerson Ripley; G, written less distinctly, is Christopher Gore Ripley (1822–81) (Harvard archives).
4. Sam Ward, whom Fuller called Raphael and Michelangelo because of his talent as an artist.

204. To Caroline Sturgis

Thursday eveg 7th Feby [1839]—
[Groton]

Dearest Cary,

I was grieved to send such a paltry answer to your last letter. I do not like to do those hurried things, but it could not be helped.— It seemed there was some superfluity in my advices, but I think they will do no harm.

What I have thought about W. S. in relation to you is too linked with other matters to be told here. I must reserve it for a personal interview.

I hope and believe that none of my comments will prevent your writing to me as freely as you have done.

Cary—I was much moved by what you say of Jesus— He will yet[n] be your best-beloved friend;—with all the blurs, that a factitious, canting world places between us and him, with all the love for liberty of the[n] speculative mind, we cannot at last dispense with,[n] we cannot get away from the divine character, the profound sympathies, the exalted ethics of that Man of Sorrows.

I partook of the communion last Sunday for the third time, and had beautiful thoughts about the bread and wine which some day[n] I may tell you.

If I do not now respond to your letter in words, I do with my heart.— I *do* consider you worthy to be my friend. You are yet to be tried, there is nothing tested in you yet, except your taste for Truth and your apprehension of what is high. I do not think your fortitude is cheerful enough to be respected as a virtue, but it is enough to give your character consistency

I have great faith in you.— And I do not wish to urge myself on you as a heroic or a holy friend. I believe it is best to receive me principally through the intellect.

Yet love me as much as you can.—

I cannot find any of Anna's letters which seem suitable to show.[1] Indeed they are so sacred to me that I dont know as I could have brought myself to send them away. When the "beautiful story of her life" as she calls it, is brought to a denouement I may then *read* you some of the letters with a running commentary. But clouds still hang about my star of stars, and none of her history is so completely past as to have become a part of Poetry.

I think I will not send you any more of Jane's letters. You have the most beautiful why should you wish to weaken the impression

Tasso you have.

I send your drawing books, but wish to look them over with you sometime.— You will find in one of the books some pencillings by J. F. C. Please give them to Sarah, and tell her James said he[n] had sent her some things that he would like me to look at, and ask her if she can give me a copy of the verses to E. Keats and the two sets on the *ring* and give her my dear love.[2]

I recommend to your perusal two articles in the last No. of the Westminster Review on Heloise[n] and Rahel von Ense. Two remarkable women indeed! In Rahel I think you may recognize well known

47

lineaments.— Observe what she says (quoted by Goethe) about being *born only to live*;[3] and what the Reviewer says of "feeling about feeling."[n] The Westminster indeed is petri de talent of late— There is Miss M's crack article too, vigorous eloquent stained with credulity, exaggeration, and man deification as ever. She has placed her abolitionist friends in the most ludicrous light, by her fine portraits; but I suppose they wont mind it. Amern Abolitionists have as little leisure to think of *good taste* as Clarkson had of *the salvation of his soul.*[4]

I shall not write to you again, unless it be a short note for several weeks. I write a great deal too much, and at this rate shall never get well. Thirty six letters, all long ones, I have dispatched beside all the other writing I have done. Tomorrow I[n] shall write two more and that closes my letter list. After that I shall not write one which is not absolutely necessary, till my translation is off my hands. Your ferns are up and their presence is cheering. I trust you will be generous and write to me, perhaps often. Do not send this parcel to Jane till you have a perfectly safe opportunity Affectionately

MARGARET F.

Lloyd is too much fascinated with Eleanor to give her up yet.

ALS (MH: bMS Am 1221 [219]). *Addressed:* Miss Caroline Sturgis / No 50 Summer St. / Boston. *Endorsed:* Feby 7th 1839.

will yet] will ↑ yet ↓
liberty of the] liberty of ⟨that⟩ the
last dispense with,] last dispense ↑ with ↓ ,
which some day] which some ⟨time⟩ ↑ day ↓
James said he] James said he⟨r⟩
on Heloise] on Heloi⟨u⟩se
about feeling."] about feeling."⟨⟩
Tomorrow I] T⟨wo⟩morrow I

1. Anna Hazard Barker was a young New Orleans beauty who became a good friend of Fuller, Sturgis, Sam Ward, and Emerson. At this time she was a frequent visitor to New England. Later in 1839 she and Ward fell in love and became engaged, an event that hurt Fuller badly.

2. George Keats (1797–1842), the poet's brother, settled in Louisville, where James Clarke came to know the family. His daughter, Emma (d. 1883), married Philip Speed (1819–82). The poem was Clarke's "To A Poet's Niece," *Western Messenger* 5 (August 1838):298–300 (*DNB* [under John Keats]; Thomas Speed, *Records and Memorials of the Speed Family* [Louisville, Ky., 1892], p. 128; *New York Times*, 11 September 1883).

3. Fuller had been reading the first number of vol. 32 of the *London and Westminster Review*. Article VI reviewed *Lettres d'Abailard et Héloise* (pp. 146–219); Article II was a review of nine volumes by and about Rahel von Ense (pp. 60–84). Rahel Levin (1771–1833) was a prominent literary hostess in Berlin before she lost her fortune. In 1814 she married Karl August Varnhagen von Ense (1785–1858), a Prussian diplomat. After 1819 Rahel again established a salon, which was frequented by such Berlin writers as Heinrich Heine, Baron Wilhelm von Humboldt, Bettina von Arnim, and La Motte-Fouqué. After her death, her husband published *Rahel: Ein Buch des*

Andenkens für ihre Freunde (Berlin, 1833) (*OCGL*). The *Westminster* reviewer quotes a Rahel letter that undoubtedly meant much to Fuller: "I am as unique as the greatest appearance in this earth. . . . To me it was appointed not to write, or act, but *to live.*" The reviewer further quotes Goethe: "'I have never *thought about thinking* [*habe nie ans Denken gedacht*]!'" "But how much wastefuller still is it to *feel about feelings!*" concludes the reviewer.

4. The lead article in vol. 32 of the *London and Westminster Review* was "The Martyr Age of the United States," by Harriet Martineau (pp. 1–59). She ranged over several topics, including William Lloyd Garrison, Maria Chapman, and Angelina Grimké, all of whom were prominent abolitionists. Thomas Clarkson (1760–1846), one of the most famous English abolitionists of the day, wrote an early attack on slavery, *The History of the Rise, Progress, and Accomplishment of the Abolition of the African Slave Trade by the British Parliament* (London, 1808).

205. To Caroline Sturgis

Thursday evening [21?] Feby 1839—

I have forgotten the day of the month; My dearest Cary, I was delighted with the box. It is just what I have been wishing for. I think the leaves are arranged with great taste; are they all from the beloved Island?— I shall put all my best letters into this one and keep it in some pretty place in my new chamber. Yet so covetous am I that I intend, if possible, to keep you up to your generous intent of making me another next summer. If you will and still feel as if you should like it, and give me a box as large as this, I think it will hold all I have had and shall have from my friend Raphael; Letters verses sketches all. I will keep it devoted to him while I live But you must line it either with a much paler blue than this, or rose color or cream color. I agree with you that this is not pretty enough for him, though quite pretty enough for me, because you say you could make a prettier, and he is such an Ariel that he deserves to be ministered to of every creature's best.

You *may* see all my verses that Jane has, if you wish. I suppose you *have* seen most of them. I am ashamed when I think there is scarce a line of *poetry* in them. All "rhetorical and impassioned" as Goethe said of Me de Stael. However, such as they are, they have been overflowing drops from the somewhat bitter cup of my existence. Will you not tax your genius to intersperse them with a few illustrations You need not "shade them into truth" for me, who am as yet but the sketch of my own possible existence. Especially should I like a symbolical frontispiece. If you could do this I should be delighted. I like to combine you and Jane, "all that's best of dark and bright."[1] I send back the book because I want Heidelberg and Drachenfels transferred to her pages.— This other book contains Halleck's Red Jacket which I think I promised to show you.[2] Keep both till I come. I am going to ask you to do every thing and do nothing for you— so I begin.

You did not tell me the name of the *transparent vase.* I want it.

What is M. Channing about?[3] She has not written to me these three weeks.

Will you buy and send me Mrs Jameson's new book, if it be not made expensive by a handsome cover or her own absurd vignette etchings.[4] I am in great haste to see it, if within the compass of my purse. Write what it cost and I will refund forthwith.

Are you not glad that I am coming to live near you? We have taken a little place, called Willow Brook, about five miles from Boston.[5] You must come out and spend Sundays there and I will come in and look over engravings at the Atheneum with you. I have not time or strength to tell you now how peaceful and promising my prospect looks at present. We shall come the 1st April.

I do not know whether I could write out your Ideal. It is more incommensurable than Jane's. I have a letter addressed to you in m[y] journal which conveys some intimations. will think it over when I can I did not understand it was James's letters you wished to see, I thought Jane's. But I cannot look over the letters again to select, and much as I have shown, there is much I have not. As to his confidence, I think he would place unlimited trust in my discretion, and that it would make no difference whether he knew the person, if *I did.* As to Anna's, I would show you the letter as soon as any one who does not know her history, but there are a mass of them in very fine hand, and, to get at any one which it would be right to show, I should have to read over what would disturb my feelings exceedingly. The letters, beside, are nothing; you should see herself, and may probably, for I shall ask her to stay with me this summer.

Will you, in addition to all other favors, find out whether W. H. Channing has lost his little daughter. There were verses in the W. Messenger, that seemed so, yet would he have put them *there.*[6]

Please say to S. Clarke I will write to her by and by, and love her *now.* Also I love E. Hoar and tell her I[n] shall pass a day or two in Concord as I come by, if they will let me.[7] Adieu, dear Cary Write whenever you can. This is no letter, but, if you knew what pain I am in, you would not wish me to write one.

M. F.

Ellery's verse is fine— Perhaps he does not like M. C's resolute efforts to make a *friend* of him and is determined not to be a friend to any fair lady.[8]

Will you send me a bit of gum arabic— I cannot get it here and some of your leaves have peeled a little.

What Appleton is it[n] to whom Miss Webster is engaged?[9]

ALS (MH: bMS Am 1221 [217]); MsCfr (MH: bMS Am 1280 [111, p. 170]). Published in *Memoirs*, 1:295, and *JMN*, 11:487–88. *Addressed:* Miss C. Sturgis. *Endorsed:* Feb 9 1839.

tell her I] tell her ↑ I ↓
is it] is ↑ it ↓

1. Byron, "She Walks in Beauty," l. 3.
2. "Red Jacket: A Chief of the Indian Tribes, the Tuscaroras," by Fitz-Greene Halleck, was first published in *The Talisman* (New York, 1828), but Fuller probably read it in Halleck's *Alnwick Castle, with Other Poems* (New York, 1836 [1835]).
3. Probably Mary Channing, Dr. William Ellery Channing's daughter.
4. Anna Jameson, *Winter Studies and Summer Rambles in Canada* (London, 1838).
5. A part of Jamaica Plain, where the Fullers lived for some months.
6. "The Child Asleep," *Western Messenger* 6 (February 1839):273. Since the poem is signed "W.H.C.," it was probably Channing's, but his daughter, Frances Maria (1837–89), was still living (*Cleveland and Cleaveland*, p. 1769).
7. Elizabeth Hoar of Concord was engaged to Waldo Emerson's brother Charles when he died. She and Fuller became close friends.
8. William Ellery Channing, son of Dr. Walter Channing, was an eccentric young man who courted Sturgis but later married Fuller's sister, Ellen. A poet, he was later Thoreau's closest friend and first biographer. M. C. is probably Ellery's cousin Mary Channing.
9. Julia Webster (1818–48), Daniel Webster's daughter, married Samuel Appleton Appleton (1811–61) on 24 September 1839 (*NEHGR* 21:8; Claude Moore Fuess, *Daniel Webster* [Boston, 1930], 2:73–74).

206. To George Ripley

Groton 21st Feby [1839]

Dear Sir,

The proofs can be sent by the mail as well as any way, though I send them back by the "virtuous man," that I may also get rid of all the M.S. which I have finished.[1] Here are a[n] hundred and fifty sheets. I shall send, in[n] a few days, perhaps twenty more including my preface and[n] the few pages of the book which remain to be translated.

As I find that two pages of my handwriting (in which the greater part of the book lies) make one of your print, I think the volume will contain about fourhundred pages. I think I have already cut out all I ought, but may, in the proofs, see some passages that could be dispensed with. You will not praise my M. S. any more, but we are so soon to remove and[n] so much is to be done, that neither my brother nor myself have time to copy. I am desirous to get this off my hands as fast as I can, without slighting it.

As to the proofs the expression "some title" corresponds with Eckermann's meaning I believe. "Habe zu betrachten *gewissermassen* als den Schmuck" is the phase[2] Tranquil *hour*[3] will do, standing for any period of time. The title Counsellor is wrong; the word Justiz,-beamt I had confounded with Justizrath.[n] It should be officer of justice, strictly; if you think it of any consequence please substitute the right phrase. I expect the chief trouble throughout will be with titles of men and books as, when I could not translate them to my mind, I have left them in German. Perhaps it would have been better not, but such combinations[n] as Upper-forest-counsellor look very formidable in English.

As to the use of[n] capitals— I have been so desirous of avoiding that copious sprinkling of great As and Bs and Cs that seems to mark the pages of every body who has learned a little German that, perhaps, I have fallen into the opposite extreme. But is it not equally correct to write— I met at the coffee house an officer of the marines, as I met at the Coffee house an Officer of the Marines—

Please mark every thing you see amiss; as I am desirous of making the publication of this book the means of drilling myself in details which, naturally, have not before attracted my attention.

Please give my love to my friend, Mrs Ripley, and ask her if she will not welcome me to the neighborhood of Boston. I shall be only five miles out, and shall see you often; that is, if you do not pass all your summers on *lakes*.— Truly yours

S. M. FULLER.

Will you do me the favor to send the other parcel to Mr Sturgis's?—

"In the year ninety" was the way the good Dr had it, and I retained it with[n] other imperfect phrases of his, because they give, at least to me, the feeling of an almost quaint simplicity.[4] 1790— is, of course, the date

ALS (VtMiM). *Addressed:* Revd George Ripley. *Endorsed:* M. Fuller.

George Ripley was a liberal Unitarian minister who was prominent in the controversy between the conservatives and liberals. A good German scholar, he was the editor of a series of translations of literary and philosophical works, *Specimens of Foreign Standard Literature.* Fuller was translating Johann Peter Eckermann's *Gespräche mit Goethe* for the series.

Here are a] Here are ⟨two⟩ a
I shall send, in] I shall send, ⟨at⟩ in
including my preface and] including ↑ my preface and ↓
to remove and] to remove ⟨that⟩ and
had confounded with Justizrath] had confounded with ⟨Justiz beamt⟩ Justizrath
but such combinations] but such ⟨words⟩ ↑ combinations ↓
the use of] the ↑ use of ↓
I retained it with] I retained it ⟨like⟩ ↑ with ↓

1. Fuller was completing her translation of Eckermann's *Gespräche mit Goethe*.
2. Fuller garbles the passage here. Eckermann wrote in his preface: "Übrigens erkenne ich dasjenige, was in diesen Bänden mir gelungen ist zu meinem Eigentum zu machen und was ich gewissermassen als den Schmuck meines Lebens zu betrachten habe, mit innigem Dank gegen eine höhere Fügung." Fuller translated the passage: "For the rest, I consider what I do possess in these two volumes, and which I have some title to regard as the peculiar ornament of my own existence, with deep-felt gratitude as the gift of Providence" (Johann Wolfgang Goethe, *Gedenkausgabe der Werke, Briefe und Gespräche*, ed. Ernst Beutler [Zurich, 1948–54], 24:12; S. M. Fuller, *Conversations with Goethe* [Boston, 1839], p. 4).
3. Eckermann's "ruhiger Stunde" (*Gedenkausgabe*, 24:61).
4. Eckermann begins his autobiographical Introduction by saying he was born "zu Anfang der neunziger Jahre" (at the beginning of the year ninety). He quotes the phrase again as Goethe used it when describing his shifting intellectual interests "in den neunziger Jahren" (*Gedenkausgabe*, 24:15, 181).

207. To Ralph Waldo Emerson

Groton 4th March 1839—

My dear friend,

I have been reading Mr Very's Hamlet.[1] I find excellent things there and its tone is[n] very noble. But the subject seems rather probed at an inquiring distance than grasped, and yet there is an attempt at mastery. I find I am displeased just in proportion, as the critic attempts to account for things in Shakspeare! His *critic* indeed has[n] never yet glorified human nature, and nothing written upon the subject deserves a higher title than that of Meditations on Shakspeare, or Studies on Shakspeare. No man knoweth his secret and failure is always signal. I am best pleased when[n] the writer confines himself to detail as Goethe did, as Mr Dana does.[2]

Mr Very is[n] *infinitely* inferior in accuracy of perception to Mr Dana, and has not so much insight, but he soars higher.— I am, however, greatly interested in Mr Very. He seems worthy to be well known.— I send you a little sketch of him by Cary on the 3d page of this which I think one of her good letters.[3] Does not the little sketch give the idea of him?— or no![n] you can keep it for me as I see you so soon.

I have only read this time Phaedrus[n] and the Banquet, but, I have had this vol several times before. I think when I am tranquil to read it. I shd like a vol of the German or Engh Plato, as this is so large that I cannot read it when I lie down to rest, and that is the only time when I do read much.

I have retained of your books a volume of Bacon, one of Plutarch, one of Ben Jonson with Underwoods, &c—you must ask me for them, if wanted, for I keep books forever.[4]

I hope you will have[n] the next Archaeus when I am within your gates. I am very much interested in this gallery. What a good attempt at a Goethe! Stirling's is just such a mind as I like.[5] The painter's eye, the poet's always listening ear, balanced by the understanding and judgment of the man of the world, all this I see in him, and though he seems like to ripen much more, he has even now a sunny flavor which fruit exposed[n] to the finest moon and star shine, *only*, will never attain.

Two of Milnes's Shadows are the gracefullest things I have seen![6] Thank you!—

It is thought by my guardians that I had best quit this mansion before it is made thoroughly desolate. I being that "extremely common character, a confirmed invalid" and likely to have the catch cold, if I sleep on the floor and sit in a draught.[n] So I shall quit someday[n] between the 20th and 30th. Please let me know[n] before the 20th whether you have engagements the week previous to the sweet day of sacred rest, for which I have already got permission to deposit an olive branch on my way to my future Ark.[7]

I shall not salute any body—for my last benediction still lingers on your roof tree; no kind wind having yet[n] blown it back to me.

I have written till I have got tired of writing the common character, and as you see, my pen inclines to the Hiero, glyphic style—

S. M. F.

I dont mean that I am going to inflict a week's visit but merely that I come some day in the week.

ALS (MH: bMS Am 1280 [2343]); MsC (MB: Ms. Am. 1450 [68]). Published in Rusk, *Letters of RWE*, 2:190–91. *Addressed:* R. W. Emerson. *Endorsed:* Margaret Fuller / March 1839.

and its tone is] and its tone ⟨d⟩ is
critic indeed has] *critic* ↑ indeed ↓ has
best pleased when] best pleased ⟨th⟩ when
Mr Very is] Mr Very ⟨in⟩ is
of him?—or no!] of him?—⟨Please send back the letter,⟩ no!
this time Phaedrus] this time ⟨p⟩Phaedrus

you will have] you will ⟨leave⟩ have
which fruit exposed] which fruit ⟨ripene⟩ exposed
and sit in a draught] and sit in ⟨the draft⟩ the draught
I shall quit someday] I shall quit ⟨b⟩ someday
let me know] let me ⟨no⟩ know
wind having yet] wind having ⟨b⟩ yet

1. Jones Very (1813–80) graduated from Harvard in 1836 and became a tutor in Greek. In September 1838 he fell prey to a religious hallucination and was committed to the McLean Hospital for the insane at Charlestown from 17 September to 17 October (*DAB*; Edwin Gittleman, *Jones Very: The Effective Years* [New York, 1967]). During his confinement Very wrote two essays on Shakespeare, which Emerson passed on to Fuller. He wrote to her on 9 November 1838, promising the essays and saying, "Talk with him [Very] a few hours and you will think all insane but he. Monomania or mono *Sania* he is a very remarkable person & though his mind is not in a natural & probably not in a permanent state, he is a treasure of a companion" (Rusk, *Letters of RWE*, 2:173).

2. Richard Henry Dana had given a series of well-received lectures on Shakespeare in Boston and New York. Goethe wrote occasionally on Shakespeare, but Fuller is probably referring to bk. 5 of *Wilhelm Meisters Lehrjahre*, where Wilhelm and Serlo debate the wisdom of condensing *Hamlet*. Wilhelm argues for a complete version, calling attention to details: "In such small matters we discover Shakspeare's greatness." He emphasizes the "external relations of the persons, whereby they are brought from place to place, or combined in various ways by certain accidental incidents" (*Wilhelm Meister's Apprenticeship and Travels*, 23:337, 333).

3. In his response, Emerson wrote, "The letter is frank & good & meets my curiosity concerning her character & raises my curiosity. So slow to speak as she is, she ought to write freely" (Rusk, *Letters of RWE*, 2:191).

4. Emerson owned Jonson's *Works* (London, 1717) in six volumes; Bacon's *Works* (London, 1824) in ten volumes; Plutarch's *Morals* (London, 1718) in five volumes. "Underwoods" is a collection of "lesser" poems by Jonson (Walter Harding, *Emerson's Library* [Charlottesville, Va., 1967]).

5. Fuller refers to John Sterling's "Onyx Ring," *Blackwood's Edinburgh Magazine* 44 (November–December 1838):664–89, 741–68, and 45 (January 1839):17–47. Her interest in "this gallery" may refer to a series of tales written by W. F. Deacon that appeared in the magazine at various times from June 1837 to March 1839.

6. "Shadows" was published in *Poems of Many Years* (London, 1838) by Richard Monckton Milnes, Lord Houghton (1809–85), who befriended numerous writers (*DNB*).

7. In his reply, Emerson urged her to come on the twentieth (Rusk, *Letters of RWE*, 2:191). Noah's dove returned to the ark, "and, lo, in her mouth was an olive leaf pluckt off: so Noah knew that the waters were abated from off the earth" (Gen. 8:11).

208. To Charles K. Newcomb

Groton 4th March 1839—

My dear Charles,

No doubt you wonder that, after taking so much pains to get a letter from you, I should so long delay to answer it.— But, alas, it came like[n] a summer bird, when old Winter has begun to seal the streams, and unclothe the trees; or a wedding guest the day after the joyful rite.— The eight weeks of tranquil reading, writing, and walking were over. I had enjoyed a holiday longer than any I have known for some years; I had quitted that element of meditation, and free communion with Nature which you and I both love so truly and passed into a condition as busy, as wearisome, though, surely, not as annoying, as I ever knew at Providence.

It was by no means a *ruse*; that saying of mine that I had many things to say to you. I have often in my walks along the banks of the now silent little stream, which I am about to leave, or through the solemn evergreen woods, whose silence, colder, if not deeper than that of summer noon, gave verge enough for reverie, addressed many remarks to you, some good, some not, but all such as you would have liked!! For Charles likes whatever rises naturally from the mind of a friend, whether it ascend till it be beautified by the Sun into a Lamb of Heaven, or curl away gray and feeble. He likes it, though[n] it be but vapor, for, however evanescent, it tells a story of intercourse between earth and the golden lamps above.

But all my tales of sudden bursts of light, tearing apart the violet curtains and casting them aside upon the distant hills who raise their gentle heads to woo the veil, all my solemn brooding twilights, less beautiful, but more poetic, and all the tales the Spirits of the trees told me by the glimpses of the moon, thoughts of books too which we had both been interested in. All is—weggeschnitten[1]—as the Germans say—and behold me—here. Every thing in such confusion— I can say nothing now except, dear Charles, I was very glad to get your letter. Do not regret writing it, because you cannot have a very good one in reply. I wanted it so much, because our last conversation had left an anxiety about you in my mind. I was fain to know whether you were tranquil in mind or only outwardly, and it pained me to have all *real* intercourse between us so suddenly checked.

Now write again or not, as you feel disposed I shall feel tranquil about you, after what you have said. As to all the good things I will say them next time I walk with you.

The task which now so engrosses me is fatiguing and melancholy, yet so interesting that I cannot think of any thing else. It is the arrangement of my father's papers. My poor father!— If I were disposed to draw a hackneyed moral, surely there never was a fitter occasion. These papers had been accumulating for forty years. College journals themes, law minutes, minutes of the most interesting debates in the Mass and U S legislature, a voluminous correspondence on almost all subjects; he had never all those years had time to examine these papers, he had just prepared the study, (at the end of the garden for we had not room in the house) in which he meant, after finally settling[n] his professional affairs to look them over when he died. He was in that building only twenty four hours before his death.

How well he was prepared to meet the fiat which went forth so suddenly, I find abundant evidence in these papers. Well as I knew my father, I know him hourly better and respect him more, as I look more closely into those secrets of his life which the sudden event left open in a way he never foresaw. Were I but so just, so tender, so candid towards man so devout towards a higher Power.—

I cannot think of any thing else, my dear Charles, and though I have been engaged with them many days there is work for many more, since well as I knew his affairs, as many documents are to be burnt I am obliged to look at each one separately. I have many many other[n] things to do, before we remove. When I am undisturbed once more, you shall hear what I think of Carlyle &c— Meanwhile this comes only to say,[n] that I am, as I was, yours affectionately

S. M. F.—

Please remember me to your mother and Lizzy, and say that I am much obliged by your mothers full response to my queries. I will see Charlotte as soon as I can after we go to Willow Brook.[2]

ALS (MH: fMS Am 1086 [10:127]). *Addressed:* To / Charles King Newcomb, / Providence, / Rhode Island. *Postmark:* Groton MS Mch 5.

Charles King Newcomb of Providence was a Brown graduate who joined Brook Farm. Both Fuller and Emerson thought he had literary talent, but he never pursued a writing career.

it came like] it came ↑ like ↓
He likes it, though] he likes it, ⟨because⟩ though
after finally settling] after finally ⟨arran⟩ settling
have many many other] have many many ⟨mtters?⟩ other
comes only to say] comes ↑ only ↓ to ⟨say?⟩ say

1. "Cut away."

2. Lizzy and Charlotte are Newcomb's sisters: Elizabeth Wright Newcomb (1818–70) and Charlotte Ellery Newcomb (1823–98), who was Fuller's pupil for some months after the Fullers moved to Willow Brook (John Bearse Newcomb, *Genealogical Memoir of the Newcomb Family* [Elgin, Ill., 1874], p. 490).

209. To Caroline Sturgis

Groton 4th March
1839—

Dearest Cary,

As this is the last day I suppose that I shall have a half hour's leisure to write to any one, I heartily wish it were in my power to write you a good letter in return for yours which always have some good thought in them. But as it is not I think I will at least tell you *why* it is not.

Last night as I was lying awake and thinking in most painful restlessness of all possible things, and among others of your designs for my poems, I thought—Thinks I to myself,—Cary supposes, I daresay that I do not love her much. She always excused my writing her such miserable letters while I was at work with my school, but now, she thinks I am in solitude and at leisure, and, if I thought of her as I ought, would write her many letters full of pictures, thoughts and sentiments.

Then thinks I to myself I'll tell her how I have passed the time since I came home. It will give her some idea of the way in which my life is drained off, and she will never be surprised at my omissions, and, perhaps, it may make her own leisure seem more valuable to her.

When I came home I was determined to take every precaution to ensure my having the whole time for myself.— I had it mentioned to all the neighbors, that I was worn out, and should not go out. I declined their invites so as not to offend them, five or six of those who knew me best, made me short calls which[n] I have not yet returned. I have never been to any house and to church only once. I have not spent two hours in the society of any person out of our own family. I stay in my own room always till about nine in the eveg; when *very* busy, I do not go down then or to meals. I have not seen half as much even of the family, as I wished.

I had several loose robes fixed to wear this winter[n] that I might lie down, whenever I have severe pain, and apply friction, when necessary. This has, really, done good, and as I have only had the trouble of keeping myself *neat* without any *fixing*, dressing has taken not a quarter the time it usually does.

Mother and Ellen have mended my clothes, when necessary. I have had no duties of the worky sort except taking care of my own room, paying some attention to Mother and Ellen when sick and teaching Ellen and Richard two afternoons in the week.

Out of this whole time I have not been confined to the bed above four or five days in all. I have had no amusement to take up my time, except that I have walked a mile or two those days when the weather permitted and five or six times have played on the piano.

For seven years I have never been able to pass two months so much as I pleased and never expect it again,[n] and I have been as industrious as any beaver. Why then will you say—no more or better letters?

I have had the curiosity to keep a list of my letters and I have written just 50 before this, since the 3d Jany, when I came home[n]— *more to you* than any one else.

As soon as I came home I arranged the first two days my books and clothes. Then my papers, which I had not been able to for more than three years. I burnt a great many, and I sent you those I selected for you.

I settled up the accts of my two little girls, wrote to them and their parents.[1]

I wrote about twenty letters then. This took about ten days, at the end of that time I was sick from fatigue. As soon as I was able to sit up, Mother and Ellen were sick While they were so and I getting better, I studied over parts of Goethe; and read two of Plato's dialogues, and a no of[n] the London and Westminster As soon as I was able I begun on my trans. Revised what had been written and compared it with the orig and wrote out the remainder All the other writing I have done has been the other letters and a very little in my journal. All the reading I did was occasionally when lying down in day time Mr Very's sonnets and pieces, Jane's letters, the Stirlings in two Blackwoods[n] and little bits of Plato, Coleridge, Goethe and Ben Jonson. After I went to bed I would read myself to sleep with chapters out of Vivian Grey, and Maryatt's novels, and I read the debates in Congress.[2] I also had talks with Mother about our future arrangements. This took up all my time till last Monday when before two o'clock, I finished my translation. In afternoon, I begun my next piece of work on which I have been engaged ever since all day and all the eveg, till to day, I felt so wearied I thought I must take a holiday.

This is the arrangement of my father's papers, the accumulation of forty years from the time he entered College till now. He brought them all here hoping to arrange them himself.

I had no idea till I began what a labor it would prove,[n] but, though I have been at work a week, and examined more than a thousand letters, I seem scarcely to have made an impression on the great heaps of paper. It is a very interesting, though very fatiguing work, and teaches me a great deal.[n]

As soon as I can get through with it, I shall pack the books which we are to take and select those we are to sell, and make many other arrangements for the auction which is to take place on the 19th. After that I shall have much to settle, before I escape to Concord where I shall pass a day or two, then to Boston, where I shall see you for some hours. Then we will talk of Poetry and Personality!— But I see I cannot write again, unless it be some short note.

Perhaps you think I might as well have written something on such subjects as all these details, but I never can speculate[n] when I am in my practical trim.

Still planning when and where, and how the business can be done,"[3] I have read of men who[n] could write on such subjects in all the stir of every day life and yet play well their parts, but I confess tis beyond me.

On the whole I feel with some sadness that I can hardly be a real friend to any one more. The claims upon me are now too many. I am always sacrificing myself more than is for my health or fame, yet I can do very little for any one person.

I know that you, my dear Cary, *ask* nothing, but I cannot help feeling you must and have a right to[n] expect it. So I think I will now say Dear Cary, Though you are much younger than I, yet I have that degree of respect for your mind and character that I can look on you as an equal friend. I also love you, and, probably, no other person you know could be so much to you as I, notwithstanding[n] all my shortcomings— Can you be contented, in consideration of your greater freedom and leisure, to do much for, receive little from me. Above all, can you be contented to write to me often and sometimes receive no reply, generally a meagre one. When I see you I shall always, I suppose, be able to talk. But writing is too fatiguing to my body, let alone the constant occupation of my mind. Yet not to hear from you often would grieve me. Indeed the week is darker hued in which I do not receive a letter. Yet they make me feel as if I ought to answer. If I am sure you do not expect it, and that you feel always that my mind answers, I shall write no letter unless I am able and then they will be good, though perhaps few.

I am ashamed when I think what letters I have written you, and I wish you would burn all the worthless business scrawls. You deserve different treatment. I think I shall like the designs very much. They are complicated, but not more so than many of the best things in ancient and modern Art. Please do them, and I will read you passages from Goethe's Propylea out at Willow Brook, as a fit expression of my gratitude

I will not tell you now wh I like best for what I think good reasons till I see them in pencil I did not ask Mrs Jameson for any thing except some local particulars, and still think her conduct ungenerous, but not so much so, since I now think her knowledge more scanty than I had[n] supposed. And the book seems to be addressed to Mrs Austen.[4] I do not wonder she thought it impertinent in an obscure stranger to propose doing what Mrs A, whom she seems so much to admire, did not feel competent to undertake. I have learnt some matters of fact from her book wh will be of use.

I send you my favorite Prince, as I believe you do not own him, and I thot you might like to read about his pictures, castles &c again.[5] If not, only let him lie in your room till I come, he is too refined to be an intruder any where, though his coat is not in the best condition.

Will you do me the favor to send the other as directed.

Do write, if you can feel like it to yrs afftely

S. M. F.

ALS (MH: bMS Am 1221 [220]). Published in part in Wade, pp. 551–54.

short calls which] short calls ⟨and⟩ ↑ which ↓

fixed to wear this winter] fixed ↑ to wear this winter ↓

pleased and never expect it again,] pleased ↑ and never expect it again ↓ ,

3d Jany, when I came home] 3d Jany, ↑ when I came home ↓

and a no of] and ↑ a no of ↓

the Stirlings in two Blackwoods] ↑ the Stirlings in two Blackwoods ↓

it would prove,] it would ↑ prove ↓ ,

Across the face of this paragraph Fuller later wrote: In all this time I can truly say I have wasted no moment.

never can speculate] never can ↑ speculate ↓

men who] men ⟨and⟩ who

you must and have a right to] you must ↑ and have a right to ↓

I, notwithstanding] I, ⟨with⟩ ↑ notwithstanding ↓

than I had] than I ↑ had ↓

1. Two girls from Louisville, Emma Keats and Ellen Clark (daughter of L. B. Clark), attended the Greene-Street School and left with Fuller to become her private pupils in Jamaica Plain (*Letters of JFC*, pp. 130, 136).

2. *Vivian Grey* (London, 1826) was Benjamin Disraeli's first novel. Frederick Marryat (1792–1848) was an English naval officer and novelist (*DNB*).

3. George Herbert, "The Church-Porch": "Let thy minde still be bent, still plotting where, / And when, and how the businesse may be done" (*The Works of George Herbert*, ed. F. E. Hutchinson [Oxford, 1941], p. 20).

4. Sarah Taylor Austin (1793–1867), English translator of German works.

5. Hermann Pückler-Muskau, *Tutti-Frutti: Aus den Papieren des Verstorbenen* (Stuttgart, 1834).

210. To Arthur B. Fuller

[10 March 1839]

[Groton]

I was very glad to get your letter, my dear Arthur, and liked it,— except the handwriting, which is *too bad* for a gentleman and a scholar! See how Ellen has improved, by *never writing in a hurry* for some months, and do likewise.

Say to Mrs Ripley with my love that I am very desirous both of seeing her and discharging some of our dues as far as specie can do it.[1] That I shall come to Waltham while staying at Concord, if possible, but if I dont get an oppory, wont she come and pass a few hours at Mr E's, as she commands a chaise and I do not? My respects also to Mr R. and love to the girls. Be sure and do my message as I shd say it

—Are not you glad we are going to that pretty place. How pleasant it will be for you to come from college and spend Saty under the blossom that hangs on the bough. You will not find us looking at all lovely here. All dust and Babel. As you pass through Concord on yr pedestrian expedition hither, you had best stop at Mr Emerson's to see if I am not there— Very afftly your sister

M.

ALS (MH: fMS Am 1086 [9:57]). *Addressed:* Mr Arthur B. Fuller. / Care of Rev ⟨ George⟩ Mr. Ripley / Waltham. / Massachusetts. *Postmark:* Groton Ms Mar 11.

Fuller's letter is a postscript to one written by her sister Ellen.

1. The Reverend Samuel and Sarah Bradford Ripley of Waltham. The girls Fuller mentions later in the paragraph were their daughters, Elizabeth Bradford, Mary Emerson, Phoebe Bliss, Ann Dunkin, and Sophia Bradford Ripley (Thayer, *Ripley,* p. 32).

211. To Eugene Fuller

Concord 31st March
1839—

My dear Eugene,

I was very glad of the encouraging prospects opened to me by your letter. I think I shall go to Jamaica Plains on Tuesday as they will then probably be so far advanced that I can work with them without overfatiguing myself.

My ride hither was by no means as tedious as I expected, for I arrived about six o'clock. The time has passed delightfully as usual with me in this mansion of peace. I have Elizh Hoar in the room with me, and like it very much, though we talk rather too much for my strength. Mrs. Ripley came on Tuesday to tea. She speaks well both of Arthur's disposition and progress in his studies, and thinks she shall have him ready to enter college in August. Mr. Wm Emerson from N. York and his wife have been staying here.[1] Mr W. E. is as unlike his brother as possible he is very gentlemanly, very amiable very clear headed, but a mere business man. He has taken Wm Pritchard into his office to assist, and[n] allows him a fourth part of the profits this first year, he said that wd probably be about twelve hundred dollars for W. P.[2] Spoke very highly of his tact, punctuality, and quiet energy. Said Charles Stuart was the reverse of all this, bustle and no execution doing little himself and getting into other peoples' way; that he could never succeed.[3]

Wm E. strikingly resembles Govr Everett in his way of speaking, gestures,[n] and attitudes.

Mr E. and Elizh both thought the airy Buchanan an uncommonly stupid, tiresome young man. John Keyes brought him to see Mr E. and had puffed him a great deal, I believe, beforehand.[4] I know not that I have aught else to tell you. In the morng I write and read. Mr E. being engaged in his study till twelve o'clock. Then he reads to me, or we talk the remaining hours. I have had no letters this week except one from S. Clarke, and know not what the world is doing. I amused Mr E. and Elizh much with the billet of D. F. jr. Has that gent. his bad cold still?— Ellen sent me my eye glass. I am very glad that I shall see you next week. Methinks Aunt Abba must be distraught or dead.[5] Shd write to R.F.F.[6] but suppose he is no longer a denizen of Groton.

Very affly yr sister

M.

ALS (MH: fMS Am 1086 [9:59]). *Addressed:* Mr Eugene Fuller, / Groton / Mass— *Postmark:* Concord Mass Apr 1.

to assist, and] to assist, ⟨him⟩ and

of speaking, gestures] of speaking, ⟨and⟩ gestures

1. William Emerson (1801–68), third child of William and Ruth Haskins Emerson, graduated from Harvard in 1818, studied in Germany, and then was admitted to the New York bar. On 3 September 1833 he married Susan Woodward Haven (1807–68), daughter of John and Ann Woodward Haven of Portsmouth, New Hampshire (*Ipswich Emersons*, pp. 264–65).

2. William Mackay Prichard (1814–97), son of Moses and Jane Hallett Prichard of Concord, graduated from Harvard in 1833 and studied with William Emerson, with whom he was a partner until the latter's retirement. At that time Prichard entered a law partnership with William G. Choate. In 1852 Prichard married Eliza Plummer of New York City (Waldo Higginson, *Memorials of the Class of 1833 of Harvard College* [Cambridge, Mass., 1883], p. 133; *Memoirs of the Social Circle in Concord*, 2d ser. [Cambridge, Mass., 1888]).

3. Charles Stuart (1811–80) was in Harvard's class of 1830, became a lawyer in New York City, then moved to Washington (*Harvard University Memoire: 1830* [Boston, 1886], p. 93; Harvard archives).

4. John Shepard Keyes (1821–1910), son of John and Ann Shepard Keyes of Concord, graduated from Harvard in 1841, became a lawyer, and was appointed judge of the Eastern Middlesex District. Emerson's son Edward married Keyes's daughter

Annie (Harvard archives). The "airy Buchanan" is unidentified, though perhaps he was Joseph Roades Buchanan (1814–99), later known for his pseudo-medicine (*DAB*).

5. Her aunt Abigail Crane of Canton.

6. Her brother Richard.

212. To Charles K. Newcomb

Jamaica Plains 18th April 1839—

My dear Charles,

I was both pleased and saddened by your letter. I am not sure that I understand your reasons for thinking it best not to write constantly to me. But you are right in supposing I could have no doubt as to their being such as would not displease me.

Indeed I think you are wise and that it could be of no profit. But, as far as regards my own convenience or leisure, my ear and heart will always be open if you desire to call upon me The tie that bound us was of a sort I never break, its hold was upon what is most real and permanent in both of us; I hope to see you true through life to the plan that pleased your youthful thought, and you, if my deed be inadequate, will not forget that my aim was high. You will always remember that what you felt in the unspoiled freshness of youth could not be delusion, and, however rarely we meet, yet when we do, if we converse less freely in words, yet there will always be a fresher flow of that inner life to which we are both, though in different ways, devoted.

You divined my estate while at Concord. After my release from *irksome* though *interesting* duties, it was happiness to give myself up to thought. I know not when I was most happy in the many hours of meditation I passed in the tangled wood-walks, or those of conversation with my friend whose serene and elevated nature I never came so near appreciating as now.

Since then I have passed a week at Dr Channing's much to my satisfaction. In their family was perfect repose and regularity. I was left to myself whenever I pleased and had conversation of real value when I wished. Many interesting topics were discussed Dr C. was reading Michelet's Life of Luther, and that naturally brought up the Reformation often.[1] We were led to fear that Luther appreciated the right of the individual to judge for himself as little as his followers do; that he only protested against the infallibility of a Pope and not against the infallibility of any *man* or *set of men*. He was a character of heroic strength, but scarce knew better how to reverence the soul than the sectarians who use his banner for their squabbles.

We talked too of this new church movement in England.[2] I allude to the Oxford coteri who share your desire for an universal church, and do not feel the force of Wordsworth's reply "When I am a good man, then I am a Christian".[3]

Dear Charles— I have spoken to your Mother of your coming to Cambridge. Why will you not? You would have access to so fine a library and would encounter a different current of opinion, and tone of thought from any you have as yet. I think a few months there might be of great use to you. You might get permission to go to the library and have sweets at will. You could walk every day in the quiet shades of Mt Auburn and think over what you had learned. You could be retired or see a great deal of the world as you liked and could at your leisure study[n] whatever of art &c Boston affords. Then sometimes you could come here, and I would show you the pretty lanes and picturesque rocks. Cambridge is the loveliest, quietest place in summer. If you are not to go to Newport I think you would be[n] far better there than elsewhere. So think of it a little.

I have seen Mr Bradley only once; but I think I should like him.[4] Your friend

S. M. FULLER—

ALS (MH: fMS Am 1086 [10:128]). *Addressed:* To / Charles King Newcomb, / Providence, / Rhode Island. *Postmark:* Jamaica Plain MS Apl 19.

leisure study] leisure ⟨see⟩ ↑ study ↓

I think you would be] I think ↑ you would be ↓

1. Jules Michelet, *Mémoires de Luther* (Paris, 1835).

2. The Oxford Movement was an attempt to return the Church of England to its Roman traditions, to infuse aesthetic qualities into its liturgy, and to remind the faithful of its historical traditions. The chief members of the "coteri" were John Henry Newman, John Keble, and Edward Bouverie Pusey (*DNB*; Owen Chadwick, *The Mind of the Oxford Movement* [Palo Alto, Calif., 1967]).

3. "I once wrote to Wordsworth to inquire if he was really a Christian," wrote Coleridge. "He replied, 'When I am a good man *then* I am a Christian'" (*Letters, Conversations, and Recollections of S. T. Coleridge* [London, 1836], p. 123).

4. Probably Charles Smith Bradley (1819–88), Brown 1838 (the class just behind Newcomb's), who was admitted to the bar in 1841, practiced law in Providence, was appointed chief justice of the Rhode Island Supreme Court, and then became professor of jurisprudence at Harvard (*The Historical Catalogue of Brown University, 1764–1934* [Providence, 1936]).

213. To [?]

Jamaica Plains
13th May, 1839—

I do nothing but go to the rocks to gather the wild columbines, or lie down by the gay little brooks, walk, ride, study and write a very little. I give myself up as much as possible to enjoyment of the fine weather, once or twice a week I visit the Allston gallery, and the pictures grow ever more beautiful to me.[1] I am sorry you were obliged to leave them so soon— [   ] I love my solitude. The picturesque part of my life has now withdrawn into the past, and the world for the future offers me nothing but work—

In the interval whh this summer offers I would do nothing but think and feel. But I delight to know what the children of my love, a fair and hopeful family, are doing—

MsCfr (MB: Ms. Am. 1450 [159]).
  1. Probably Harding's Gallery on School Street, which began an exhibition of Washington Allston's paintings on 24 April 1839 (*Boston Daily Advertiser,* 24 April 1839).

214. To Elizabeth Hoar

Jamaica Plains. May 15, 1839[n]

It is Blossom Sunday. The apple trees are full of blossoms, the golden willows too. I have found new walks, and a waterfall, and a pond with islands. But my feeling of beauty is superficial now, all these fair things are dumb compared with the last year. I long to feel them too. I feel near a faithful breast, yet gently put back by an irresistible power. I am like Ulysses near the loved shades. Write to me, dear E. I like when a friend has left me, to take up the next links. Since you went away, I have thought of many things I might have told you, but I could not bear to be eloquent and poetical. It seems all mockery thus to play the artist with life, and dip the brush in one's own heart's blood. One would fain be no more an artist, or a philosopher, or a lover, or a critic, but a soul ever rushing forth in tides of genial life, or retiring evermore into precious crystals, too pure to be lonely. A life more intense, you say, we pine to have. But we mount the heights of our being, only to look down into darker colder chasms. It is all one earth, all under one heaven—but the moment—the moment.

66

MsCfr (MH: bMS Am 1280 [111, pp. 57–59]). Published in part in *Memoirs*, 1:294; published entire in *JMN*, 11:469.

May 15 did not fall on Sunday in 1839. Emerson may have mistakenly changed the date from 12 or 19 to 15.

215.   To Hiram Fuller

Jamaica Plains
May 29th 1839—

My dear Mr Fuller,

I do not know that this book will be very interesting to you for its own sake, but, as being of the same date with my labours in Greene St, I thought it seemed to belong to your library there, and would look like a friend to yourself and those of my former pupils who are still with you.[1]

I cannot write at length in reply to your letter as I am today much fatigued and very busy— With affectionate remembrances to Mr Grinnell's family[2] yours

S. M. FULLER.

Please say to my former friends in the school that I think of them often and hope to see their pleasant faces again in the autumn.

ALS (ViU). *Addressed:* Mr Fuller.

Hiram Fuller (not Margaret's kin), a disciple of Bronson Alcott, conducted the Greene-Street School in Providence, where Fuller taught in 1837–38.

1. Her translation *Conversations with Goethe* had just been published in Boston.
2. William Taylor Grinnell of Providence was a merchant and prominent patron of the arts. He and his wife Abigail were friends of Fuller's during her stay in Providence.

216.   To Charles K. Newcomb

Jamaica Plain—
May 29th 1839—

My dear Charles,

I think you were right at first and that we had best not correspond. But, as I hope not to be forgotten for sometime, I shall hold myself in readiness to answer whenever you appeal to me for sympathy, or, if such I am able to give, for information.

Meanwhile I hope to see you here soon, to show you one of my beautiful walks, and to talk with you of the revelations which Nature has made and is making— I fear I do not know any English book that would be of use to you

How lovely is this weather! The frequent showers keep the earth fresh and delicate as a bride! You need not send me wildflowers, for I never saw them in such profusion as now. The columbine wreathes the foot of every rock, the wild geranium[n] purples the lanes, and the woods are absolutely paved with violets!— You will be very happy I am sure in seeing Mr Allston's pictures. To me the gallery has been a home.

I have time only for a note but you will soon be here. Believe me always yours affectionately

S. M. FULLER.

ALS (MH: fMS Am 1086 [10:129]). *Addressed:* To / Charles King Newcomb, / Providence / R.I.

the wild geranium] the wild ⟨p⟩ geranium

217. To Ralph Waldo Emerson

Jamaica Plains
June 3d 1839—

It is in vain, dearest friend, to hope that any letter will write itself to you. Many float through my mind, but none will stay long enough to be fixed on paper by Daguerroscope or elsehow. I am just at present, indeed, walking through Creation in a way you would nowise approve. The flowers peep, the Stars wink, the books gaze, the men and women bow and curtsey to me, but nothing nor nobody speaks to me, nor do I speak. Yet I seem to receive a great deal though I cannot call it by name, nor could I, at present utter it forth again unless I had the gift of doing so by "lyrical glances."— Mais le bon tems viendra, perhaps I might say *reviendra*[1] since you have deigned to be pleased with former letters of mine I heartily thank you for your encouraging word about my work and I pray you always to encourage me whenever you can.[2] But in truth I find much more done for me than I expected. To arrange with discretion rather than to divine will be my task. I find daily new materials and am at present almost burthened by my riches. I have found for instance all the Frankfort particulars in letters to Meyer. And Goethe's Darstellung-gabe lends such beauty to the theme that I shall often translate, and string rather than melt my pearls.[3] I do not write steadily for the subject keeps fermenting and I feel that the hour of precipitation is not arrived. Often a study is suggested and I pass several days in the woods with it before I resume the pen. It would make quite a cultivated person of me, if I had four or five years to give to my task. But I intend to content myself with doing it inadequately rather than risk living so long in the shadow of one mind.

I am about to oblige you to read Döring by asking you to send it me in two or three weeks.[4] You shall have that or any other of the books in a few months, but now I wish to see what is in it.

Thank you for the accompanying papers. The Ghosts spoke very lifelike to me who understand the language of Hades.[5] I grieved I had fettered myself by a promise so that I could not steal several sentences I liked. I have marked them and, if you be one half as generous, and sweet, and confiding as I, you will copy and send them to me.

There is a piece on Music in the last London and Westminster better than that by Dr Park which I showed you.[6] There does not seem to be any deep insight into the secrets of the art, but high cultivation, a very liberal and delicate taste and great descriptive power.

I have just recd a letter from Mrs Whitman of Providence, which I think so good that I would send it you if there were not so many compliments that it would make you quite faint and ill.[7] But I wish to quote one little passage about Goethe's Helena which pleases me.[8]

"A great part of this beautiful poem which is getting to be a great favorite with me is still an enigma, and perhaps will ever remain so, but it wins upon me so much that I often repeat pages of it to myself in the middle of the night and ever with increasing pleasure. When I first turned from Faust to Helena, it was like plunging into a cold stream when burning with fever— But the coolness soon becomes refreshing and the rich varied imagery of the flower fringed shores sooths and charms us as we float languidly down the current."

If your Blackwoods are at hand will you mark in your next letter the Nos in which Sterling has written.[9] I want them for Mr Ward.

Will you not come to see me. If you will come this week I will crown you with something prettier than willow, or any sallow. Wild geranium stars all the banks and rock clefts, the hawthorn every hedge. You can have a garland of what fashion you will Do but come. Has not Elizabeth told you fine things of our piney mountain.

Please give much love to Lidian, and your dear Mamma and the son and daughter.[10]

S. M. FULLER.

ALS (MH: bMS Am 1280 [2344]). Published in Rusk, *Letters of RWE,* 2:202–3. Endorsed: Margaret Fuller / June 1839—

1. "But the good time will come, perhaps I might say will come again." In his
journal, Emerson commented that *"lyrical glances* was a favorite expression" of Fuller's.
"It came from George Sand, who speaks of an artist whose ambition outwent his
genius;—'He always found himself obliged at last to translate into the vulgar language
"les élans lyrique de son âme"'" ("the lyrical bursts of his soul") (*JMN,* 11:497).

2. On 1 May Emerson wrote to her, "I know that not possibly can you write a bad
book a dull page, if you only indulge yourself and take up your work somewhat
proudly" (Rusk, *Letters of RWE,* 2:197).

3. Fuller had long admired the work of Johann Wolfgang von Goethe. At one point
she had planned a biography of Goethe but could not get the material she needed for
the book. She refers here to "Goethe an J. H. Meyer," in the sixth volume of *Über
Kunst und Altertum,* which Fuller would have found in vol. 3 of *Nachgelassene Werke,*
ed. J. P. Eckermann and F. W. Riemer (Stuttgart, 1832–42). Darstellunggabe: "power
of dramatic presentation."

4. As early as 1837, Emerson appears to have borrowed Heinrich Döring's *Goethe's
Briefe in den Jahren 1768 bis 1832* (Leipzig, 1837), for he quotes from the volume in his
journal for April of that year (*JMN,* 5:316). It is possible, however, that he had a copy
of Döring's *J. W. v. Göthe's Leben* (Weimar, 1828).

5. Possibly a reference to Emerson's manuscript of "Demonology," the last lecture
of his "Human Life" course, read in Boston on 20 February (*Emerson Lectures,* 3:151–71).

6. "The Pianoforte," *London and Westminster Review* 32 (December–April 1838–
39):306–56, a survey of piano music from Elizabethan England to the nineteenth
century. Dr. Park is probably John Park (1804–65), a Scottish minister and poet who
wrote songs (*DNB*).

7. Sarah Helen Power Whitman of Providence was a poet whose work and critical
opinions Fuller admired.

8. "Helena, zwischen Spiel zu Faust" had originally appeared in pt. 1 of vol. 6
of *Über Kunst und Altertum* in 1827.

9. Sterling had frequently contributed to *Blackwood's* in 1838 and early 1839: "Crystals from a Cavern" (March), "The Sexton's Daughter" (July), "Thoughts and Images" (August), "Land and Sea" (September), "The Onyx Ring" (November–January
1838–39).

10. Lydia (Lidian) Jackson married Emerson in 1835. His mother, Ruth Haskins
Emerson, lived with them in Concord. His son, Waldo Emerson, was a favorite of
Margaret Fuller's; the daughter was Ellen Emerson.

218.   To Eugene Fuller

Saturday eveg June 8th 1839—

My dear Eugene,

As your shirts have been returned today and Mother proposes

sending them on Monday, I will give you our journal up to this time. I think you left us overshadowed by clouds of surpassing blackness, which did not dissipate till the following Tuesday. At Cambridge Port you heard the history of poor Ellen Messenger. This made me really sad, though I did not know her, and did it not bring up in your mind a thought of Mary T.?[1]

I do not know that any thing occurred that would interest you till Monday. Sunday eveg J. Balch and Gardiner Weld called here to invite Ellen and myself to go out in their boat the following eveg.[2] They also wished me to invite all my former pupils from Miss T.'s.[3] I did so and her manner of refusing to let them come was such as to bring on the eclaircissement,[4] which, however, as I was otherwise engaged and could not see her did not take place till the following Wednesday.

We went in the boat with the Welds, Balchs and a Miss Jarvis to whom Dr Weld is *engaged*. The engagement came out this week. She is said to be a good girl, and, though far from pretty will, as you know, be a suitable pendant in that respect to her fiancé—

The row was pleasant enough, but the walk to and fro the pond so long, and, to me, so stupid that I shall rarely, if ever, tempt the wave with them, though the Dr was really most assiduous in pointing out the beauties of the margin,—or marginal beauties.

On Tuesday we were blest at last with a sunny day, and I did joy in it. I thought we had had enough of the weather you found so propitious to reflection. C. Sturgis came out in the aftn, we took a delightful walk and she staid all night. That night, too, Mrs Newcomb, from whom I had recd a letter to announce her advent, came. She was desirous to have some conversation with Miss T. about Charlotte and Miss T. coming here for that purpose and opening a conversation with me[5] We were led to discuss the past in presence of Ellen.

She was disposed to impute the chief blame to you and says you treated her very sadly when you went there last winter. She owned, however, to her desire to prevent our getting the house, and even to asking Mr Green to get the refusal for that purpose! But she gives as a reason her unwillingness to have Mary disquieted.— She was exceedingly shocked that I could suppose she would be unwilling to have the girls influenced by me, or intimate with Ellen, (towards whom however she showed in my opinion a decided dislike and hostility.) She had expected so high-souled a person as I to understand her better!! She loves Mother now, did love Ellen once, admires me and supposes she should love me if she knew me!!

I cannot, of course, give the particulars of a conversation that lasted more than three hours, and surely never lady talked more nimbly or with more force of epithet than she. The result of it was that I thought better of her inasmuch as I thought she had been able to justify her conduct to herself all through, but considered it according to my notions, unhandsome, indirect, and bespeaking a sort of character I do not like. I told her as gently and courteously as I could what I thought, but said that I regretted the pain I gave and would not, if I could avoid it, give any in future. She was quite overwhelmed at last, though thinking herself much aggrieved by these *base suspicions*. I told her I would not agree with her as I considered there had been cause enough to warrant or suggest them. Mother also stood her ground manfully considering that tears were shed. We patched up a hollow peace, and I trust there will in future be little or no intercourse. I feel much relieved that all has been said, at least on our part. I think I shall take back Emma and Charlotte the next winter.[6]

Wednesday, Thursday. Rain but Caroline Kuhn came here on Thursday and staid all night Friday, (yesterday) it was fair.[7] I went to Boston in the morng and went first to the Allston gallery. There I saw the Misses Ward from N York of whom I have heard so much. They were accompanied by their tutor, Mr Cogswell, and Miss Hall who paints miniatures so beautifully and their cousin and brother, so cried up for talent.[8] The eldest of these swains was frightfully ugly, both walked as if their backs were out of joint (which I take to be the present fashion) and wore their hair very long and curled at the edges, whether by the hand of Nature or Art I know not. The second Miss W. is not to be compared with Ellen for beauty, and if I could judge from the little I saw of the well known Julie she is inferior to E. in mind and as affected as she can be. I was inclined to be more worldly and low-minded than is my wont, and to murmur at the attention these wealthy damsels attracted when if poor Ellen had been there nobody would have noticed her, despite her beautiful face. I was introduced to Miss Julie, and Miss Hall, but went no farther. Mr Dana and Charlotte were there and the fair Anna Shaw—[9] I dined at Mr Ward's (S's father) with whom the dames and knights of the N. York exchange returned that P. M. Mrs Ward brought me home in aftn and went in to see Mother.[10] Charles Newcomb passed the night here. To day had been very fine and I have been very happy with my books. Rebecca Tillinghast is engaged to Dr Willing of Phila, large fortune, first conections, age 25, further the deponents say not as yet.[11]

Revd H. Bellows is engaged to some lady in N. York.[12]

Richard and Lloyd have both made short visits to Chelsea, and returned much edified. R. recd from Mr T. a silver pencil case "as a mark of esteem"! Jane is very unwell.

Mother is pretty well and in good spirits. Ellen's eyes are no better and she has a great deal of headach.

I have not seen the Ripleys yet and do not know how my book sells. In Providence all the copies sold immedy, and the people like it very much. I have recd a letter of praise from Mr Emerson which I value more than I should a voucher from any other quarter.[13] S. Ward says his father is reading it with great devotion and likes it much. I should think if he did, most would. When I write again I shall, probably, know more.

I will add a few lines tomorrow eveg—

Sunday eveg—

Nothing particular has transpired— I send the London and Westminster, wishing you to read and send it back in the course of a week if poss. It may be left with Belinda or I will go there for it.[14]

I should also like you to write me whether you should have time or money to go to Niagara, if I wished it. I have only the slightest notion of it and do not really think I can go, but shd like you to tell me whether it would be poss for you, if for me. I shd also like you to ascertain what would be the exact expense for each of us, and answer me on this subject *by Saty next*.— Very afftly yr sister

M.

A letter from Wm to Uncle A. more plausible than ever.[15] He will be home in a week or two.

ALS (MH: fMS Am 1086 [9:172]). *Addressed:* Mr Eugene Fuller / Groton, / Mass.

1. Ellen Gould Messinger (1819–39), daughter of Henry Messinger, died "suddenly" at Cambridgeport on 30 May (*CC*, 5 June 1839; "List of Baptisms and Deaths, Cambridgeport Parish, 1814–1820," MHi). Mary T. is not identified.

2. Probably Joseph Williams Balch (1819–91), son of Joseph and Caroline Williams Balch (she was a cousin of Margaret's father), and Christopher M. Weld (1812–78), a homeopathic physician in Roxbury. In 1841 he married Mary Ann Jarvis (1815–98), daughter of Edward and Nabby Porter Jarvis of Boston (Balch: Galusha B. Balch, *Genealogy of the Balch Families in America* [Salem, 1897], p. 310; Weld Harvard archives; MVR 483:511).

3. Catherine Brown Tilden (1807–82), daughter of Bryant P. and Zebiah Brown Tilden, conducted a school in Jamaica Plain (Linzee ms. genealogy, NEHGS, box 1, sec. 1; MVR 339:285; C. B. Tilden to James F. Clarke, 26 May 1840, MHi).

4. Clearing up, explanation.

5. Rhoda Mardenbrough Newcomb, Charles's mother, was a strong-willed woman who was part of the intellectual circle in Providence. Miss T. is Catherine Tilden; Charlotte is Mrs. Newcomb's daughter.

6. Emma Keats and Charlotte Newcomb.

7. Caroline Kuhn was the daughter of Nancy Weiser Kuhn, the half sister of Margaret Fuller's mother.

8. This is the first meeting between Fuller and the New York Wards (who are not to be confused with the Boston Wards—Thomas Wren and his son, Samuel Gray). Julia, later Julia Ward Howe (1819–1910), Louisa Cutler (1823–97), Ann Eliza (1824–95), and Francis Marion Ward (1820–47) were the children of Samuel (1786–1839) and Julia Cutler Ward (d. 1824). The cousin was Henry Hall Ward (1820–72); Miss Hall was Ann (1792–1863), daughter of Dr. Jonathan and Bathsheba Hall. The tutor was probably Joseph Green Cogswell (1796–1871), who had been librarian at Harvard and who later became superintendent of the Astor Library in New York City (Ward: *DAB*; *NAW*; Clifford B. Monalton, "Genealogy of the Ward Family," in *Correspondence of Governor Samuel Ward, May 1775–March 1776*, ed. Bernard Knollenberg [Providence, 1952], pp. 219–25; Hall: Clarence Winthrop Bowen, *The History of Woodstock, Connecticut: Genealogies of Woodstock Families* [Norwood, Mass., 1935], 6:550; Cogswell: *DAB*). Despite her cool reaction here, Fuller later became quite friendly with Julia Ward.

9. Richard Henry Dana, Sr., and his daughter Ruth Charlotte (1814–1901) (*Dana Family*, p. 505). Anna Blake Shaw (1817–1901), daughter of Robert Gould and Elizabeth Parkman Shaw of Boston, married William Batchelder Greene (1819–78) in 1845 (Francis G. Shaw, "Hon. Robert Gould Shaw," *Memorial Biographies*, 2:38–61; Hodgman, "Elias Parkman," p. 55).

10. Thomas Wren Ward and his wife, Lydia Gray Ward.

11. Rebecca Tillinghast married Dr. Charles Willing (1805–87) in 1840. Willing, the son of Thomas Mayne Willing of Philadelphia, graduated from Harvard in 1825 and from the Medical School at the University of Pennsylvania in 1828 (Harvard archives).

12. On 18 August the Reverend Henry Bellows (1814–82) married Eliza Townsend (1818–69), daughter of Elihu Townsend, a New York merchant. Bellows graduated from Harvard in 1832, attended the Divinity School, and was ordained in 1839. He was pastor at the First Congregational Church in New York City until his death. A gifted, often controversial orator, Bellows was prominent in reform movements (Thomas Bellows Peck, *The Bellows Genealogy* [Keene, N.H., 1898], p. 319; *Heralds*, 3:23–34).

13. On 7 June Emerson thanked her for her *Conversations with Goethe* by saying, "The translating this book seems to me a beneficent action for which America will long thank you. . . . The Preface is a brilliant statement" (Rusk, *Letters of RWE*, 2:201–3).

14. Belinda Randall, daughter of Dr. John Randall of Boston, was a long-time friend of Margaret Fuller's.

15. Abraham Williams Fuller, Margaret's uncle, was executor of her father's estate. She and Mrs. Fuller had quarreled with Abraham over the distribution of the money.

219. To Sarah Helen Whitman

Jamaica Plains
10th June 1839—

The very magnificient sunset of tonight—a violet curtain drawn aside to display a golden city with its citadel built up into the very central heaven, and the slight shower which came to melt all these gorgeous fabrics into one glistening canopy reminded me of a sunset we saw at Stetsons last summer and impels me to write to you, my dear Mrs Whitman. And speaking of sunsets, Have you read the Onyx Ring in Blackwood and do you remember the "violent and resplendent hour" there described. Mr Emerson thought it too theatrical. I liked it. This author, Sterling, who wrote also the Crystals from a Cavern and the fine poetical pieces signed Archaeus is a great encouragement to me. I see that the force of the human intellect is not all turned yet to tact and accomplishment, but that meditation broods and Genius flashes still. In the Onyx Ring there is an admirable side view of Goethe in the character of Walsingham. It shows a degree of refinement and insight beyond any thing I know on the same subject.— I am much pleased by your remarks on the Helena—pray give me your impressions whenever you can, in reading these works; they are just and delicate and will revive my interest. I hope you have read my translation of Eckermann, as there you will find several of your questions about Faust answered. I shd like also to know what you think of Goethe at eighty after having seen him (in Werther) at twenty three.

Your description of P. virtu amused me much. If you will come to Boston you shall see a genuine "Rambert" or what Mr Allston vouches for as such.[1] It is at the Atheneum Gallery and is called the Shipmaster of Amsterdam. There are also better copies than we are wont to see from Salvator, Poussin, Ruysdael, Claude Lorraine and Vandyke, and one very sweet picture, a copy from one of Raphael.[2]

I am nowise inclined to *faint* when I go to the Allston gallery, being always much exhilarated to see that any man has been able in our society to live true to such a standard. But I staid there too long one day, got one of my nervous spasms in the head and was obliged to send for a physician while on a visit. This[n] I suppose gave rise to the story, which, however, do not contradict as I think it makes me appear very interesting, something like the Chevalier Mozart[3] or— Amanda Fitzal [   ] Child of an Abby! But you really ow it to yourself to come to Boston and see Mr Allston's pictures. It is a bath of roses, potent enough to perfume one's earth for days and years of after life.

You wish to know my condition. I am as happy as I can be. My health is much improved. I have beautiful Nature, beautiful books, beautiful pictures, beautiful engravings, and retirement and leisure to enjoy and use them. My mind flows on its natural current and I feel that I have earned this beautiful episode in my Crusade. Nevertheless I doubt not that you, my dear Mrs Whitman are wise enough to enjoy the summer more than I do. The description of your unbought pleasures, was to me inexpressibly pathetic. O how equal is Nature, is

Fortune, could we but see, rather could we *feel* it— I *see* it well enough. But, for me, my desires dilate with my horizon! However I feel myself blest now in living at harmony with myself which I never did in your city. Your city however I think of with affection. I hear the fair Rebecca T. is to be married, pray present her my affectionate congratulations and please tell me about it when you write If you visit Boston, you must come and see me. I will show you my wild rocky walk, my grove of whispering pine, my little waterfall and answer all your questions. How is Susan?[4] She does not send me any message? Afftly yours

S. M. FULLER.

ALS (ViU). *Addressed:* Mrs S. H. Whitman. / Providence / R.I.— *Postmark:* Jamaica Plain MS Jun 10.

on a visit. This] on a visit. ⟨which⟩ This

1. Among the three Rembrandts on exhibition at the Boston Athenaeum Gallery was *The Master Shipbuilder and His Wife of Amsterdam*, dated 1633 (*Catalogue of the Thirteenth Exhibition of Paintings in the Athenaeum Gallery* [Boston, 1839]).

2. The exhibition had two paintings by Salvator Rosa, one each by Nicholas and Gaspard Poussin, one by Jacob Ruysdael (1628?–82), three by Claude Lorrain (1600–1682), seven by Sir Anthony Vandyke (1599–1641), and three by Raphael (1483–1520), including *The Holy Family*, which may be the one Fuller singles out.

3. Wolfgang Amadeus Mozart was named Chevalier of the Golden Spur by Pope Clement XIV in 1770.

4. Mrs. Whitman's sister, Susan Anna Power (1813–77) (John O. Austin, *One Line of the Power Family* [n.p., n.d.], p. 22).

220. To Jane F. Tuckerman

Jamaica Plains, [ca. 21?] June. 1839.

I have had a pleasant visit at Nahant, but was no sooner there, than the air braced me so violently as to drive all the blood to my head. I had headache two of the three days we were there, still I enjoyed my stay very much. We had the rocks and piazzas to ourselves, and were on sufficiently good terms not to destroy, if we could not enhance, one another's pleasure.

The first night we had a storm, and the wind roared and wailed round the house that Ossianic poetry of which you hear so many strains. Next day was clear and brilliant, with a high North-west wind. I went out about six o'clock and had a two hours' scramble before breakfast. I do not like to sit still in this air, which exasperates all my nervous feelings; but when I can exhaust myself in climbing, I feel delightfully; the eye is so sharpened, and the mind so full of thought. The outlines of all objects, the rocks, the distant sails, even the rippling of the ocean were so sharp that they seemed to press themselves into the brain. When I see a natural scene by such a light, it stays in my memory always, as a picture; on milder days it influences me more in the way of reverie. After breakfast, Mrs R. Ellen and I walked over the beaches.[1] It was quite low tide, no good waves, and the fine sand eddying wildly about. I came home with that frenzied headache that you are so unlucky as to know, and went to bed, and covered my eyes with wet towels. After dinner I was better, and we went to the Spouting-Horn. Cary was perched close to the fissure, far above me, and in a pale green dress she looked like the nymph of the place. I lay down on a rock low in the water, where I could hear the twin harmonies of the sucking of the water into the spout and the washing of the surge on the foot of the rock; I never passed a more delightful afternoon. Clouds of pearl and amber were slowly drifting across the sky, or resting awhile, to dream like me, near the water; opposite me at considerable distance, was a line of rock, along which the billows of the advancing tide chased one another, and leaped up so exultingly, as they were about to break. That night we had a sunset of the gorgeous, autumnal kind, and in the evening very brilliant moonlight, but the air was so cold I could enjoy it but a few minutes.— Next day which was warm and soft, out on the rocks all day. In the afternoon I was out alone and had an admirable place, a cleft between two vast towers of rock with turret-shaped tops. I got a ledge of rock at their foot, where I could lie and let the waves wash up round me, and look up at the proud turrets rising into the prismatic light. This evening was very fine; all the sky covered with crowding clouds, profound but not sullen of mood, the moon wading, the stars peeping, the wind sighing very softly. We lay on the high rocks and listened to the plashing of the waves. The next day was good, but the keen light was too much for my eyes and brain, and though I am glad to have been here, I am as glad to get back to our garlanded rocks and richly-green fields and groves; I wish you could come to me now, we have such wealth of roses.

MsCfr (MH: fMS Am 1086 [Works, 1:99–103]). Published in *WNC*, pp. 361–63.
1. Ellen may be either Ellen Fuller or Ellen Sturgis Hooper; Mrs. R. is unidentified.

Sarah Helen Whitman. Courtesy of the Rhode Island Historical Society.

221. To Caroline Sturgis

Tuesday eveg—
25th June 1839,

My dear Caroline,

I have this evening received your letter.[1] If I were to answer it according to my present feelings I should give you pain. And as I have never voluntarily done so for a moment from the hour you first came to seek me to the present, neither will I now!

I will let time pass and write when the hour seems to me to have arrived. It is not necessary that there should be any mutual understanding at present. I understand from Marianne that you are going to Mr Swain's soon, and we shall meet but little.[2]

But I asked[n] Marianne to come here to tea with you, during your visit to her[n] and I hope to see you both.

Whatever may be my opinion of future intercourse I have read too fair a page in your soul ever to cease offering for you the prayer of kind wishes and thoughts of honor.

MARGARET F.

ALS (MH: bMS Am 1221 [222]). *Addressed:* Miss Caroline Sturgis. / Summer St. *Endorsed:* 25th June 1839.

But I asked] ↑ But ↓ I asked
with you, during your visit to her] with you, ↑ during your visit to her ↓

1. The letter, now lost, clearly discussed some quarrel the two women had during their vacation at Nahant. Fuller was under great stress during this time, for her romance with Sam Ward was disintegrating.

2. The William Swain family in New Bedford, where Sturgis often visited.

222. To Caroline Sturgis

[28? June 1839]
Friday—

Your letter goes to my heart. Yet let me not answer it hastily. For reflections have passed in my mind which do make it doubtful to me whether we can continue *intimate*; *friends* we shall always be, I hope, after all we have known of one another.

It is not because I shrink from the pain or trouble, or because I am not willing to say the whole truth that I do not come out with all that has passed in my mind. It is because I have so much pride that I am always in danger of being unjust. And I have always wished to be not merely generous and tender but scrupulously just to you, Caroline. I feel that you have character enough to claim that I should think about you, and judge you by your own nature. In order to this I must put time and other objects between you and me. You, too, will know the state of your own mind better by and by. Let us wait. And meanwhile why should we avoid seeing one another? We cannot be, more estranged than we were at Nahant. And as I have asked Marianne, I hope you will come. So much as we have to control ourselves in life a lesson never comes amiss. We need not be false, nor need we be cold, and it is not desirable to attract the attention of others to any misunderstanding.

May heaven be with you and your soul be wise duly to appreciate its own position!

AL (MH: bMS Am 1221 [213]). *Addressed:* Miss Caroline Sturgis / ⟨Care of Wm Sturgis Esq. / Boston⟩ Brookline. *Endorsed:* 1839.

223.   To Caroline Sturgis[?]

July 1839

Could a word from me avail you, I would say that I have firm faith that Nature cannot be false to her child who has shown such an unalterable piety towards her.

MsCfr (MH: bMS Am 1280 [111, p. 82]). Published in *Memoirs*, 1:282, and *JMN*, 11:473.

224.   To Samuel G. Ward

July 1839.

No, I do not distrust you, so lately as you have spoken the words of friendship. You would not be so irreverent as to dare tamper with a nature like mine, you could not treat so generous a person with levity.

The kernel of affection is the same, no doubt, but it lies dormant in the husk. Will ever a second Spring bid it put forth leaf and flower? I can make every allowance. The bitterness of checked affections, the sickness of hope deferred, the dreariness of aspirations broken from their anchorage. I know them all, and I have borne at the same time domestic unhappiness and ruined health.

I know you have many engagements. What young man of promising character and prosperous fortunes has not one waiting his every hour? But if you are like me, you can trample upon such petty impossibilities; if you love me as I deserve to be loved, you cannot dispense with seeing me.

J'attendrai.¹ I will not think of you, but fix my mind on work. I cannot but see that never, since we were first acquainted, have we been so far removed from one another as at present.—

We did not begin on the footing of rational good-will and mutual esteem, but of intimacy; and I should think, if we ceased to be intimate, we must become nothing to one another.

We knew long ago that age, position, and pursuits being so different, nothing but love bound us together, and it must not be *my* love alone that binds us. I want a friend that could realize to me what is expressed in Byron's—"Though the day of my destiny's over, &c" And above all the line "Though loved, thou forborest to grieve me!"²

MsCfr (MH: fMS Am 1086 [Works, 1:179–81]).

Though the copy bears no salutation, the letter is clearly meant for Ward.

1. I shall wait for you.
2. "Stanzas to Augusta," stanzas 1 and 4:

> Though the day of my destiny's over,
> And the star of my fate hath declined,
> Thy soft heart refused to discover
> The faults which so many could find. . . .

> Though human, thou didst not deceive me,
> Though woman, thou didst not forsake,
> Though loved, thou forborest to grieve me,
> Though slander'd, thou never couldst shake. . . .

225.   To Caroline Sturgis

11 July 1839

[   ] one another, do justice to one another. If Fate has in store

81

for my Caroline a friend of soul and mind like mine of more equal age and fortunes, as true and noble, more beautiful and pure, I should accept what I have known of her as an equivalent for the little one situated like me can give. Otherwise I shall be faithful to you in my own way.

One word more lest my letter seem cold and rigid. Your letters move m unspeakably and, if I wrote wha I feel from one, my words would flow as balmy soft as tears. But I feel it is best to drop the heart for the present. I might—no matter what now. Let it be so.— Write to me when you feel like it. I also will write to you sometimes, but not always when I feel like it; it is not permitted me to make *that* my law. The hours of this summer, the first leisure summer since I I was of your age, and perhaps the last truly leisure hours of my life are to me the gold of Ophir, the spices of Ceylon. Since I came from Nahant I have been almost entirely well. I can use the whole day, and I am steeped in my thoughts no less than my occupations. Every now and then the grim face of Care peeps in at my casement, smiling ghostly at the hopes and plans I dare again indulge. She seems to say "I am called elsewhere now but do not think thou hast escaped; I shall have thee again soon." But I know that in each of these moments I put forth [   ]

ALfr (MH: bMS Am 1221 [223]). *Addressed:* Miss Caroline Sturgis, / Care of Wm Swain Esq. / New Bedford, / Mass.— *Postmark:* Jamaica Plain MS. July 12. *Endorsed:* July 11th 1839.

226. To Jane F. Tuckerman

Jamaica Plains August, 1839.

I returned home well, full of earnestness, yet, I know not why, with the sullen boding sky came a mood of sadness, nay, of gloom, black as Hades, which I have vainly striven to fend off by work, by exercise, by high memories. Very glad was I of a painful piece of intelligence which came the same day with your letter, to bring me an excuse for tears. That was a black Friday, both above and within. What demon resists our good angel, and seems at times to have the mastery? Only *seems*, I say to myself, it is but the sickness of the immortal soul, and shall bye and bye be cast aside like a film. I think this is the great step in life, to change the nature of our self-reliance; we find that the will cannot conquer circumstances, and that our temporal nature must vary its hue here, with the food that is given it. Only on the mulberry-leaves will the silk-worm spin its thread fine and durable. The mode of our existence is not in our own power, but behind it is the immutable essence that cannot be tarnished; and to hold fast to this conviction, to live as far as possible by its light, cannot be denied us, if we elect this kind of self-trust. Yet is sickness wearisome, and I rejoice to say that my demon seems to have been frightened away by this day's sun. But, conscious of these diseases of the mind, think that I can sympathize with a friend when subject to the same. Do not fail to go to Concord and stay with Elizabeth. Few live, so true, so sensitive, so penetrating, and yet so kind; she is the spirit of Love, as well as of Intellect.

MsCfr (MH: fMS Am 1086 [Works, 1:95–97]). Published in *WNC*, pp. 363–64.

227. To Elizabeth Hoar

Jamaica Plain—
17th August 1839—

Dearest Elizabeth,

I intended writing you[n] a letter to be enclosed in the pacquet I have been making up for Mr E. when it occurred to me that I had better write by post and ask you[n] to tell him that it shall be found as well as the Brentano vols. at Mr Adams Thursday by 10, morning.[1]

What I wished to say to you is this— I hear you are very unwell, and that, though you have had leisure this summer, it has done you no good. So I want you to go to the sea-side. I believe you have never been there, and you ought to try it, in the expectation that it may make an era for your mind. But when there is a chance that it may brace you again to strength and healthy sensation, and when you may combine the delight of renewed bodily health with that of new thought— O do try it—if only for the chance.

When my head is oppressed and a dry feverish heat irritates my skin and blood so that each touch and sound is scorpions and trumpets to me, take me, kind fairies, if ye can find a flower bell sufficiently large to hold me and carry me[n] in my sleep to where the tall rock casts its grotesque shadow on the yellow sand. There let the plash of the waves and the fanning of the sea-breeze awake me. That breeze is healing and cheer, mild and earnest it cools my brow, it soothes my brain, and new strings every sense. I can open my eyes for the lids are no longer heavy; I can gaze where brightest light loves to linger on the swelling waters, those streams of gold, those myriad diamonds are not too much for me who blinked but now at a sunbeam. You would feel so too, I think. And there how happy you will be when first embraced by the very arms of nature, your ear and mind filled, needing no thought but of the solemn harmonies of sky and sea, you will feel as if the mighty Mother had always before kept you like a little child studying the hornbook at her knee and that never till now[n] had you been near enough to feel the beating of her heart. And then, when the first raptures are over and you are no longer entranced but only wide awake in soul and eye what happiness to sit upon the rocks and see the beautiful poetic shapes, the phantoms of your hope advancing on the distant surge to greet you. It seems that they will be borne to your very feet, but no, not so shall Beauty be given us, but you shall see with your eyes Venus, sea born, of whom before you have only dreamed and love ever after foam and sea weed better than the reddest roses—which celebrate the loss of Adonis.

Will you not go, dear Elizabeth, and feel and see these things and others of which I know not yet. Could I give you any feeling what the Sea has been to me you would go. But go before it is cold, or you will not be happy.

I rejoice Jane is to visit you.

But do not have her while Mr E is gone I want him to know her.

I shall not come to C. till Mr E's return as Mr Alcott has been so lately, and it is not convenient to me.

Mr E can show you my Bristol journal if he think it worth your reading. But it does not tell the marvels of the sea, for there you do not get at it.

The Basilikum is in great glory; I have not worn any of it yet; reserving it for some fair hour, but have put a sprig as a book-mark into the Life of Raphael.[2] Will you not come to see it? I want to see you very much. Love to Lidian, to dear Mamma, and dear little Waldo. Is he lovely still? I almost fear to ask, for it is time for his human nature to be showing its ugliness.

Your faithful friend

MARGARET F.

ALS (ViU). *Addressed:* Miss Elizabeth Hoar, / Care Hon. Saml Hoar, / Concord / Mass— *Postmark:* Boston MS Aug 19.

Boston from Dorchester Heights, ca. 1839–40. From *American Scenery*, ed. N. P. Willis (London, 1840). Courtesy of the Pennsylvania State University Libraries.

intended writing you] intended writing ⟨t⟩ you
by post and ask you] by post ↑ and ask you ↓
and carry me] and carry m⟨y⟩e
never till now] never till ⟨k⟩now

1. Fuller sent Emerson an essay she had written on modern French literature, her journal of a trip to Bristol she had just made, and some journal observations on art and music (Rusk, *Letters of RWE*, 2:220; Robert N. Hudspeth, ed., "Margaret Fuller's 1839 Journal: Trip to Bristol," *Harvard Library Bulletin* 27 [October 1979]:445–70). She completed her package with Bettina Brentano von Arnim's *Goethes Briefwechsel mit einem Kinde* (Berlin, 1835). Bettina Brentano (1785–1859) was a peripheral figure in Goethe's literary circle from 1807 to 1811, the year she married Joachim von Arnim. Both *Goethes Briefwechsel* and her later *Günderode* (Grünberg, 1840) were fabrications. During Fuller's lifetime both books were widely read and admired (*OCGL*). Abel Adams (1793–1867) was Emerson's long-time friend and financial adviser (MVR 203:276).

2. Antoine Quatremère de Quincy, *Histoire de la vie et des ouvrages de Raphaël* (Paris, 1824).

228. To [Sophia Ripley?]

[I] Jamaica Plain,
27th August, 1839—

My dear friend,

I find it more difficult to give on paper a complete outline of my plan for the proposed conversations than I expected.[1] There is so much to say that I cannot make any statement satisfactory to myself within such limits as would be convenient for your purpose. As no one will wish to take the trouble of reading a long manuscript, I shall rather suggest than tell what I wish to do, and defer a full explanation to the first meeting. I wish you to use this communication according to your own judgment; if it seems to you too meagre to give any notion of the plan, lay it aside and interpret for me to whomsoever it may concern.

The advantages of such a weekly meeting might be great enough to repay the trouble of attendance if they consisted only in supplying a point of union to well-educated and thinking women in a city which, with great pretensions to mental refinement, [II] boasts at present nothing of the kind and where I have heard many of mature age wish for some such means of stimulus and cheer, and these people for a place where they could state their doubts and difficulties with hope of gaining aid from the experience or aspirations of others. And if my office were only to suggest topicks which would lead to conversation of a better order than is usual at social meetings and to turn back the current when digressing into personalities or commonplaces so that—what is invaluable in the experience of each might be brought to bear upon all. I should think the object not unworthy of an effort. But my own ambition goes much farther. Thus to pass in review the departments of thought and knowledge and endeavor to place them in due relation to one another in our minds. To systematize thought and give a precision in which our sex are so deficient, chiefly, I think because they have so few inducements to test and classify what they receive. To ascertain what pursuits are best suited to us in our time and state of society, and how we may make best use of our means for building up the life of thought upon the life of action.

Could a circle be assembled in earnest desirous to answer the great questions. What were we born to do? How shall we do it? which so few ever propose to themselves 'till their best years are gone by. I should think the undertaking a noble one, and if my resources should prove sufficient to make me its moving spring, I should be willing to give it a large portion of those coming years which will as I hope be my best. I look upon it with no blind enthusiasm, nor unlimited faith, but with a confidence that I have attained a distinct perception of means which if there are persons competent to direct them, can supply a great want and promote really[?] high objects. So far as I have tried them yet they have met with success so much beyond my hopes, that my faith will not be easily shaken, or my earnestness chilled.

Should I however be disappointed in Boston I could hardly hope that such a plan could be brought to bear upon general society in any other city of the U.S. But I do not fear if a good beginning can be had, I am confident that twenty persons cannot be brought together for better motives than those of vanity or pedantry to talk upon such subjects as we propose without finding in themselves great deficiencies which they will be very desirous to supply. Should the enterprize fail, it will be either from incompetence in me or that sort of vanity in others [III] which wears the garb of modesty. On[n] the first of these points I need not speak. I can scarcely have felt the wants of others so much without feeling my own still more deeply. And from the depth of my feeling and the earnestness it gave such power as I have thus far exerted[n] has come. Of course those who propose to meet me feel a confidence in me. And should they be disappointed I shall regret it not solely or most on my own account, I have not given my gage without weighing my capacity[n] to sustain defeat. For the other I know it is very hard to lay aside the shelter of vague generalities, the cant of coterei criticism and the delicate disdains of *good society* and fearless meet the light although it flow from the sun of truth. Yet, as without such generous courage nothing can be done, or[n] learned I cannot but hope to see many capable of it. Willing that others should think their sayings crude, shallow or tasteless if by such unpleasant means they may secure real health and vigor which may enable them to see their friends undefended by rouge or candlelight.

Since I saw you I have been told that several persons are desirous to join, if only they need not talk. I am so sure that the success of the whole depends on conversation being general that I do not wish any one to join who does not intend, *if possible*, to take an active part. No one will be forced, but those who do not talk will not derive the same advantages with those who openly state their impressions and consent to learn by blundering as is the destiny of Man here below. And general silence or side talks would paralyze me. I should feel coarse and misplaced if I were to be haranguing too much. In former instances I have been able to make it easy and even pleasant to twenty five out of thirty to bear their part, to question, to define, to state and examine their opinions. If I could not do as much now I should consider myself unsuccessful and should withdraw. But I should expect communication to be effected by degrees and to do a great deal myself at the first meetings.

My method has been to open a subject as for instance *Poetry* as expressed in
External Nature,
The Life of man
Literature
The Fine Arts
or History of a nation to be studied in[n]
Its religious and civil institutions
Its literature and arts,
The characters of its great men
and after as good a general statement as I know how to make select a branch of the subject and lead others to give their thoughts upon it.

When they have not been successful in verbal utterance of their thoughts I have asked for them in writing. At the next meeting I read these aloud and canvassed their adequacy without mentioning the names of the writers. I found this less and less necessary as I proceeded and my companions acquired greater command both of thoughts and language, but for a time it was useful. I hope it may not be necessary now, but if it should great advantages may be derived from even this limited use of the pen.

I do not wish at present to pledge myself to any course of subjects. Except generally[n] that they will be such as literature and the arts present in endless profusion. Should a class be brought together, I should wish first to ascertain our common ground and in a few meetings should see whether it be practicable to follow up the design in my mind which would look as yet too grand on paper. Let us see whether there will be any organ and if so note down the music to which it may give breath.

I believe I have said as much as any one will wish to read. I am ready to answer any questions which may be proposed Meanwhile put and will add nothing more here except always yours truly

S. M. FULLER.

I. Alfr (MH: fMS Am 1086 [9:61]); II: Msfr (MH: fMS Am 1086 [9:61]); III: AlfrS (MH: fMS Am 1086 [9:62]). MsCfr (MH: fMS Am 1086 [Works, 1:197–201]); MsCfr (RPB). Published in part in *Memoirs*, 1:324–28 and Higginson, *MFO*, pp. 112–13.

Sophia Dana Ripley, daughter of Francis and Sophia Dana of Cambridge, married George Ripley in 1827. She was a force behind the creation of Brook Farm and a participant at Fuller's conversations.

Though the middle part of the letter is not in Fuller's hand, the paper and ink are the same in all three parts. Possibly this is a draft, part of which Fuller dictated.

garb of modesty. On] garb of modesty. ⟨Of the⟩ On
thus far exerted] thus far ⟨has⟩ exerted
weighing my capacity] weighing my ⟨power⟩ capacity
can be done, or] can be done, ⟨learned⟩ or
studied in] studied in ⟨Religion⟩
Except generally] Except ⟨such⟩ generally

1. Each fall and spring from 1839 to 1844, Fuller conducted a series of "conversations" in Boston. These gatherings were designed to give women a forum for the development and exchange of ideas. Fuller led the discussions, giving her views and then drawing out the other participants. The conversations were highly successful, save for the one time when she included men in the group. Her audience included many of her friends, a number of women writers and reformers, and the wives of men prominent in social and literary causes. (Emerson provides a list of participants in *Memoirs*, 1:338.) The meetings were, by any measure, distinguished gatherings of minds. Sarah Clarke noted, however, that "there had been some fear expressed about town that it was a kind of infidel association, as several noted transcendentalists were engaged in it." A month later Clarke described how Fuller managed the meetings: "One lady was insisting upon her sex's privilege to judge of things by her feelings, and to care not for the intellectual view of the matter. 'I am made so,' says she, 'and I cannot help it.' 'Yes,' says Margaret, gazing full upon her, 'but who are *you*? Were you an accomplished human being, were you all that a human being is capable of becoming, you might perhaps have a right to say, "I *like* it therefore it is good"—but, if you are not all that, your judgment must be partial and unjust if it is guided by your feelings alone.' Thus she speaketh plainly, and what in her lies; and we feel that, when she so generously opens her mind to us, we ought to do no less to her" (Sarah Clarke, "Letters of a Sister," 17 November and 14 December 1839, MH: bMS Am 1569.3 [12]).

229. To Samuel G. Ward

[I] I believe,
in the first days of
Septr 1839

To—

You love me no more— How did you pray me to draw near to you! What words were spoken in impatience of separation! How did you promise to me, aye, and doubtless to yourself, too, of all we might be to one another.

We are near and with Spring's fairest flower I poured out my heart to you.— At an earlier period I would fain have broke the tie that bound us, for I knew myself incapable of feeling or being content to inspire an ordinary attachment. As soon as I saw a flaw I would have broke the tie. You would not— You resented, yet with what pathetic grace, any distrust on my part. *Forever, ever* are words of which you have never been, are not now afraid.

—You call me your best of friends, your dearest friend, you say that you always find yourself with me. I doubt not the depth of your attachment, doubt not that you feel my worth. But the confiding sweetness, the natural and prompt expression of attachment are gone—are they gone forever?

You do not wish to be with me; why try to hide it from me, from yourself? You are not interested in any of my interests. My friends, my pursuits are not yours. If you tell me of yours, it is like a matter of duty, not because you cannot help it, and must write or speak to relieve the full heart and mind.

The sympathizing contemplation of the beautiful in Nature, in Art is over for us. That for which I loved you first, and which made that love a shrine at which I could rest upon my weary pilgrimage.— Now—moons wax and wane, suns rise and set, the summer segment of the beautiful circle is filled, and since the first flush on the cheek of June we have not once seen, felt, admired together. You come here—to go away again, and make a call upon me in the parlor while you stay! You write to me— to say you could not write before and ask me why I do not write.— You invite me to go and see Michel's work—by myself! You send me your books and pictures—to ask me what I think of them! Thus far at least we have walked no step together and my heart deceives me widely if this be love, or if we live as friends should live:

Yet, spite of all this, sometimes I believe when I am with you, and, come what may, I will be faithful myself. I will not again draw back:

it shall be all your fault if we break off again. I will wait— I will not complain— I will exact nothing— I will make every allowance for the restlessness of a heart checked in its love, a mind dissatisfied with its pursuits. I will bear in mind that my presence is like to recal all you have need to forget and will try to believe that you would not be with me lest I "spoil you for your part on life's dull scene," or as you have said "call up the woman in you"

You say you love me as ever, forever. I will, if I can, rely upon your word, believing you must deem me entitled to unshrinking frankness.

You have given me the sacred name of Mother, and I will be so indulgent, as tender, as delicate (if possible) in my vigilance, as if I had borne you beneath my heart instead of in it. But Oh, it is waiting like the Mother beside the sepulchre for the resurrection, for all I loved in you is at present dead and buried, only a light from the tomb shines now and then in your eyes. But I will wait, to me the hardest of all tasks, will wait for thee whom I have [II] loved so well. I will never wound thy faith, nor repel thy heart, never, never! Only thyself shall have power to divorce my love from its office of ministry,— not even mine own pride shall do it. So help me God, as I keep this vow, prays

ISOLA.

I: ALfr (MH: fMS Am 1086 [9:60]); II: MsCfr (MH: fMS Am 1086 [Works, 1:87]). MsC (MH: fMS Am 1086 [Works, 1:183–87]). Published in part in Miller, pp. 50–52, and Chevigny, pp. 109–10.

Although the manuscript is folded in letter form, it is not addressed, and the To— in place of a salutation suggests that this is Fuller's copy of her original letter. The contents clearly show that Ward was the intended recipient.

230. To Elizabeth P. Peabody

Jamaica Plain
24th Sept. 1839—

My dear Miss Peabody,

I have been trying to answer your last letter, but have been so busy.

The Democratic Review is not what I want, yet I might like to put something there occasionally, and should like to be asked.[1] As to what my answer would be I would only ask of you, in addition to what you have already told me, an answer to these queries. Are they good pay (for I have heard the contrary)—?

Will they pay me *unasked*? or torture all my lady like feelings as almost all[n] other persons have with whom I have been concerned.— I thank you for thinking of me.

I have not been able to look at Mary's room yet, but think I shall probably accept your kind offer. My thanks to Mrs Park—[2]

Mr. Emerson's lectures are to be on Wednesday[n] eveg?[3] Why is Thursday preferred for the conversations, and was it so by you or Mrs Lowell?[4] for she, I understand, has not given her name.

In great haste yours

S. M. FULLER.

ALS (DLC). *Addressed:* Miss E. P. Peabody / Care Dr Peabody / Salem / Mass *Postmark:* Jamaica Plain MS.

Fuller met Elizabeth Palmer Peabody in the 1820s and apparently did not care for her. Their lives continued to mingle, however, for Fuller became Bronson Alcott's assistant at the Temple School after Peabody resigned. Fuller was also a part-time assistant to Dr. Channing, just as Peabody had been. Both women were members of the Transcendental Club. Peabody published the *Dial* for a time and also published Fuller's translation of Bettina von Arnim's *Die Günderode*. In 1840 Peabody opened a bookshop on West Street in Boston, where Fuller held her conversations.

feelings as almost all] feelings as ↑ almost ↓ all
to be on Wednesday] to be on ⟨Thursda⟩ Wednesday

1. *The United States Magazine and Democratic Review*, founded by John Louis O'Sullivan and S. D. Langtree, first appeared in 1837 and quickly became known for its literary quality by publishing Hawthorne, Bryant, and Whittier, and for its enthusiasm for Democratic politics. Sophia Hawthorne later remembered that, despite O'Sullivan's high ideals, the magazine was financially troubled, paying only $20 "for an article of what length soever" in 1837. O'Sullivan (1813–95), who became Hawthorne's good friend, coined the phrase "manifest destiny" (Frank Luther Mott, *A History of American Magazines 1741–1850* [New York, 1930], 1:677–84; Julian Hawthorne, *Nathaniel Hawthorne and His Wife* [Cambridge, Mass., 1884], 1:219; *DAB*).

2. Mary is probably Mary Peabody, Elizabeth's sister, who later married Horace Mann, the educational reformer. Fuller was on good terms with all three Peabody sisters: Elizabeth, Mary, and Sophia. Mrs. Park is unidentified.

3. Emerson began his "Present Age" lectures on Wednesday, 4 December 1839, and concluded the ten-part series on 12 February 1840 (*Emerson Lectures*, 3:175–315).

4. Harriet Spence Lowell (d. 1850), daughter of Keith and Mary Traill Spence, married the Reverend Charles Lowell (1782–1861) in 1806 (*Lowells of America*, p. 64).

231. To Caroline Sturgis

Jamaica Plains
7th Octr 1839.

My dear Caroline,

Your letter, for which I had often wished in calmer days, arrived nearly a week ago in the very first days of Anna.[1] At that time I could not even read it.— I could not think of our relation, so filled was I so intoxicated, so uplifted by that eldest and divinest love.

Yesterday she went away to stay two or three days, and I was obliged to take immedy to my bed, and am not yet really well enough to be up. The nights of talk and days of agitation, the tides of feeling which have been poured upon and from my soul have been too much for my strength of body or mind.— Even yet I cannot think of you, my Caroline. I cannot tell what I shall think or feel.

I write now" because else" you would not know why I was silent.

I do not know whether any time soon I shall recover from all the fatigue and various excitements of the past six weeks. I know not when I can free my thoughts from the poems which have oermastered them of late," but of this be sure, the first hour when I can meet you in a way worthy of us I will.

I loved you, Caroline, with truth and nobleness. I counted to love you much more. I thought there was a firm foundation for future years." In this hour when my being is more filled and" answered than ever before, when my beloved has returned to transcend in every way not only my hope, but my imagination, I will tell you that I once looked forward to the time when you might hold as high a place in my life as she. I thought of all women but you two as my children, my pupils, my play things or my acquaintance. You two alone I would have held by the hand. And with Mr E for the representative of religious aspiration and one other of Earth's beauty I thought my circle would be as complete as friendship could" make it.

How this hope was turned sickly, how deeply it was wounded you know not yet, you do not fully understand what you did or what passed in my mind.—" I will own that in no sacred solitary wood walk, in no hour of moonlight love had I been able to feel that that hope could recover from its wound. My feelings had not changed since you went away. I had not been able, much as I desired it, to take a different view of the past or future. But your letter has changed it. Your vow is registered in heaven.— I know not yet whether I can avail myself of it, but, oh, my Caroline, for mine you must ever be in memory of your first hours of real youth, blessed the Great Spirit, that it has been offered, that you have not been permitted to quench a flame upon so lonely, so ill sustained an altar.

Whatever is done shall be noble, be true. Only for a moment did I cease to love you. I wept at the loss you were to sustain in me. I would have given all but self-respect to save you. I said, World-wise, at least I can always be her friend in the spirit realm I will wait for her. O may it be that on earth I can walk with you.

—Write again and tell me when you will return and if it is not to be soon I will write to you when the good hour comes though I would much rather talk, there is so much to be told—

MARGARET F.

About the class it is of no consequence *to* decide. If after your return and knowing *from me* all the circumstances you wish it, I will receive you then. Mr E. has not asked why you did not write to him. He asked me of you, but I merely told him we were silent now by mutual consent.

ALS (MH: bMS Am 1221 [224]). *Addressed:* Miss Caroline Sturgis / Care Wm Swain Esq. / New Bedford / Mass. *Endorsed:* 7th Oct. 1839. *Postmark:* Jamaica Plain MS Oct 8.

I write now] I write ⟨y⟩ now
because else] because ↑ else ↓
oermastered them of late] oermastered them ⟨ut⟩ of late
for future years] for future ⟨hours⟩ years
more filled and] more filled ⟨than⟩ ↑ and ↓
as friendship could] as friendship ⟨would⟩ could
mind.—] *At this point Sturgis wrote in the margin: "At Nahant Margaret asked me if I loved her but I could not at once say yes"*

1. Anna Barker, who had been visiting just as Sam Ward rejected Fuller.

232. To A. Bronson Alcott

Oct 10th 1839.
[Jamaica Plain]

Dear Sir,

As you desired me to fix the day for our visit to Concord I write now to say that I can go a week from next Sunday, if that time would be agreeable to you.—[1] And if you should like to go then will you send me a note through the postoffice to let me know at what hour to expect you. The address is simply Miss S. M. Fuller Jamaica Plain. No Roxbury—when that is put on, the letters always go to the wrong office.

I am afraid the leaves will have fallen and the sweet South West be^n weary of blowing before this long expected Sunday arrives. But our friend at least will not disappoint us. He was here a day or two since and looked in much better health than on the day of many words at Watertown.[2]

yours with great regard

S. M. FULLER.

ALS (MH: 59m-312 [123]); MsCfr (MB: Ms. Am. 1450 [1b]). *Addressed:* Mr Alcott. / Boston.

sweet South West be] sweet South West⟨,⟩ be

1. Beginning in September 1839, Fuller, Alcott, Ripley, and Emerson discussed the possibility of a new literary journal. On 20 October, the day she here proposes, Fuller and Alcott went to Concord to discuss the planned journal. They returned the morning of the twenty-first. That evening Emerson wrote in his journal: "They brought nothing but good spirits & good tidings with them of new literary plans here" (*JMN*, 7:273). Thomas Wentworth Higginson, drawing on notes made by Alcott, says that the meeting was in response to a suggestion by Orestes Brownson that the writers contribute to his *Quarterly* rather than start a new periodical. The suggestion, if it was made, was declined (Higginson, *MFO*, pp. 147–48; Rusk, *Letters of RWE*, 2:225). By the end of the year, plans for the *Dial* were under way.

2. The Transcendental Club met on 16 September at Convers Francis' home in Watertown. Emerson ("our friend"), Alcott, and Fuller were among those who attended (Myerson, "Calendar," p. 204).

233. To Samuel G. Ward

15th Octr 1839—

My dearest S.—

Although I do not feel able[n] at present to return a full answer to your letter I will not do myself[n] the injustice of preserving entire silence.

Its sincerity of tone is all I asked.— As I told you hastily the last time I had any real conversation with you— I never should make any claim upon the heart of any person on the score of past intercourse and those expressions of affection which were the flower and fruitage of its summer day. If autumn has come, let come also chill wind and rain like those of today. But on the *minds* of those who have known me once I have always a claim. My own entire sincerity in every passage of life gives me a right to expect that I shall never be met by u[n]meaning phrases or attentions.

For the rest believe me I understand all[n] perfectly.[1] In some future step of our being you will feel that I did so. And, though I might grieve that you should put me from you in your highest hour and find yourself unable to meet me on the very ground where you had taught me most to expect it, I would not[n] complain or feel that the past had in any way bound either of us as[n] to the present. If I had not been able to sympathize with you, I should have felt myself free to show it, should have thought it unworthy of myself or you to do otherwise, of course I am willing you should do the same.

Truth and honor noble natures owe to one another, but love and confidence are free gifts or they are nothing.—

"The world has separated us as intimates and may separate us more"— 'tis true, but no more than I had expected though you, dear friend, were more hopeful as became the sweetness of your earlier age.— I had thought too, that in ceasing to be intimates we might cease to be friends. I think so no longer. The knowledge I have of your nature has become a part of mine, the love it has excited will accompany me through eternity. My attachment was never so deep as now, it is quite unstained by pride or passion, it is sufficiently disinterested for me to be sure of it. Time, distance, different pursuits may hide you from me, yet will I never forget to be your friend or to visit your life with a daily benediction. Nor can you, I feel it, while true to yourself be otherwise than true to me.

For these nearest[n] coming days—I cannot of course dictate to your spirit, yet as far as I can see I would say think of me no more at present. Give yourself up to the holy hour and live in the celestial ray which shines on you at present. O I could weep with joy that real life is lived. Do you not feel how I should grieve to be the ghost to cross the path of true communion in the Elysian grove. Live without me now. Do not bid yourself remember me, but should an hour come by and by when the curtain shall be dropped and the lights extinguished and you have any need of me, you[n] will find me in my place and find me faithful to you.

If you would wish to hear aught else of me, I may say that the day is "solemn and serene" as is its wont after a flood of noonday light and I am tranquil after the season when "many a feeling long, too long, repressed Like autumn flowers dared blossom out at last"

That I am very busy with affairs I had deferred till I could bend my mind to them, and so prayerful that I do not for the present need though I might be grateful for even your prayers.

With unchangeable affection

MARGARET F.

ALS (MH: fMS Am 1086 [9:63]); MsC (MH: fMS Am 1086 [Works, 1:187–93], MsCfr bMS Am 1280 [111, p. 160]). Published in part in *Memoirs*, 1:304 and in *JMN*, 11:487.

At the top of the first page, in Fuller's hand, is the notation: Copy, but not verbatim.
feel able] feel ⟨myself adequate⟩ able
do my self] do my ⟨heart⟩ self
I understand all] I understand ⟨it⟩ all
I would not] I ⟨could never⟩ would not
either of us as] either of us ⟨fr⟩ as

For these nearest] For these ⟨present⟩ nearest
of me, you] of me, ⟨it is well known that my ear and heart are always open to
you—⟩ you
    1. By this time it was becoming known that Ward was engaged to Anna Barker.
In his journal for 21 October, Emerson obliquely mentions the news Fuller gave him:
"To my private ear a chronicle of sweet romance, of love & nobleness" (*JMN*, 7:273).

234. To [?]

[ca. Autumn? 1839?]
[Jamaica Plain?]

The circle I meet interests me. So even devoutly thoughtful seems
their spirit, that, from the very first I took my proper place, and
never had the feeling I dreaded, of display, of a paid Corinne.[1] I
feel as I would, truly a teacher and a guide. All are intelligent; five
or six have talent. But I am never driven home for ammunition; never
put to any expense; never truly called out. What I have is always
enough; though I feel how superficially I am treating my subject.

ELfr, from *Memoirs*, 1:332.
    1. Heroine of Madame de Staël's *Corinne*.

235. To Ralph Waldo Emerson

Nov, 1839

I could not make those ladies talk about Beauty: they would not
ascend to principles, but kept clinging to details.[1] I have let it drop,
and shall take it up again by and by, if they get in train.

MsCfr (MH: bMS Am 1280 [111, p. 104]). Published in *JMN*, 11:477.
May be part of letter 234.
    1. At her conversation.

236. To Ralph Waldo Emerson

Nov 12 1839

Had the first meeting with my class last Wednesday and gave them a brief statement of my views and aims apparently not without success for they were intent and many (some strangers to me) said words of faith and cheer to me afterwards But tomorrow comes the real trial of whether they will talk themselves. There are some fine faces.

MsCfr (MH: bMS Am 1280 [111, p. 100]). Published in *JMN*, 11:476.

237. To Ralph Waldo Emerson

Jamaica Plain,
24th Novr 1839—

My dear friend,

Your letter brought me joy;— Mr Alcott was here when I recd it. He came out to pass three or four hours and it would have been a very pleasant interview but that I was under the influence of the concluding headach of a three weeks course. I have not now been troubled with one for nearly a week so that I feel both happy and wise, and could bring[n] the Finite much more resolutely in face of the Infinite than on that day! I had thought of going into town tonight to hear Mr A. discourse on *Genius,* but it rains and I will talk with you, instead of hearing him.[1]

I send you the canto in the poem[n] of Caroline which I half promised. I have had[n] many doubts about it, but finally I see so much beauty here that I cannot be willing not to share it with you, especially as I cannot hope to share it with any other person. I have given her last letter of the winter that you may better appreciate the flux and reflux of mind. Next to this read the two passages in my journal where I have turned the leaf, they were read by her and to the conversations which sprung from them several passages in her[n] letter refer. To make the whole complete you should see a letter of mine upon the wind; but neither C. nor I has that now. The little poem of Drachenfels in the marble paper book[n] also had much effect on her thoughts, it is to that she refers about the dragon voice![2]

I thought this chapter[n] out of my poetical journal might interest you now all the the verses, even the translns[n] bear some reference to Anna, W. and myself.

Those on Beethoven &c are very bad, but not without glimmers of my thoughts. If you wish to read the rest of the Winter Clouds, you must remember that it was a cloudy time; my sufferings last winter were almost constant and I see the journal is very sickly in its tone. Now I am a perfect Phenix compared with what I was then and it all seems Past to me.[3]

I hesitated about sending you any papers now because you are busy writing, but then I reflected that you would not wish your mind strained up to your subject all the day, but might like some grove of private life, into which you might step aside to refresh yourself from the broad highway of philosophy. All these papers I commend to your most sacred safe-keeping wherein they may continue for three or four weeks.—

I have not prepared Rakemann's programme as I intended.[4] He is coming here again and I will then send you *two!*[n] I shall not tell Caroline that I have shown you the letters till by and by when all is as past to her as to me.

I am sorry you read the wrong Sands first though in André there is a vein of the best in the two others is seen her[n] worst. Mauprat is at the shop now; it is worth your reading, but not your buying and they let them out by the week.[5] I shall get for you Les Sept Cordes de la Lyre, if ever it is in my power[n]

What is the Harleyan Miscellany; an account of a library?—[6]

Mille mercis for the tickets. I am too happy to think it will probably be in my power to use mine this year the others were delivered according to direction! You have really cheated me to send no notes on the pictures I shall expect very good lectures to make up for it

Will you not send me my friend Mr Sterling's letter. I will return it promptly![7]

M. F.

I thought to send Tennyson this time, but I cannot part with him, it must be for next pacquet. I have been reading Milnes; he is rich in fine thoughts, but not in fine poetry, and his Christianity is often forced in till it becomes what Mr Alcott calls noxious.[8]

ALS (MH: bMS Am 1280 [2345]); MsC (MB: Ms. Am. 1450 [69]). Published in part in Higginson, *MFO*, pp. 69, 94; published entire in Rusk, *Letters of RWE*, 2:238–40. *Endorsed:* Margaret Fuller / Nov. 1839—

could bring] could ⟨?⟩ bring
the canto in the poem] the canto ↑ in the poem ↓
I have had] I have ↑ had ↓
passages in her] passages in ⟨my⟩ her
the marble paper book] the marble ↑ paper ↓ book
thought this chapter] thought this ⟨book⟩ chapter
even the translns] even the trans ↑ lns ↓

then send you *two*!] then send you ⟨Here?⟩ ↑ *two*! ↓
seen her] seen ⟨here⟩ her
I shall get for you Les Sept Cordes de la Lyre, if ever it is in my power] ↑ I
shall get for you Les Sept Cordes de la Lyre, if ever it is in my power ↓

1. Emerson's letter of 14 November, which Fuller mentions here, discussed the new periodical, her conversations, and his reading of George Sand (Rusk, *Letters of RWE*, 2:234–35). Alcott and Fuller were exchanging journals at this time: he had given her his for the first half of 1839 when they met on 2 November; she gave him hers for 1837 when they met on the sixteenth. Alcott gave a series of lectures, "Interpretations of Christianity," beginning on Sunday, 3 November (Alcott, Journal, July–December 1839, MH: 59m-308 [13], pp. 377, 409–11). His subjects were "Conscience" on 10 November, "Incarnation" on the seventeenth, and "Inspiration" the night Fuller wrote her letter. ("Rained, not many came," wrote Alcott in his journal.) The "Genius" lecture was not given until 1 December (Alcott, Letter Book, 1836–50, MH: 59m-305 [2], p. 18; Journal, July–December 1839, pp. 392, 407, 429, 445).

2. Fuller's poem.

3. Here Fuller added later, "I have taken out some leaves."

4. During the 1840s both Ludwig and his brother Frederic William Rackemann (or Rakemann), sons of Daniel Rackemann of Bremen, Germany, gave concerts in Boston and New York. However, Frederic, the younger of the two, did not arrive in America until 16 October 1842, so Fuller's reference is to Ludwig. In much demand, both men played the pianoforte and the violin; John Sullivan Dwight called them "pioneers to us of the best classical and modern piano-forte music." In 1855 Frederic William (1821–84 married Elizabeth Dwight Sedgwick (1826–91), daughter of Charles and Elizabeth Buckminster Sedgwick (Hubert M. Sedgwick, *A Sedgwick Genealogy* [New Haven, 1961]; MVR 355:45; *Boston Evening Transcript*, 29 November 1842; Dwight, "History of Music," p. 428; Charles Sedgwick Rackemann, *Frederic William Rackemann: A Memoir* [n.p., 1885]).

5. In his letter, Emerson had given his reaction to Sand's *André* (Paris, 1835), *Leone Leoni* (Paris, 1835), and *Indiana* (Paris, 1832), but noted that he could not find *Mauprat* (Paris, 1837), which Fuller had recommended he read. He liked Sand's sometimes "authentic revelations of what passes in man & in woman," but he objected to her "sickness of the French intellect" (Rusk, *Letters of RWE*, 2:235). *Les sept cordes de la lyre* had, like many of Sand's novels, appeared in *Revue des Deux Mondes*, where Fuller had read it the previous summer.

6. Emerson's reading included two essays in *The Harleian Miscellany* for 1809. The *Miscellany* was a reprint of some of the tracts from the library of Edward Harley, second earl of Oxford. The original tracts had been edited by William Oldys and Samuel Johnson and published from 1744 to 1746.

7. Emerson told Fuller that he had received "the other day" a letter from Sterling, "which you shall see" (Rusk, *Letters of RWE*, 2:235).

8. Richard Monckton Milnes had published *Memorials of a Tour in Some Parts of Greece, Chiefly Poetical* (London, 1834), *Memorials of a Residence on the Continent, and Historical Poems* (London, 1838), and *Poems of Many Years* (London, 1838).

238. To Charles K. Newcomb

Monday eveg
Nov 25th [1839]

My dear Charles,

The past sunset brought you to my mind.— There had been all day a warm rain plashing in big drops from the South West. Just at sunset rolled back vast draperies of pure gold all over the sky and every leafless tree stood as if carved from Eldorado mine in the last glance of the divine Charioteer.

I often wish for you at sight of these glorious pageants. For it is most true, as you say, that you not merely *saw* but *felt* nature with me. And I think that we should sympathize even more now that your mind is freer and you have pierced nearer to the spiritual presence.

When we meet I think to have many things to tell you for my mind has been radiant with visions of beauty. But I do not know now when that will be. Meanwhile, my dear Charles, if you still value my friendship do not rashly lay yourself open to others. I valued your delicacy about intercourse and the sacredness of your life more than almost anything, do not let me suppose it infringed.

I take pleasure in forming your sister. I hope she will be your friend and companion, since I cannot be myself. I flatter myself she will be more to y[ou] for having been wi[th] me.

Let me introduce a new friend to you, Milnes, in whose poems I have of late been interested. If you read, write me what you think of them. Always, dear Charles yours affectionately

MARGARET F.

ALS (MH: fMS Am 1086 [10:131]). *Addressed:* Charles King Newcomb.

239. To [?]

25 Nov 1839

M[y] class is singularly prosperous I think. I was so fortunate as to rouse at once the tone of simple earnestness which can scarcely, when once awakened, cease to vibrate. All seem in a glow and quite as receptive as I wish They question and examine, yet follow leadings; and thoughts (not opinions) have been trumps every time. There are about 25 members, and every one, I believe, full of interest. The first time, ten took part in the conversation; the last still more. Mrs Bancroft came out in a way that surprized me.[1] She seems to have shaken off a wonderful number of films. She showed pure vision, sweet sincerity, and much talent. Mrs Josiah Quincy keeps us in good order and takes care yt "Xy" and "morality" are not forgotten.[2] The first time was the genealogy of heaven and earth, then the will (Jupiter); the Understanding, (Mercury)

Second, the celestial inspiration of genius, perception and transmission of divine law (Apollo) the terrene inspiration the impassioned abandonment of Genius (Bacchus) of the thunderbolt, the Caduceus, the ray, and the grape having disposed of as well as might be, we came to the wave, and the seashell it moulds; to Beauty, and Love, her parent her child

I assure you there is more Greek than Bostonian spoken at the meetings, and we may have pure honey of Hymettus to give you yet. I have been happy *a mourir.*[3] Four hundred and seventy designs of Raffalle in my possession for a week.

MsCfr (MH: bMS Am 1280 [111, pp. 101–(3)]). Published in part in *Memoirs,* 1:266, 331–32; published entire in *JMN,* 11:476–77.

1. George Bancroft's first wife, Sarah Dwight, died in 1837. In August 1838 he married Elizabeth Davis Bliss (1803–86), the widow of Alexander Bliss, Daniel Webster's junior partner (*DAB*; Davis, *Ancient Landmarks,* p. 83; *Boston Evening Transcript,* 16 March 1886).

2. Eliza Morton (1773?–1850), daughter of John Morton of New Jersey, married Josiah Quincy in 1797 (Edward Elbridge Salisbury, *Family Memorials* [New Haven, 1885], p. 366).

3. "Unto death."

240. To Caroline Sturgis

Tuesday 24th [December 1839]

My Caroline—

I think these are the verses you wanted. How are you this week? I am in one of my lazy studious moods, dreading my own thoughts, devouring those of others; today I have been so absurd as to read nearly a volume of Plato, and naturally I feel rather discomposed tonight.[1] I feel as if I had lost the day and want to use the night, if I could avail myself of my machines never to go regularly to bed I should like it. But I will not write any more of this, truly I am in danger of being a peevish one at last— this piece of ennui is almost too much.— But what I was to say is this.— Mr Schmidt proposes to bring Rakemann here next Thursday P. M. and to bring his own violin and play to us.[2] Will you come out in the morng omnibus and stay that day and night. There is a slight but I believe very slight uncertainty. Mr [Schmidt? said?] R. wished to come, but he doubted wh[ether] they could stay the eveg. I am sorry th I am not quite sure for I shd like to invite several persons. I hope you will come at any rate.— And I want you to see Mrs Ripley from whom I got a *jocose* invite to go to Rakemann's concert. Tell her it is to be Friday eveg, ask her if she is going and would like to take me and Ellen Grinnell with her; Ellen has an aunt in town with whom she can stay at night, but I want to take her with me to the concert. If she is not going cannot you make an arrangement (c'est a' dire secure a brother Hooper or Cousin Isaac and take us with you, for Eugene cannot go that night.[3] You can tell Mrs R. that I expect Rakemann here. I should like to have her come if she could, but I suppose she could not in the day. Farewell—if you cannot come on Thursday write me through the post about the concert. Tell Mary I am straining every nerve to raise two dollars Boston money for her, me[an]while she must *suspend payment*! [   ]

> The Bible is a book worthy to read,
> The life of those great prophets was the life we lead
> From all delusive seeming ever freed—
>
> Be not afraid to utter what thou art
> Tis no disgrace to keep an open heart,
> A soul free, frank, and loving friends to aid,
> Not even does this harm a gentle maid.
>
> Strive as thou canst thou wilt not value o'er
> Thy life. Thou standest on a lighted shore
> And from the waves of an unfathomed sea
> The noblest impulses flow tenderly to thee—
> Tell them as they arise and take them free.
>
> > Better live unknown
> >   No heart but thy own
> > Beating ever near,
> >   To no mortal dear
> > In thy hemisphere.
> >   Poor, and wanting bread,
> > Steeped in poverty,
> >   Than to be in dread,
> > Than to be afraid,
> >   From thyself to flee:
> > For it is not living

To a soul believing
All the noble joys
Which our strength employs
In a guise half rotten
To give a life to toys—
Better be forgotten
Than lose equipoise!⁴

ALfr (MH: bMS Am 1221 [232]). *Endorsed:* 1840.

1. The letter is dated by its contents. Fuller mentions here her reading of Plato, the same reading she reports in her next letter. Rackemann did play in Boston on Friday, 27 December 1839 (*Boston Daily Advertiser,* 27 December 1839). The only other "Tuesday 24th" would have been 24 November 1840, but by that date Eugene had already left for New Orleans.

2. Henry Schmidt, a violinist and piano teacher, began his career in New York, but moved in 1837 to Boston, where he became director of instrumental music at the Boston Academy of Music and led the orchestra until the 1842–43 season (Kinkeldey, "Beginnings of Beethoven," pp. 242–43).

3. Brother Hooper is probably Sturgis' brother-in-law, Robert Hooper; Cousin Isaac is probably Isaac Hinckley (1815–88), son of Hannah Sturgis Hinckley. Young Hinckley graduated with Eugene Fuller from Harvard in 1834 and became a railroad manager (Hingham VR; Thomas Cushing, *Memorials of the Class of 1834 of Harvard College* [Boston, 1884], pp. 76–78).

4. The verses are from Ellery Channing, "The Bible Is a Book Worthy to Read," later published in *Dial* 1 (October 1840):229–31.

241. To Ralph Waldo Emerson

26 December 1839
[Jamaica Plain?]

If you could look into my mind just now, you would send far from you those who love and hate. I am on the Drachenfels, and cannot get off; it is one of my naughtiest moods. Last Sunday, I wrote a long letter, describing it in prose and verse, and I had twenty minds to send it you as a literary curiosity; then I thought, this might destroy relations, and I might not be able to be calm and chip marble with you any more, if I talked to you in magnetism and music; so I sealed and sent it in the due direction.

I remember you say, that forlorn seasons often turn out the most profitable. Perhaps I shall find it so. I have been reading Plato all the week, because I could not write. I hoped to be tuned up thereby. I perceive, with gladness, a keener insight in myself, day by day; yet,

after all, could not make a good statement this morning on the subject of beauty.

ELfr, from *Memoirs*, 1:230–31. One sentence in MH: bMS Am 1280 (111, p. 101)
and published in *JMN*, 11:476.

242. To Caroline Sturgis

[1840?]

My dear Caroline,

When the thoughts connected with that page in my journal to which
I referred shall have ripened more fully I will tell them to you and
show you that record. I thought of doing so now, but on looking at
the passage I find that, standing alone, it would not make a true
impression on your mind.

When I am dissatisfied or feel repelled by any trait of yours I feel
also that I can wait. I see that your nature is as yet very little brought
out in proportion to its capacity. As eldest and most experienced I
ought to be willing to wait. I am rejoiced to meet a nature that
makes it worth my while to wait, to watch, to study. I promise myself to see you sometime both grateful and tender as now you are
sacred and true. I think the intimacy one of life-long promise even to
me; I know none at present of which I feel so rational a hope. For[n]
this has been redeemed from the search after Eros, and, in the pas-
sive repulsion on your side which sometimes grieves or chills me now,
I see a promise of future reaction which beings more liberal or more
yielding do not give.

W. also at times resists or leaves me, though in a different way
from you. He always returns, and so I think will you. I am of too
ardent and sympathetic a nature not to feel these mental raptures
keenly at the time, but where I see good reason I can be patient,
indulgent, attentive. And, apart from friendship, I feel it due to
myself to do justice to all fine natures.

With you, I would have no pedantry of nobleness or justice. I
would be spontaneous and free, but I would also feel that my years
more of life command me not to be rash, and sometimes to be silent
till I can[n] be sure you know and I know what is in[n] your mind.

I hope you will always write to me when such a letter as that of
Sunday rises in your mind, even when, as today, my response is

inadequate.[n] I think of you much. I believe I apprehend the secret of your nature, and that I shall know you as far as it is given to friendship to know. When my answer is not full; it is that the mind bids me bide mine own time.

I send the vol of Plato. If you find you wish to keep it more than two or three weeks, borrow it again of Mr Ripley in your own name. Theatetus I read with attention and great profit. In the midst of Philebus I was compelled to stop.[1] My mind seems to be revenging itself for the force it was kept under so long by all sorts of freaks. I console myself for so much unfinished work in the[n] consciousness that I never had so many thoughts as now.

Yesterday was the worst day! I could do nothing But in the night I awoke and thought out my problems with considerable success.

This question before the class of the process of composition with the poet interests me deeply. It is one on which I have thought much and now all seems fermenting to a new state. But I am writing too much. Adieu, my dear Caroline in faith and hope yours

MARGARET F.

ALS (MH: bMS Am 1221 [234]). *Addressed:* Miss Caroline Sturgis / Summer St. *Endorsed:* 1840–

hope. For] hope. ⟨?⟩ For
till I can] till I ⟨was⟩ can
what is in] what ⟨was⟩ is in
my response is inadequate] my response is ⟨inaquate⟩ inadequate
work in the] work ⟨by⟩ in the

1. Fuller's reading included the late dialogue "Philebus," an examination of pleasure and knowledge as good.

243. To Caroline Sturgis

Monday eveg, [1840?]

Dear Caroline,

I think what is poetical in your verses is of the purest tone. And even where most unmusical and unfinished they have the great beauty of being written to the dictation of Nature. The most irregular pulses beat with the mighty heart.

I hope you will be induced to perfect yourself in this mode of expression for the degree to which you have succeeded surprizes me. Your verse is almost as good as your best prose; with practice I think you would be most free in rhythm. Self-adopted chains well suit ambitious natures.

Some of these strains are to me of ineffable pathos. To live in your life is soothing and mystical to me even as the pine forest.— Show me whenever you can what you write, what you do. I shall not often answer it directly, for such is not my way, but each drop will swell the wave of thought, of life,—till you hear the rebound.

One thing I admire at in you is your steadiness of nature, how I am often and not least tonight tired to death of the earnestness of my life. I long to do something frivolous to go on a journey or plunge into externals somehow. I never can, my wheel whirls round again.

I build on our friendship now with trust, for I think it is redeemed from "the search after Eros"[1] We may commune without exacting too much one from the other.— Intercourse may be suspended at times, but not eventually broken off. Believe me worthy to know your nature as I believe you worthy to know mine. Believe as I do that our stars will culminate at the same point.

But think not, my Caroline, that thought can save thee from the grand mistake of sometime fancying that you love a mortal. Only *that* fire can burn away some useless parts of your being and leave the pure gold free! But it shall not beggar, nay it shall not impoverish you, for to a soul which has been true so long its horoscope stands sure.

I write hastily. I know not what daemon hurries my pen and makes me feel as if I stole time now when I write to my companions. I will not often write to you—directly, but will at times show you leaves from my journal. Of Ellery's verse I think not much; I am ill at appreciating a nature so noble, yet with no constructiveness and no force of will. Yet I take no vulgar view of him either. If clear thoughts come I will write them to himself. In hope that this night is a happy one to you, yours—(*how* you know.)

M. F.

ALS (MH: bMS Am 1221 [235]); MsCfr (MH: bMS Am 1280 [111, p. 82]). Published in part in *JMN*, 11:473. *Endorsed:* 1840.

1. Probably a reference to the poet Klingsohr's tale of Eros and his foster sister, Fabel, in chap. 9 of Novalis' *Heinrich von Ofterdingen*. After searching for Eros, Fabel finds him and commands him to end his destruction by awakening his lover, Freya. Fabel then rides the Phoenix in a celebration of love and rebirth.

244. To William H. Channing[?]

1840

Since the Revolution, there has been little, in the circumstances of this country, to call out the higher sentiments. The effect of continued prosperity is the same on nations as on individuals,—it leaves the nobler faculties undeveloped. The need of bringing out the physical resources of a vast extent of country the commercial and political fever incident to our institutions, tend to fix the eyes of men on what is local and temporary, on the external advantages of their condition. The superficial diffusion of knowledge, unless attended by a correspondent deepening of its sources, is likely to vulgarize rather than to raise the thought of a nation, depriving them of another sort of education through sentiments of reverence, and leading the multitude to believe themselves capable of judging what they but dimly discern. They see a wide surface, and forget the difference between seeing and knowing. In this hasty way of thinking and living they traverse so much ground that they forget that not the sleeping railroad passenger, but the botanist, the geologist, the poet, really see the country, and that, to the former, "a miss is as good as a mile." In a word, the tendency of circumstances has been to make our people superficial, irreverent, and more anxious to get a living than to live mentally and morally. This tendency is no way balanced by the slight literary culture common here, which is mostly English, and consists in a careless reading of publications of the day, having the same utilitarian tendency with our own proceedings. The infrequency of acquaintance with any of the great fathers of English lore marks this state of things.

New England is now old enough,—some there have leisure enough, —to look at all this; and the consequence is a violent reaction, in a small minority, against a mode of culture that rears such fruits. They see that political freedom does not necessarily produce liberality of mind, nor freedom in church institutions—vital religion; and, seeing that these changes cannot be wrought from without inwards, they are trying to quicken the soul, that they may work from within outwards. Disgusted with the vulgarity of a commercial aristocracy, they become radicals; disgusted with the materialistic working of "rational" religion, they become mystics. They quarrel with all that is, because it is not spiritual enough. They would, perhaps, be patient if they thought this the mere sensuality of childhood in our nation, which it might outgrow; but they think that they see the evil widening, deepening,—not only debasing the life, but corrupting the thought of our people, and they feel that if they know not well what should be done, yet that the duty of every good man is to utter a protest against what is done amiss.

Is this protest undiscriminating? are these opinions crude? do these proceedings threaten to sap the bulwarks on which men at present depend? I confess it all, yet I see in these men promise of a better wisdom than in their opponents. Their hope for man is grounded on his destiny as an immortal soul, and not as a mere comfort-loving inhabitant of earth, or as a subscriber to the social contract. It was not meant that the soul should cultivate the earth, but that the earth should educate and maintain the soul. Man is not made for society, but society is made for man. No institution can be good which does not tend to improve the individual. In these principles I have confidence so profound, that I am not afraid to trust those who hold them, despite their partial views, imperfectly developed characters, and frequent want of practical sagacity. I believe, if they have opportunity to state and discuss their opinions, they will gradually sift them, ascertain their grounds and aims with clearness, and do the work this country needs. I hope for them as for "the leaven that is hidden in the bushel of meal, till all be leavened."[1] The leaven is not good by itself, neither is the meal; let them combine, and we shall yet have bread.

Utopia it is impossible to build up. At least, my hopes for our race on this one planet are more limited than those of most of my friends. I accept the limitations of human nature, and believe a wise acknowledgment of them one of the best conditions of progress. Yet every noble scheme, every poetic manifestation, prophesies to man his eventual destiny. And were not man ever more sanguine than facts at the moment justify, he would remain torpid, or be sunk in sensuality. It is on this ground that I sympathize with what is called the "Transcendental party," and that I feel their aim to be the true one. They acknowledge in the nature of man an arbiter for his deeds,—a standard transcending sense and time,—and are, in my view, the true utilitarians. They are but at the beginning of their course, and will, I hope, learn how to make use of the past, as well as to aspire for the future, and to be true in the present moment.

My position as a woman, and the many private duties which have filled my life, have prevented my thinking deeply on several of the great subjects which these friends have at heart. I suppose, if ever I become capable of judging, I shall differ from most of them on important points. But I am not afraid to trust any who are true, and in intent noble, with their own course nor to aid in enabling them to express their thoughts, whether I coincide with them or not.

On the subject of Christianity, my mind is clear. If Divine, it will stand the test of any comparison. I believe the reason it has so imperfectly answered to the aspirations of its Founder is, that men have received it on external grounds. I believe that a religion, thus received, may give the life an external decorum, but will never open the fountains of holiness in the soul.

One often thinks of Hamlet as the true representative of idealism in its excess. Yet if, in his short life, man be liable to some excess, should we not rather prefer to have the will palsied like Hamlet, by a deep-searching tendency and desire for poetic perfection, than to have it enlightened by worldly sagacity, as in the case of Julius Caesar, or made intense by pride alone, as in that of Coriolanus?

After all, I believe it is absurd to attempt to speak on these subjects within the limits of a letter. I will try to say what I mean in print some day. Yet one word as to "the material," in man. Is it not the object of all philosophy, as well as of religion and poetry, to prevent its prevalence? Must not those who see most truly be ever making statements of the truth to combat this sluggishness, or worldliness? What else are sages, poets, preachers, born to do? Men go an undulating course,—sometimes on the hill, sometimes in the valley. But he only is in the right who in the valley forgets not the hill-prospect, and knows in darkness that the sun will rise again. That is the real life which is subordinated to, not merged in, the ideal; he is only wise who can bring the lowest act of his life into sympathy with its highest thought. And this I take to be the one only aim of our pilgrimage here. I agree with those who think that no true philosophy will try to ignore or annihilate the material part of man, but will rather seek to put it in its place, as servant and minister to the soul.

ELfr, from *Memoirs*, 2:26–31; also in Miller, pp. 62–66.

1. Perhaps a modification of 1 Cor. 5:6–7. "Your glorying is not good. Know ye not that a little leaven leaveneth the whole lump? Purge out therefore the old leaven, that ye may be a new lump, as ye are unleavened."

245. To Ralph Waldo Emerson

1840

I do not wish to talk to you of my ill-health, except that I like you should know when it makes me do anything badly, since I wish you to excuse and esteem me. But let me say, once for all, in reply to your letter, that you are mistaken if you think I ever wantonly sacrifice my health. I have learned that we cannot injure ourselves without injuring others; and besides, that we have no right; for ourselves are all we know of heaven. I do not try to domineer over myself. But, unless I were sure of dying, I cannot dispense with making some exertion, both for the present and the future. There is no mortal, who, if I laid down my burden, would take care of it while I slept. Do not think me weakly disinterested, or, indeed, disinterested at all.

ELfr, from *Memoirs*, 1:301.

246. To William H. Channing

Jamaica plain
1st Jany 1840.

My dear Mr Channing,

Enclosed is a subscription from Mrs Newcomb, Providence, R I, for the W. Messenger this year; will you see that it is forwarded for her?[n]

I write to inform you that there is now every reason to hope that a first number of[n] the much talked of new journal may be issued next April and to ask what you will give.[1] I have counted on you for the first number because you seemed so really in earnest and said you had articles ready written. But I want to know what part you propose to take in the grand symphony and I pray you to answer me directly for we must[n] proceed to tune the instruments. Mr Emerson is warmly interested and will give active assistance for a year. Mr Ripley and Mr Dwight are also in earnest for others I know not yet.

Will not Mr Vaughan give us some aid. His article on the Chartists excited interest here and we should like some such "large sharp strokes" of the pen very much.[2]

This is a business letter— Mr Ripley would have written you a better, but he is too busy fighting the battles of Spinoza and other infidels. I am going to Mr Emerson's lecture and have only one hour to write three letters.[3] So with best wishes for the coming year farewell,

S. MARGARET FULLER.

At Newport you prophecied a new literature; shall it dawn on 1840.

William Henry Channing. Courtesy of the Unitarian-Universalist Association.

ALS (MB: Ms. Am. 1450[36]). Published in part in Higginson, *MFO*, p. 149, and Wade, p. 555.

her?] *The salutation and opening paragraph have been heavily canceled by a later hand.*

that a first number of] that ↑a first number of↓

we must] we ↑must↓

1. Though the *Dial* had been actively planned since 18 September 1839, publication was delayed until July 1840. An infrequent contributor to the early issues of the journal, Channing did send "Ernest the Seeker" for the first two issues.

2. John Champion Vaughan (1806–92), a native of South Carolina, was practicing law with Edward P. Cranch in Cincinnati (typescript biography of Vaughan, OCHP). He wrote "The Chartists," *Western Messenger* 7 (October 1839):365–95.

3. For Ripley's latest controversy, see letter 247, note 3. Emerson read "Politics," the fourth lecture in his series "The Present Age," on this day at the Masonic Temple (*Emerson Lectures*, 3:238–47).

247. To Frederic H. Hedge

Jamaica plain
1st Jany 1840.

My dear Henry,

I write this new years day to wish you all happiness and to say that there is reason to expect the new journal (in such dim prospect when you were here) may see the light next April. And we depend on you for the first No. and for solid bullion too. Mr Emerson will write every number and so will you if you are good and politic, for it is the best way to be heard from your sentry box there in Bangor.— My friend, I really hope you will make this the occasion for assailing the public ear with such a succession of melodies that all the stones will advance to form a city of refuge for the just. I think with the greatest pleasure of working in company with you. But what will it be? will you give us poems or philosophy or criticism, and how much, for we are planning out our first No. by the yard. Let me hear from you directly.[1]

Except one scrap of a letter to Mr Ripley I have seen no word from you since you left us. But in the journal you will write to us constantly and of your best life.— I have little taste, myself, for this epistolary medium. It does not refresh like conversation, it does not stimulate, like good serious study or writing.

Were we near I should have a vast deal to tell you, but my life is rather a subject for a metaphysical romance than a gazette. I waste much time in sickness and am now again under medical care. Also I have a good deal of domestic care which I like quite as little. I have three young ladies with me to be carved into roses "with flowers and foliage overwrought." My class in town succeeds very well I think, but it breaks up my time a good deal. They talk as much as I could expect and seem deeply interested in the subjects. I think also of giving readings in Boston from Goethe's Miscellanies, if they collect a circle large enough to make it worth my while.—[2] When I am at home I write all I can, to what purpose time will show!

Mr Emerson is lecturing well; his introductory was noble. He makes statements much nearer" completeness than ever before; this all the audience feel.

The world is somewhat occupied with Mr Norton and Mr Ripley. The seeming mildness of Mr N's late rejoinder gives him at present the advantage, but Mr R. comes out again this week.[3]

I write in haste pray you write at leisure and forth with. With best wishes of the new year to Lucy,[4] believe me in hope, trust, and love always your friend

Margaret F.

ALS (MH: fMS Am 1086 [10:103]). Published in part in Higginson, *MFO*, pp. 149–50. *Addressed:* Revd F.H. Hedge, / Bangor, / Maine. *Postmark:* Jamaica Plain Jany 2.

Frederic Henry Hedge was the person Fuller most often turned to for help with her studies in German literature. When Emerson and his friends started a discussion group, they called it "Hedge's Club," for they met when he came to Boston from his pastorate in Bangor. Fuller was counting on Hedge to support and contribute to the *Dial*, but he became increasingly remote from her and the other Transcendentalists.

He makes statements much nearer] He makes ↑ statements ↓ much ⟨more⟩ nearer

1. On 16 January Hedge replied, abruptly setting himself apart from the new *Dial*. "You frighten me with your sudden announcement. I had scarcely thought of our project since I saw you last. . . . I should like now, if possible to have no other part in it than that of reader & subscriber. Forgive me therefore, if my first feeling after reading your letter was not one of unmingled satisfaction." Hedge then recovered himself enough to offer an essay for the first issue and to give Fuller advice on how to run the journal. He concluded by saying: "If I speak despondingly of my own share in this business, it is only that you may not count on me too confidently or too largely. For the rest, I need not tell you that my whole heart is with you, & that all I have of intellectual energy & of literary resource is at your command" (Hedge to Fuller, 16 January 1840, MH). The first of his four contributions, "The Art of Life,—The Scholar's Calling," was published in the second issue of the *Dial*.

2. In her journal, Fuller commented briefly on her readings from Goethe and Lessing. Describing the evenings as experiments that may lead to larger future meetings, she mentions Goethe's *Propyläen*, Lessing's *Laokoon*, and smaller essays and letters on painting and sculpture. Fuller met the group at least four times (Margaret Fuller journal, n.d., MH).

3. Andrews Norton and George Ripley had been quarreling in print for over three years. The professor had taken it upon himself to defend conservative Unitarianism against the heresy of such writers as Emerson and Ripley. In 1836 Ripley had written an essay on James Martineau for the *Christian Examiner*. Norton denounced the essay, and an exchange followed in the newspapers (*Christian Examiner* 21 [1836]:225–54;

Boston Daily Advertiser, 6 November 1836; *Christian Register*, 12 November 1836). Then in 1838 Emerson touched off an explosion with his address to the Divinity School. The following summer Norton replied in his own Divinity School address, which was published as *A Discourse on the Latest Form of Infidelity* (Cambridge, 1839). Ripley, in turn, attacked Norton; the two exchanged a series of "replies." On 4 January 1840 James Munroe advertised Ripley's *Reply to Norton's Remarks on Spinoza: A Second Letter*, the pamphlet Fuller mentions here.

4. Lucy Pierce married Hedge in 1830.

248. To Richard F. Fuller

Boston.
Jany 14th, 1840.

My dear Richard,

Always I am pleased with your letters, but am now also grieved at hearing from Mr E. that you take little or no exercise.— Why is this? knowing as you do, from the testimony of all men, that neglect on this score is sure of punishment. Do not fancy it will not hurt you, merely because you do not feel it at the time. For the sake of your own good sense and your affection for us, I beg of you [   ] before leaving Concord, you had better ask for it then. Of course you will want some to settle up your bills, but I suppose you will come here, be examined to see if you can be admitted and, if you can, return there to make arrangements for depart[ing] when you can also take the money. You come here to be examined by the middle of Feby,— do you not?

I cannot answer you yet about summer arrangements, as for many reasons I am still undecided about them. [   ]

ALfr (MH: fMS Am 1086 [9:52]); MsCfr (MH: fMS Am 1086 [Works, 2:641–43]).
The letter is torn in half across the page.

249. To Ralph Waldo Emerson

20 Jan 1840

The plan of selling the Journal by merit rather than by subscription strikes me very favorably. Shall you not have some pages on Shakspeare to give?[1] I wish each of us who knows anything about Shakspeare might give leaves on him, and see if there could not be some good comment if not criticism.

Since I came home, for very cold, I cannot read. I sit and look at the fire, or scribble pencil notes on little books, but my thoughts have a frostbitten meanness also; no flowers beneath the snow for me.— Yet here is a fine one on Shakspeare.

It has been justly remarked by Schlegel and other apprehensive critics, that, as all the world was in our Shakspeare, and he expressed the gift of the bard or seer with the tact of the man of the world, so there lies beneath very slight expressions of his thought a double meaning like that supposed in the Swedenborgian construction.[2] So that while the obvious meaning covers but a point, a line may be drawn from it to the limit of the Universe: As in this passage, so slight to a vulgar observer. "Old Signior, walk aside with me. I have studied eight or nine wise words to speak with you, which these hobby horses must not hear."[3] Are not all audiences assembled in hall of state, saloon, or lecture-room described in this fine compound term with a picquancy which requires the illustration of no other word. Is it not this term, and none other, which must ever after being once acquainted with it, rise in the mind, on each day's intercourse with the world? O admirable Shakspeare, who, having not even for a hobby thyself, didst not disdain to write for hobby horses.

MsCfr, in Emerson's hand (MH: Os 735Laa 1840.1.20). Published in Rusk, *Letters of RWE*, 2:248–49.

1. In the middle of January, Emerson had written Fuller telling her of his negotiations about the publication of the *Dial* with James Brown. Brown refused to publish the magazine if it depended solely on a subscription list; he insisted that it should "stand on the same footing as all the books they publish" (Rusk, *Letters of RWE*, 2:249). Emerson wrote no essay on Shakespeare for the *Dial*, but he did contribute his brother Charles's "Notes from the Journal of a Scholar," which contained a section headed "Shakspeare."

2. Between 1797 and 1810, August Wilhelm von Schlegel (1767–1845) translated seventeen of Shakespeare's plays into German. This labor, which contributed greatly to the study of Shakespeare in Germany, was accompanied by a series of lectures Schlegel gave in Vienna in 1808, later published as *Vorlesungen über dramatische Kunst und Literatur* (Heidelberg, 1809–11) (*OCGL*). The work of Emanuel Swedenborg developed a theory of "correspondence" in which physical facts were emblems of spiritual realities, an idea that became the foundation for the "Language" section of Emerson's *Nature*.

3. *Much Ado About Nothing*, III.ii.70–73.

Richard Frederick Fuller. Courtesy of Willard P. Fuller, Jr.

250. To Sarah Helen Whitman

Jamaica plain
21st Jany 1840.

My dear Mrs Whitman,

It has always seemed to me unnatural to write to more than one person at a time. Either I am quite engrossed in a correspondence or good for nothing in it. I am not excited by the thought as by the[n] face of a companion. I pray you forgive my being a bad correspondent in consideration of my being a ready talker.

Your article looks very fair in print and is, I am told, much commended, but I fear Orestes B. pays in nought more solid than praise.[1] Such was the case and, on beginning this year when he applied to several persons to aid him, I know[n] he offered no more glittering bait. But I will inquire.

There are few German books for sale in Boston, now Burdett has given up his shop. You will be more likely to find them at Behr's in New York.[2] The vol of Tieck could not I presume, be bought, you might get it from the library of Harvard university, if you have a friend there. I send you a book[n] of mine, one of Richter's finest works.[3] I think its fancy, humor, and sweet humanity will delight you. You can keep it till April, you will find it quite a study, for Richter loves to coin words, and seeks his thought even in the most distant mint.

You joke about my Gods and Goddesses but really my class in Boston is very pleasant. There I have real society, which I have not before looked for out of the pale of intimacy.[n] We have time, patience, mutual reverence and fearlessness eno' to get at one another's thoughts. Of course our treatment of topics is superficial but good, I think as far as it goes. I took up the Grecian mythology[n] as a good means of opening a vista to[n] the plain I sought and the topics were pursued thus.

Jupiter—	Creative Energy, Will.
Apollo—	Genius.
Bacchus,	Geniality
Venus Urania—	Ideal Beauty.
Cupid and Psyche,	Redemption of the soul by human experience.
Venus again	on which they wrote as well as talked.
Pallas.	very inadequately treated.

I then availed myself of a good oppory to drop the Mythology, and begin again by dividing the universe into Poesy,[n] Philosophy, Prose then Poesy (following Coleridge's classification) into Poetry, Music, Painting, Sculpture, architecture and the histrionic art.[4] We then took up Poetry and, after some consideration of its different forms, are taking up the poets. Shakspeare and Burns next time This in reference to some discussion of the words satire wit and humor called up by the question given out for last time, Whether there be any such thing as satirical poetry? I wish you would write and send me *your* definitions of poesy, poetry, wit and humor, fancy and imagination.

I wish you could come to town and be present at one of these conversations.

As soon as Mr Emerson's lectures are over I am to take that eveg to give readings from Goethe's works on the Fine Arts to a small circle.

These sort of things suit me very well. I also read some fine books, have now and then some thoughts and see some good people. So I am more good-natured than when you knew me, for then I had less leisure, less sympathy and less congenial pursuits. I still[n] intend to come to P. in order to show myself in this more favorable light, in April or May, probably. You must invite Lorenzo [Da Ponte][n] to meet me.—[5] By the way Belshazzar tarried on his way—did he see any fresh script of Upharsin—where is he!.[6]

I am sorry to hear such reports of my friend Miss—— I trow it is no part of Xty to deny your neighbor's claim to be religious his own way. But I dare[n] say she does herself injustice as was the case in the days of my acquaintance with her. She was inclined to insist, persist, and dogmatize too much in conversation, but in her heart I thought very desirous to do justice and find truth. Your circle at P. is too narrow and you are too close together and jostle too often to see one another fairly. I used to be much annoyed while there by habits of minute scrutiny unknown in wider circles and, meseems, very injurious to fairness of view.

I have now written all day and my poor fingers are sadly tired. This is a longer, if not a better letter than you ever before recd from me. I hope you will not be ungrateful but write soon to yours truly

MARGARET F.—

ALS (RHi). Published in *American Literature* 1 (January 1930):419–21. *Addressed:* Mrs S. H. Whitman / Providence / R.I.

as by the] as ↑ by the ↓
I know] ↑ I know ↓
you a book] you ↑ a book ↓ ⟨one⟩
the pale of intimacy] the pale of ⟨?⟩ intimacy

the Grecian mythology] the ↑ Grecian ↓ mythology
a vista to] a vista ⟨for⟩ ↑ to ↓
Poesy,] ⟨Poetry,⟩ ↑ Poesy, ↓
I still] I ↑ still ↓
"Da Ponte" is added by another hand.
But I dare] But ↑ I ↓ dare

1. Orestes Brownson was a minister and writer who often changed his intellectual position. He began as a Universalist and ended a Roman Catholic. He was known for his radical economic and political ideas in 1840. He founded, edited, and wrote almost everything in the *Boston Quarterly Review*. Whitman, however, reviewed Fuller's translation of Eckermann in the January 1840 issue (pp. 20–57).

2. James W. Burditt (1780?–1847) opened his stationery business in Boston in 1803. At various times he was a partner with James White and Joseph Roby (Boston VR; Rollo G. Silver, *The Boston Booktrade, 1800–1825* [New York, 1949], p. 22). Charles de Behr's bookshop at 94 Broadway, New York City, was the home of *Le Courrier des États Unis* and two other French papers (*New York City as It Is* [New York, 1840], p. 190).

3. Which of Tieck's books Whitman wanted is not clear, but presumably the Richter is *Titan*.

4. "On Poesy or Art," the thirteenth of Coleridge's 1818 lectures, was published in vol. 1 of *Literary Remains* (London, 1836). He grouped painting, sculpture, architecture, and music under the term "art," then called the fine arts "mute poetry, and so of course poesy (*Biographia Literaria*, ed. J. Shawcross [London, 1907], 2:253–55).

5. Lorenzo L. Da Ponte (1803–40), son of the poet who wrote librettos for Mozart, was professor of Italian literature at the University of the City of New York (Joseph L. Russo, *Lorenzo Da Ponte: Poet and Adventurer* [New York, 1922], pp. 104–5).

6. In the fifth book of Daniel, King Belshazzar sees a hand writing on a wall, "Mene, Mene, Tekel, Upharsin," which the prophet Daniel interprets as prophesying the king's doom. Whom Fuller means here is not known.

251. To Caroline Sturgis

Monday Feby 10th [1840]

My dear Caroline,

I begun this morning to mark those of your verses which I wished you to copy for me. But I soon found I was marking them all, for there were none which either for their own sakes or as marking *you* I did not wish to keep, did not feel that the moment would come when it would give me pain that I could not recal it distinctly.— Such being the case I must ask either that you will copy them all for me, or if that be too much exertion, choose yourself.— Do not omit at any rate those I sent to Anna. But if you can be generous *on great occasions* (as we hope always from those of your Spartan strain) I shall expect them all. If you can write as well on the paper I send, will you. I cannot read writing so well on the blue paper.

I restore Ellen's sweet though pale buds of daily life.[1] I should like

to see more of them, and wished I had been at liberty to keep these—
I have sent a letter of Dr Channing's which Ellen wished to see sometime since, and I have forgotten to show her. It does not contain
much, but I do not wish any other to see it.

I have copied for you (without leave) a little piece of S. W's to
which I am partial.

I do not feel like speaking of myself or my works today so fare
well.

I am not sure whether I can see you on Wednesday, but if I do
will read you two letters one from Charles Newcomb and one from
Michel Angelo!!

AL (MH: bMS Am 1221 [236]). *Addressed:* Miss Caroline Sturgis. *Endorsed:* Monday
Feby 10th 1840.

1. Caroline Sturgis' sister Ellen frequently contributed poetry to the *Dial*.

252. To Ralph Waldo Emerson

23 February 1840
[Jamaica Plain?]

I am like some poor traveller of the desert, who saw, at early morning,
a distant palm, and toiled all day to reach it. All day he toiled. The
unfeeling sun shot pains into his temples; the burning air, filled with
sand, checked his breath; he had no water, and no fountain sprung
along his path. But his eye was bright with courage, for he said,
"When I reach the lonely palm, I will lie beneath its shade. I will
refresh myself with its fruit. Allah has reared it to such a height,
that it may encourage the wandering, and bless and sustain the faint
and weary." But when he reached it, alas! it had grown too high to
shade the weary man at its foot. On it he saw no clustering dates,
and its one draught of wine was far beyond his reach. He saw at
once that it was so. A child, a bird, a monkey, might have climbed to
reach it. A rude hand might have felled the whole tree; but the
full-grown man, the weary man, the gentle-hearted, religious man,
was no nearer to its nourishment for being close to the root; yet he
had not force to drag himself further, and leave at once the aim of
so many fond hopes, so many beautiful thoughts. So he lay down
amid the inhospitable sands. The night dews pierced his exhausted
frame; the hyena laughed, the lion roared, in the distance; the stars

smiled upon him satirically from their passionless peace; and he knew they were like the sun, as unfeeling, only more distant. He could not sleep for famine. With the dawn he arose. The palm stood as tall, as inaccessible, as ever; its leaves did not so much as rustle an answer to his farewell sigh. On and on he went, and came, at last, to a living spring. The spring was encircled by tender verdure, wild fruits ripened near, and the clear waters sparkled up to tempt his lip. The pilgrim rested, and refreshed himself, and looked back with less pain to the unsympathizing palm, which yet towered in the distance.

But the wanderer had a mission to perform, which must have forced him to leave at last both palm and fountain. So on and on he went, saying to the palm, "Thou art for another;" and to the gentle waters, "I will return."

Not far distant was he when the sirocco came, and choked with sand the fountain, and uprooted the fruit-trees. When years have passed, the waters will have forced themselves up again to light, and a new oasis will await a new wanderer. Thou, Sohrab, wilt, ere that time, have left thy bones at Mecca. Yet the remembrance of the fountain cheers thee as a blessing; that of the palm haunts thee as a pang.

So talks the soft spring gale of the Shah Nameh.[1] Gentle Sanscrit I cannot write. My Persian and Arabic you love not. Why do I write thus to one who must ever regard the deepest tones of my nature as those of childish fancy or wordly discontent?

ELfr, from *Memoirs*, 1:289–91.

1. The *Shah Nameh* of the Persian poet Firdawsi (spelled variously in English translations) was an epic poem recalling the adventures of Persian kings. By 1840 numerous editions, versions, and paraphrases were in print. Fuller probably knew the translation by James Atkinson, *The Shah-Nameh of the Persian Poet Firdausi* (London, 1832).

253. To Charles K. Newcomb

Jamaica Plain,
24th Feby 1840.

My dear Charles,

Your letter gave me great pleasure and I have been hoping for time and thought to answer it as I would, but since I cannot find these I will e'en answer it from mere feeling that you may not wait too long.— You know how earnest I am in my pursuits and though I can turn at will to any subject in conversation, yet I cannot write upon any without getting deeply engaged. The questions you asked in your letter to me involved views so important that I must wait till I can talk with you in full; yet thus much let me say, that I deem if the religious sentiment is again to be expressed from our pulpits in its healthy vigor it must be by those who can speak un-fettered by creed or covenant; each man from the inner light— And as to baptism if it were the means of binding me to any sect I should reject it, for all sects as sectarian are unworthy, but, received sym-bolically, the rite is beautiful in my eyes. Would life indeed permit us to be purged by water instead of fire!

I rejoiced to hear you speak so steadfastly of your intercourse with other minds, and will be uneasy no longer. Charles will not disappoint me and profane his nature as some I had looked to have done.— But not often—my faith has sorely been wounded.

Do *you* not rejoice in this premature spring? I do, yet feel as if I scarce deserved it— This winter has not been to me very productive I know not— I have been so deeply engaged it would seem somewhat must have been done yet there is little outward token. My mind is always bright yet restless and[n] languid too. I feel tired of being always ill, always interrupted. I am sometimes[n] ready to wish for health as the one thing needful, yet then I check myself and am wise enough to reflect that no mortal will be over well pleased in this world who deserves another. Yet I know few can suffer at falling short of the ideal standard so much as I, for few have had occasion to raise it so high. O to achieve nobleness. Dear Charles, tarry not, sleep not, build up a palace in your life. Let me see others do it, others younger, sooner acclimated. But I will not talk lyrics on this key.

Remember me affecty to your mother and sisters. Charlotte is im-proving rapidly. I shall write about her when I have time. Expect to see me the second week in May. Your friend

M. F.

ALS (MH: fMS Am 1086 [10:132]). *Addressed:* To / Charles King Newcomb, / Provi-dence, / Rhode Island.

yet restless and] yet restless ⟨l⟩ and
I am sometimes] I am ↑ sometimes ↓

254. To Caroline Sturgis

Tuesday, [ca. March 1840]

My dear Cary,

The storm here is so violent that I shall not go to town.[1] Will you yet this once more let Mrs Channing know, and yr sister Annie too, if necessary, that I shall not come, but as I must be in town tomorrow shall give the reading tomorrow eveg[2]

I am better, but still not well at all, and I do not like to be exposed as I think I should be.

O this long snowy day! Had but one genius what works of beauty might be done! I have been writing a long essay. Here are Chapman and Tennyson, and Mr E's letter which give me tomorrow. Please keep this other parcel. I think I shall come to your house when I first get in tomorrow morng, and pardon trouble from your affte

M. F.

Perhaps this Sand will amuse you this eveg. I afterwards thought I would not send my other books.

ALS (MH: bMS Am 1221 [233]). *Addressed:* Miss C. Sturgis. Endorsed: 1840

1. The snowstorm Fuller mentions places the letter either in late winter or in the fall of 1840, but other details suggest the earlier rather than the later date: in her letter to Sarah Helen Whitman on 21 January, Fuller mentions her plan to conduct readings from Goethe as soon "as Mr. Emerson's lectures are over." His "Present Age" series ended on Wednesday, 12 February. He had sent her a copy of Chapman's *Homer* on 18 February (a Tuesday) (Rusk, *Letters of RWE*, 2:254). Then, since she was in Concord, not Jamaica Plain, that Tuesday, this letter must have been written on the twenty-fifth or later. On 24 February, however, Fuller wrote Charles Newcomb commenting on the "premature spring" weather. Thus the letter probably was written on one of the Tuesdays in March.

2. Ruth Gibbs of Rhode Island married Dr. William Ellery Channing in 1814. Anne Sturgis (1813–84) was Caroline's older sister (*Sturgis of Yarmouth*, p. 43).

255. To Frederic H. Hedge

Jamaica Plain. 10th March 1840

Henry, I adjure you, in the name of all the Genii, Muses, Pegasus, Apollo, Pollio, Apollyon, ("and must I mention"——) to send me something good for this journal before the 1st May. All mortals, my friend, are slack and bare; they wait to see whether Hotspur wins, before they levy aid for as good a plan as ever was laid.[1] I know you are plagued and it is hard to write, just so is it with me, for I also am a father. But you can help, and become a godfather! if you like, and let it be nobly, for if the first number justify not the magazine, it will not find justification; so write, my friend, write, and paint not for me fine plans on the clouds to be achieved at some future time, as others do who have had many years to be thinking of immortality.

I could make a number myself with the help Mr. E. will give, but the Public, I trow, is too astute a donkey not to look sad at *that*.

ELfr, from Higginson, *MFO*, p. 150.

1. *I Henry IV*, II.iii.16–18. Fuller's allusion to Hotspur's "By the Lord, our plot is a good plot as ever was laid, our friends true and constant," is ironic, for Hedge, like Glendower, failed to further the cause. This letter is her answer to his of 16 January, in which he offered his large family and low income as reasons for refusing to write for the *Dial*.

256. To William H. Channing

Jamaica Plain,
22d March, 1840—

My dear friend,

This eveg is not a very good time to answer your letter, but I must take it, *faute de mieux*, because I want to say to[n] you. Though your plan be a brave one, and I would wish to become acquainted with Ernest as speedily as possible, yet if you be not ready at once to commence your pilgrimage with him, send some short pieces.[1] I do not ask as James was wont for "bundles" of fine original compositions but make use of the modester words *some* or *several* and I pray you heed my request, for with[n] this first number we want room for choice. I have myself a great deal written but as I read it over scarce a word seems pertinent to the place or time. When I meet people I can adapt myself to them, but when I write, it is into another world, not a better one perhaps, but one with very dissimilar habits of thought to this where I am domesticated. How much those of us who have been much formed by the European mind have to unlearn and lay aside, if we would act here. I would fain do something worthily that belonged to the country where I was born, but most times I fear it may not be.

What others can do, whether all that has been said is the mere restlessness of discontent, or there are thoughts really struggling for utterance will I think be tested now. A perfectly free organ is to be offered for the expression of individual thought and character. There are no party measures to be carried, no particular standard to be set up. A fair calm tone," a recognition of universal principles will, I hope pervade the essays in every form I hope there will neither be a spirit of dogmatism nor of compromise. That this periodical will not aim at leading public opinion, but at stimulating each man to think for himself, to think more deeply and more nobly by letting them see how some minds" are kept alive by a wise self-trust. I am not sanguine as to the amount of talent which will be brought to bear on this publication. I find all concerned rather indifferent, and see no great promise for the present. I am sure we cannot show high culture, and I doubt about vigorous thought. But I hope we" shall show free action as far as it goes and a high aim. It were much if a periodical could be kept open to accomplish no outward object, but merely to afford an avenue for what of free and calm thought might be originated among us by the wants of individual minds.

James promises nothing but if I can get him here I shall expect some sound rough fruit of American" growth.[2] From Mr Emerson we may hope good literary criticisms, but his best thoughts must, I suppose take the form of lectures for the present.

But you will see I wish you were here that I might talk with you once. I cannot write well to any one to whom I do not write constantly. But we shall write constantly to our friends in print now. When I have finished "Ernest" I will seal and send a letter I writ you last summer provided it seems fit for an appendix to the record of your search.

My dear friend," you speak of your sense of "unemployed force."— I feel the same. I never, never in life have had the happy feeling of really doing any thing. I can only console myself for these semblances of actions by seeing that others seem to be in some degree aided by them. But Oh! really to feel the glow of action, without its weariness, what heaven it must be! I cannot think, can you, that all men in all ages have suffered thus from an unattained Ideal. The race must have been worn out" ere now by such corrosion." May you be freed from it! for me, my constant ill-health makes me daily more inadequate to my desires and my life now seems but a fragment. At such hours we take refuge in the All, we know that somewhere in Nature this vitality stifled here is manifesting itself. But individuality is so dear we would fain sit beneath our own vines and fig trees.

Farewell, pray write to me again if it suits you so to do. I should answer all the letters, a compliment I do not always pay. My respects to Miss Channing.[3] Mother and sister are not near me now, but they think of you ever with respect and love.

Yours

S. MARGARET FULLER.[n]

ALS (MB: Ms. Am. 1450 [37]). Published in part in *Memoirs*, 2:24–25, and Higginson, *MFO*, p. 309. *Addressed:* Rev. W. H. Channing / Cincinnati, / Ohio. *Postmark:* Jamaica Plain Mar 23.

to say to] to say ↑ to ↓
for with] for ↑ with ↓
fair calm tone,] fair calm tone, ⟨calm without⟩
how some minds] how ⟨a few⟩ ↑ some ↓ minds
I hope we] I hope ⟨wel⟩ we
American] *Three lines have been canceled heavily by a later hand.*
dear friend,] *this salutation and the previous paragraph have been canceled heavily by a later hand.*
have been worn out] have ⟨seemed⟩ ↑ been worn out ↓
ere now by such corrosion] ere now ⟨beneath⟩ ↑ by ↓ such corrosion
Mother . . . FULLER] *The final paragraph and the closing have been heavily canceled by a later hand.*

1. Channing's "Ernest the Seeker" appeared in *Dial* 1 (July 1840):48–58 and (October 1840):233–42.

2. Though they were close friends and aspiring writers, Fuller and Clarke wrote little for each other's journals: Fuller contributed nine essays and poems for Clarke's *Western Messenger*; he wrote the same amount for the *Dial*.

3. Apparently his sister, Lucy Ellery Channing (1809–77), went with Channing to Cincinnati (Higginson, *Reverend Francis Higginson*, pp. 31–32).

257. To Ralph Waldo Emerson

Apr 1840

When I look at my papers I feel as if I had never had a thought that was worthy the attention of any but myself, and some fond friend; and tis only, when, on talking with people, I find I tell them what they did not know, that my confidence at all returns.

MsCfr (MH: bMS Am 1280 [111, p. 88]). Published in *Memoirs*, 1:295, and *JMN*, 11:474.

258.   To Ralph Waldo Emerson

Jamaica plain,
12th April 1840.

My dear friend,

I received your letter, for which, as usual, thanks. They tell me in Boston that E. H. was much pleased with the medallion and I hope you are too.[1]

Caroline Sturgis has given consent that we should have the poems, and they will be sent from you that you may choose ethically or lyrically?[2]

I went last week to see Forest in Metamora.[3] I had forgotten till I came into the box that this was the same as King Phillip and then the contrast between[n] these paltry apparitions and my Mount Hope reveries made me laugh well. But Forrest is not paltry. He is a nobly formed man, and seemed to have the true Indian step and tone. 'Tis true I am not the best judge never having seen a fine specimen of the race but it seemed much nearer one's ideal than Cooper's or Miss Sedgwick's fancy sketches, and they say he[n] studied the Sioux carefully at Washington.[4] There was something tragic in the contrast between him and the people round him. The six or eight candlesnuffers who[n] represented the Yankee nation when they caught the hero at last looked like rats and weazels round a lion, and you felt as if any one might say in this present world, "I would not turn on my heel to save my life."

I should like very much to visit one of the tribes. I am sure I could face the dirt, and discomfort and melancholy to see somewhat of the stately gesture and concentred mood.

Yesterday was the first day of spring we have had since Feby. I went into the woods and read a little book called "Nature" through for the first time. 'Tis strange that it should be the first, but you read it to me originally, and so since whenever I have opened it I missed the voice and laid it aside. I was pleased to feel how much more truly I understood it now[n] than at first. Then I caught the melody now I recognize the[n] harmony. The years do not pass in vain. If they have built no temple on the earth they have given a nearer vi[ew] of the City of God. Yet would I rather, were the urn tendered to me, draw the lot of Pericles than that of Anaxagoras.[5] And if such great names fit not the occasion I should[n] delight more in thought living, than in living thought. That is not a good way of expressing it either. But I must[n] correct the press another time!

Knowest thou that a, young, publicly styled Reverend, has discharged[n] a paper-pellet from the intellectual stand-point of Charlestown, which doth cause several of that peculiarly nervous sect styled Transcendentalists to wink the eye-lid as one who feareth to be wounded.[6] Also that Rev A. Norton has been amusing his learned retirement by preparing more furniture for the book-sellers shelves.[7] Also that a new pamphlet cometh forth next week of which I have read some pages whilk seemed, to use Scotch Caution, *weel aneugh.*—[8] Also,—what would Mr Landor say who thinks those who love religion most speak of her least,[9] and would it not be well to go to Florence for a while, "Thither, Oh thither"[n] nor return till the dust be laid, and the champions had hurtled together in the arena. Truly people must have great care for their neighbors souls or great need of their neighbor's sympathy—tell me which. And tell me who is *my* neighbor. And tell about *your* neighbor, Mr Alcott's prospects, for I have a regard for him in my own way.[10] Yours always

M. F.

ALS (MH: bMS Am 1280 [2346]); MsC (MB: Ms. Am. 1450 [71]). Published in part in Higginson, *MFO*, p. 310; published entire in Rusk, *Letters of RWE*, 2:280–81. *Addressed:* R. W. Emerson, / Concord / Mass. *Postmark:* Jamaica Plain MS Apl 13. *Endorsed:* Margaret Fuller / April 1840.

contrast between] contrast ⟨p⟩ between
they say he] they say ⟨t⟩he
candlesnuffers who] candlesnuffers ⟨which⟩ ↑ who ↓
understood it now] understood it ⟨?⟩ now
I recognize the] I recognize⟨d⟩ the
occasion I should] occasion I ↑ should ↓
But I must] ↑ But ↓ I must
has discharged] has ⟨fire⟩ discharged
a while, "Thither, Oh thither"] a while, ↑ "Thither, Oh thither" ↓

1. Emerson wrote on 8 April discussing the contents of forthcoming issues of the *Dial*. Sophia Peabody had modeled a bas-relief medallion of Charles Emerson that pleased Waldo Emerson enough to have six copies cast (Rusk, *Letters of RWE*, 2:274–75; Louise Hall Tharp, *The Peabody Sisters of Salem* [Boston, 1950], p. 131). E. H. is Elizabeth Hoar of Concord, who was engaged to Charles Emerson when he died.

2. Caroline Sturgis became a frequent contributor to the *Dial*, but none of her poems was included in the first issue.

3. John Augustus Stone (1800–1834) wrote *Metamora or The Last of the Wampanoags* in 1829; Robert Bird revised it in 1836 for Edwin Forrest (1806–72). The play, a huge success with Forrest playing the lead, was performed on 6 April at Boston's Tremont Theatre (*DAB*; *Boston Daily Advertiser*, 6 April 1840).

4. Fuller had the story confused. Forrest had lived with the Choctaws. He became a close friend of Push-ma-to-ha, the tribe's chief, and became a student of the Indians' history (William R. Alger, *Life of Edwin Forrest* [Philadelphia, 1877], 1:126–28, 240). Catharine Sedgwick's Indians appear in *Hope Leslie* (New York, 1827) and in *Tales and Sketches* (Philadelphia, 1835).

5. The philosopher Anaxagoras renounced wealth and public honors in favor of meditation and philosophy. His student Pericles became the leader of Athens, making the city a center of art and literature.

6. With an uncharacteristic pun, Fuller alludes to the Reverend Alexander Young (1800–1854), whose wife was Caroline James, Fuller's roommate at the Prescott School in Groton. Young had delivered the discourse at George Ellis' ordination in Charlestown in March 1840. At that time, Young—the pastor of New South Church—aggressively attacked Platonism, intuition, and all the "naturalism, mysticism and pantheism" afflicting the church. He specifically claimed that "the truths of Christianity are not instinctive or intuitive, and consequently are not to be derived and communicated from one mind to another." It was indeed an attack on the Transcendentalists. The sermon was published as *The Church, the Pulpit, and the Gospel* (Boston, 1840) and offered for sale on 2 April 1840 (*DAB*).

7. Andrews Norton edited *Two Articles from the Princeton Review, Concerning the Transcendental Philosophy of the Germans and of Cousin, and Its Influence on Opinion in This Country* (Cambridge, 1840).

8. Fuller must have seen *A Letter to Andrews Norton, on Miracles as the Foundation of Religious Faith*, published by Weeks, Jordan and Company on April 24, though just how she got the pamphlet is unclear. The anonymous pamphlet was written by Richard Hildreth (1807–65), later known for his *History of the United States* (*DAB*).

9. Walter Savage Landor, "Washington and Franklin": "[God] has placed us where our time may be more beneficially employed in mutually kind offices, and he does not desire us to tell him, hour after hour, how dearly we love him" (*The Works of Walter Savage Landor* [London, 1927–36], 7:28–29). Landor (1775–1864) was a poet, dramatist, and author of numerous fictional "conversations" that Fuller read with enthusiasm (*DNB*).

10. The Alcotts had just moved to Concord. According to Emerson's answer to Fuller's query, Alcott "is thus far very well pleased with his house & his new condition & says that for the first time for years Mrs A. goes singing about the house. Only he finds this step he has taken so popular that he distrusts it" (Rusk, *Letters of RWE,* 2:281).

259.   To William H. Channing

Jamaica Plain
19th April 1840

My dear friend,

I received and read[n] a day or two since your folio sheet with great delight.[1] I am very glad you have begun at once on your new plan instead of sending last year's fallen leaves; I am much pleased with the first chapter and hope you will keep Constant in Rome some time. I want to send you some notes of my own on the Sybil and Prophet you speak of, but there is not room on this little sheet. When I can afford to buy one of those large ones, perhaps I will, unless indeed I publish them with a string of other Americanisms upon Michel; I will not promise to correct well for you myself, for I am ignorant and careless in these details, but you may be sure Mr R. will be miserable if there is a comma amiss, and he is to be the corrective as I the [*illegible*] element in this new organization. I do not expect to be of much use except to urge on the laggards, and scold the lukewarm, and act Helen Mac Gregor to those who love compromise, by doing my little best to sink them in the waters of Oblivion!![2]

Things go on pretty well, but I dare say people will be disappointed, for they seem to be looking for the gospel of transcendentalism. It may prove as your Jouffroy says it is with the French ministry; the public wants something positive, and finding such and such persons excellent at fault finding raises them to be the rulers, when lo! they have no noble and full Yea, to match their shrill and bold Nay, and are hurled down again—[3] Mr Emerson knows best what he wants but he[n] has already said it in various ways.— Yet I deem the experiment is well worth trying; hearts beat so high, they must be full of something, and here is a way to breathe it out quite freely.— It is for dear New England that I wanted this review; for myself, if I had wished to write a few pages now and then, I had ways and means of disposing of them. But in truth I have not much to say, for since I have had leisure to look at myself I find that, so far from being a great original genius, I have not yet learned to think to any depth, and that the utmost I have done in life has been to form my character to a certain consistency, cultivate my tastes, and learn to tell[n] the truth with a little better grace than I did at first. For this the world will not care much, so I shall only hazard a few critical remarks, or an un[pre]tending chalk sketch now and then, till I have learned to do something. There will be some beautiful *poesies* about prose I know not yet so well. We shall be the means of publishing the little Charles Emerson left as a mark of his noble course, and though it lies in fragments you will think yourself a gainer by it I am sure.[n4]

Please when you write to James tell him he must write me a better letter before I write to him, for that I thought when I opened his last some[n] one had sent me a leaf from a copy book, the lines were so far apart, also that I sit here at my window waiting for his poem. I hope James will come here and live, albeit he must leave you to do it.

I suppose you hear all that would interest you that is doing here, for I know you have excellent correspondents, so I have egotized quite at my ease. Your dear mother I did see *often* and had hoped to see *much,* but though I was with her so often, yet, on those evegs when I gave the readings at her room I never once was well enough to talk with her after. But it is a pleasure to me even to see her face which lights up with the same noble, youthful earnestness—as in former days when there is any good thought living near her. But she rather slandered you, I think, for she spoke of you as a man of more plan than[n] performance. I shall go and tell her what admirable promptitude you have shown. My dear Mr Channing, you must not write to me again unless you wish, for I remember you told me you did not like to write letters, but, if you do, I hope you will tell me about yourself and your various relations. You will not now misunderstand me or think I live in a mere intellectual curiosity surely, yet ah! how many more times you must misunderstand before ever you know me, I felt when last we met. But I shall have your true friendship sometime, I am sure, in faith and hope yours

M F

ALS (MB: Ms. Am. 1450 [38]). Published in part in *Memoirs*, 2:25–26, and Higginson, *MFO*, p. 151. *Addressed:* Rev W. H. Channing / Cincinnati, / Ohio. *Postmark:* Jamaica Plain MS Apr 20.

The entire first page has been canceled by a later hand.
I received and read] I received ↑ and read ↓
he wants but he] he wants ⟨and⟩ ↑ but ↓ he
and learn to tell] and ↑ learn to ↓ tell
sure.] *Three lines are here canceled by a later hand.*
I opened his last some] I opened ⟨it⟩ ↑ his last ↓ some
than] *One and one-half lines are here canceled by a later hand.*

1. Channing's manuscript of "Ernest the Seeker."
2. Helen MacGregor, Rob Roy's wife in Scott's novel (Edinburgh, 1818), is a fierce woman who threatens destruction to any who oppose her or her husband. Fuller's reference is probably to chap. 32, where Helen demands Rob Roy's release in extreme terms.
3. Channing's translation of Théodore Jouffroy's *Introduction to Ethics, Including a Critical Survey of Moral Systems* (Boston, 1840), vols. 5 and 6 of Ripley's *Specimens of Foreign Standard Literature*, was reviewed by W. D. Wilson in the first *Dial*, pp. 99–117.
4. "Notes from the Journal of a Scholar," *Dial* 1 (July 1840):13–16.

260. To Ralph Waldo Emerson

Jamaica plain
Saturday eveg [25 April] 1840—

My dear friend,— I have received the parcel.[1] It is no wish of mine to have an introduction or to write it, and all that you say on that score[n] had occurred to me, but Mr Ripley and the publishers both thought it very desirable. I shall show Mr R. what you have written and talk with him once more— Those parts you thought too fierce, he thought not sufficiently so. I know not whether I can find the golden mean between you. What you have written pleases me greatly. But if we call on you for a prologue, it will be in a few days for they want it, I think the[n] week after the next. I shall write again after I have seen Boston.

I have been reading over the "Notes" which please me more and more. The omission of that verse in the poem mars it greatly. But I suppose[n] I would not that you had[n] done differently; these journals have something of the market-place vulgarity after all, and I like to see that these priests[n] of the Universal Soul have also respect for the shrine and the reliquary as well as we Romanists.

Tis pity I should not write in straight lines. But I merely let my hand write. I feel delightfully indolent.— Is not this weather "gar zu lieblich"?[2] It has taken away all my pain and raised me at once to the heights of bliss where I passed so much of last summer. Yet with all the sweetness I am somewhat saddened to find that[n] high and beautiful mood was from a state of health.— It is quite the same as if I had died and the spirit had put on a new elastic form without losing one of its memories. Yet every thought is fragrant with the new sweetness. It is like rising out of the busy crowded streets of Babylon into the hanging gardens. This belongs to your chapter of Compensations, for I never felt so when I was well. I suppose even if I could go to a warm climate this happiness would not last, for I have been reading in Shelley's journals how he continued to suffer in Italy and he was affected very much as I am. I wish you would read his Essay "The defence of poetry" Mr Wheeler will lend it you.[3] I have his copy now. The Letters I think you would not like yet I never can tell what you *will* like, so that sometimes it seems I was not born to be your friend, but then again the flowers spring up and I am sure I was.[4]

I wish you could see the flowers I have before me *now*. A beautiful bouquet brought me this evening, multifloras, verbenas, fusias, English[n] violets and a lemon branch of the liveliest green. There is but a very little bit of the Heliotrope. It is the flower I love best, but it is rarely given me. I suppose I do not look as if I deserved it.— When I am a Queen, if so unfortunate as to come to the throne in a northern climate, I will have greenhouses innumerable, and I will present every person of distinguished merit with a bouquet every week and every person of delicate sensibility with one every day. If you are there I shall only give you sweet pea or lavender because you are merely a philosopher and a farmer, not a hero, nor a sentimentalist

Adieu, dear friend. I have another letter from Anna but—had not arrived—

M. F.

The Persius shall go into the first number.[5] I am sure they ought to be glad of it! How beautiful, how appropriate is your motto. I should think you would always have a regard for Persius who has furnished you with it.

I see Shelley in his letter to Gifford makes the same distinction in favor of Keats's Hyperion over his other works that you did.[6]

ALS (MH: bMS Am 1280 [2347]). Published in Rusk, *Letters of RWE*, 2:290–91. *Addressed:* R. W. Emerson, / Concord, / Mass. *Postmark:* Jamaica Plain / MS / Apr 26. *Endorsed:* Margaret Fuller / Apr. 1840.

you say on that score] you say ↑ on that score ↓
I think the] I think ↑ the ↓
I suppose] I ⟨p⟩ suppose
would not that you had] would not ⟨have⟩ ↑ that ↓ you ↑ had ↓
that the priests] that the⟨se⟩ priests
to find that] to find ⟨that all⟩ that
fusias, English] fusias, ⟨and⟩ English

1. Fuller's letter clearly answers the two that Emerson sent her that week. (Rusk, *Letters of RWE*, dates the first 21? and 23? April; the second is dated the twenty-fourth.) With the letters came some manuscripts related to the first issue of the *Dial*: a draft of their introductory essay, a copy of Edward Palmer's *Letter to Those Who Think* for possible review, Thoreau's "Persius," some Emerson poetry, Charles Emerson's "Notes," and Edward Bliss Emerson's "Last Farewell" (with the fifth stanza omitted) (Rusk, *Letters of RWE*, 2:285–88).
2. "Entirely too lovely."
3. Charles Stearns Wheeler (1816–43), son of Charles Wheeler of Lincoln, Mass., graduated in 1837 from Harvard, where he had been Thoreau's roommate. Wheeler became a tutor in Greek in 1838 when Jones Very resigned and then became an instructor of history. Wheeler helped Emerson edit Carlyle's *Sartor Resartus* and the *French Revolution*. He went to Germany and sent back letters that Emerson published in the *Dial*. His promising career ended abruptly when he died in Germany (Harvard archives; Myerson, *New England Transcendentalists*, pp. 219–24).
4. Mary Shelley had published the two-volume *Essays, Letters from Abroad, Translations and Fragments, by Percy Bysshe Shelley* (London, 1840). Here Fuller had found Shelley's descriptions of the difficulties of European travels, his essay on poetry, and his letters.
5. Emerson had received a rewritten draft of Thoreau's "Persius." The essay was published as "Aulus Persius Flaccus," *Dial* 1 (July 1840):117–21.
6. Shelley evaluated Keats's "Hyperion" in a letter to William Gifford, editor of the *Quarterly Review:* "The great proportion of this piece is surely in the very highest style of poetry. I speak impartially, for the canons of taste to which Keats has conformed in his other compositions are the very reverse of my own" (*Essays . . . by Percy Bysshe Shelley*, 2:289).

261. To Ralph Waldo Emerson

[I] Jamaica plain,
May 31st 1840.

My dear friend,

I take this large sheet without being sure I shall fill it. This weather makes me, too, very impatient of the artificial life of reading and writing, though I dont think that "weeding onions" would be the way I should take of linking myself to Nature in this her liebersvollste Tag.—[1] You did wrong not to come here. I had a great deal to say to you which I shall not write. However I dont wonder you economize your time if you are to have your house full of company all the beautiful, solitary summer.[2] I will try not to wish to see you.

I cannot write down what the Southern gales have whispered.— I shall talk mere gossip to you now.— Of Providence, you have really got up a revival there, though they do not know it.[3] Daily they grow more vehement in their determination to become acquainted with God. If they pursue the chase with such fury a month or two longer I think they will get some thoughts about—themselves. I was much pleased by the correctness of their impressions about you and about Mr Ripley. Charles gave as good a sketch of you as I could draw[n] myself— Mr Greene said some piquant things Mrs Burges had expanded like a flower in[n] your light.[4] She has[n] received at last just the impulse she[n] needed. I sympathized in her happiness on my celestial side, and, on the demonical, I amused myself with annihilating Mr Pabodie who offered himself as a prey to the spoiler.[5] I wish you had been there I think you would not have been too sweet to be amused; he provoked it from such a low vanity.— Susan, the Recluse, was absent on a journey, and she goes to the theatre now in the costume I formerly described to you.[6] She will be the founder of an order of lay nuns!— I was much pleased with the way in which some of my girls received the lectures. They understood at once.

I had a (to me) very pleasant visit from Mr Alcott. I saw him[n] by the light of his own eyes. With me alone he is never the Messiah but one beautiful individuality and faithful soul. Then he seems really high and not merely[n] a person of high pretensions. I think his "Sayings"[n] are quite grand, though ofttimes too grandiloquent.[7] I thought he bore my strictures with great sweetness for they must have seemed petty to him.— Tell him that Mr Ripley verified at once my prophecy and said what I told him would be said about the Prometheus.

Mr Ripley is most happy in the step he has taken.[8] He seems newborn. The day you went to town with me as we were talking about it, I told him what is thought of him as a preacher, and expressed doubts as to his being able to build up a church here. I told him I had hoped when he broke away he would enter on some business and leave preaching. But he said he could not without a trial; that he knew as well as any body that he never had preached, but that was because he had never been on his true ground, that he had much he longed to say and was sure that in suitable relations he should be able to breathe out what was so living in him. He showed himself a fine, genial, manly person that day. I feel that he has many steps to take before he arrives at his proper position. There is to me a manifest inconsistency in his views. But this will be a valuable experiment to him. He will yet be free and fair, I hope *complete* in his way.

There are only thirty names on the Boston subscription list to the "Dial"; I hope you will let me have your papers by next Friday or Saty. Send Ellen Hooper's too if you have done with them.[9] And will you not send me Carlyle's letter containing the sketches of Landor and Heraud.[10] And tell me a little what you said to Milnes of his review.[11] I thought you might like to see this letter from Miss Martineau[n] Mr Sumner says she is not likely to live, but I suppose she knows the exact truth. No one would be willing to deceive one who looks on death with such a bright and rational calmness.[12] Do not show it to any unless Lidian or Elizabeth, for though I believe every one here now knows what her illness is, I would regard her wishes as far as I am concerned.

Farewell, dear friend, yours always,

M F.

You do not speak of "Man in the Ages." Have you looked at it, and will you send it with yours.[13]

Did I not leave at your house my copy of Chartism you gave me, and, if so, will you send it me? when the proofs come.[14]

[II] Looking at your letter again I am reminded to say a few words of Shelley. You disappoint me a little. How can you, who so admire beautiful persons when you see[n] them in life, fail to be interested in this picture of so beautiful person. I do not look at Shelley's journals &c for me, but for him He inspires tenderness. I do not care whether I knew the thought before or not. I am interested to know what *he* thought. But even from your point of view the Defence of Poetry seems to me excellent It seems to me not "stiff" but dignified, and no otherwise "academical" than as showing a high degree of culture. If there are many statements as good I do not know them. But I am afraid you will abide by your say. tell me if by and by you look my way.[15]

I send you a few slight notes I made on the Life of Michel, if you look at them when you read it, it will be as if I read it with you.— I send you a leaf of James Clarke.[16] What he says of me is akin to what I expressed to you while at Concord. What he says of Landor is good, I think. I send you a leaf from my journal to give Mr

Alcott. Tell him it was written long ago, but will give him some idea of the feeling he has always excited in me For he would have it the other day that "there was nothing but a veil of words between us. Will you send me André by Cary, And tell me if you like Mr Briggs.[17]

I: ALS (MH: bMS Am 1280 [2348]); II: AL (MH: bMS Am 1280 [2383]). MsCfr (MB: Ms. Am. 1450 [72]). Published in part in Higginson, *MFO*, p. 151, and Rusk, *Letters of RWE*, 2:297–98. *Addressed:* Mr Emerson. *Endorsed:* Margaret Fuller / May 1840.

I could draw] I could ↑ draw ↓
a flower in] a flower ⟨f⟩ in
She has] She ⟨had⟩ ↑ has ↓
the impulse she] the impulse ⟨g⟩ she
I saw him] ⟨though⟩ I saw him
and not merely] and not ↑ merely ↓
his "Sayings"] his "⟨s⟩Sayings"
this letter from Miss Martineau] this letter ⟨of⟩ ↑ from ↓ Miss Martineau⟨'s⟩
when you see] when you ⟨l⟩ see

1. In his letter to Fuller of the same week, Emerson said wearily, "I have come to think it a piece of extreme good nature to read twenty pages in any volume and do think weeding onions a better employment" (Rusk, *Letters of RWE*, 2:299). Liebervollste Tag: "most charming day."

2. George P. Bradford and George Ware Briggs had been visiting at Emerson's home (Rusk, *Letters of RWE*, 2:299). Briggs (1810–95), the associate pastor at the First Church, Plymouth, from 1838 to 1852, was a Rhode Island native and a graduate of Brown (1825) and of the Harvard Divinity School (1834). He married Lucretia Archbald Bartlett (1812–46) in 1835; after her death, Briggs married Lucia J. Russell (1821–81) of Plymouth (*Heralds*, 3:37–40; Medford VR; *Plymouth Church Records*, p. 686; Mary LeBaron Stockwell, *Descendants of Francis LeBaron of Plymouth, Massachusetts* [Boston, 1904], p. 148).

3. Emerson had lectured in Providence from 20 March to 1 April, drawing from the six lectures in the "Human Life" and "Present Age" series. He was enthusiastically received and pressed often to expound the "Transcendentalist" philosophy as the most luminous New Light thinker (*Emerson Lectures*, 3:176; Rusk, *Letters of RWE*, 2:266).

4. Mrs. Burges may be Mary Arnold Burges (1774?–1851), wife of Tristam Burges, but it is more likely that Fuller refers to Eleanor Burrill Burges (1804?–65), daughter of the Honorable James Burrill of Providence and wife of Tristam's nephew, Walter Snow Burges (1808–92). Letters of Mrs. Newcomb make frequent reference to the Walter Burgeses as members of the literary set Fuller knew in Providence. The younger Mrs. Burges was the aunt of George Curtis, later a member of Brook Farm. (*NEHGR* 5:371; *The Biographical Cyclopedia of Representative Men of Rhode Island* [Providence, 1881], p. 251; Edwin Snow et al., *Alphabetical Index of the Births, Marriages and Deaths Recorded in Providence* [Providence, 1879–]; Rhoda M. Newcomb letters, RPB archives).

5. William Jewett Pabodie (1813–70), son of William and Jane Jewett Todd Peabody, was a Providence poet. According to the *Providence Journal*, he committed suicide after "long continued use of morphine." Pabodie commented coolly on Fuller in his review of the *Dial* in the *Providence Journal*, 27 July 1840 (*Peabody Genealogy*, p. 478; *Providence Journal*, 18 November 1870).

6. Susan Anna Power, Sarah Helen Whitman's sister.

7. Neither Fuller nor Emerson was surprised when Alcott's "Orphic Sayings" were mocked by many unsympathetic *Dial* readers. Two sets of the "Sayings" appeared, each a series of oracular, if foggy, pronouncements. When he sent the manuscript to

Fuller on 8 May, Emerson observed, "One grave thing I have to say, this, namely, that you will not like Alcott's papers; that I do not like them; that Mr Ripley will not; & yet I think, on the whole, they ought to be printed pretty much as they stand, with his name in full" (Rusk, *Letters of RWE*, 2:294). The willingness of the editors to include Alcott's work testifies to their faith in his potential.

8. George Ripley had just resigned his pulpit at the Purchase Street Church, a pastorate he had held since 1826.

9. In response to this prompting, Emerson sent Fuller his manuscript essay "Thoughts on Modern Literature," which opened the second issue of the *Dial*, but Ellen Hooper's poems did not come from Emerson until 21 July (Rusk, *Letters of RWE*, 2:303, 315).

10. In his letter to Emerson of 1 April, Carlyle had tartly commented on John Heraud ("a loquacious scribacious little man, of middle age, of parboiled greasy aspect") and Walter Savage Landor ("a soul ever promising to take wing into the Aether, yet never doing it, ever splashing webfooted in the terrene mud, and only splashing the worse the more he strives!") (*Emerson–Carlyle Correspondence*, pp. 264–65). Heraud (1799–1887), a poet, dramatist, and editor, was at this time editing the *Monthly Magazine*. Despite Carlyle's description, the two were friends, and the Carlyles took Heraud's advice when he suggested that they move into a house in Chelsea (*DNB*).

11. Richard Monckton Milnes had reviewed Emerson in "American Philosophy.—Emerson's Works," *London and Westminster Review* 33 (March 1840):345–72. Milnes sent Emerson a copy of the essay with a letter. Emerson replied on 30 May, saying, as he paraphrased it to Fuller, that he "hoped yet to win his assent to far broader & bolder generalizations than any of those he esteems so rash" (Rusk, *Letters of RWE*, 2:304). Martineau's letter has not survived, but Emerson reported to his brother William that the subject was a favorable view of Milnes's essay (Rusk, *Letters of RWE*, 2:302).

12. Charles Sumner had just returned from a European trip. During the summer of 1840 he was the social rage of Boston as he brilliantly recounted his successes in European society (David Donald, *Charles Sumner and the Coming of the Civil War* [New York, 1960], pp. 70–71). Harriet Martineau was suffering a protracted illness that began in 1839 and confined her to her room, often under sedation, until 1844, when she was cured by mesmerism.

13. Thomas Treadwell Stone, "Man in the Ages," *Dial* 1 (July 1840):273–89. The essay had passed back and forth between Emerson and Fuller during April and May. In response to Fuller's query, Emerson called the essay "a high statement, though a little verbose, & careless sometimes in expression" (Rusk, *Letters of RWE*, 2:304). Stone (1801–95), a native of Maine, graduated from Bowdoin in 1820 and was ordained at Andover, Maine, in 1824. He then served at East Machias from 1832 to 1846 (*Heralds*, 3:358–62).

14. When she attended a meeting of the Transcendental Club at Emerson's on 13 May, Fuller had received a copy of Carlyle's *Chartism*, which had first been published in December 1839. Emerson arranged for an American edition, which appeared in 1840 (Myerson, "Calendar," p. 205; *Emerson–Carlyle Correspondence*, p. 266; *Boston Daily Advertiser*, 29 April 1840).

15. Having read Shelley's letters and journals at Fuller's urging, Emerson dismissed the poet: "All that was in his mind is long already the property of the whole forum and this Defence of Poetry looks stiff & academical" (Rusk, *Letters of RWE*, 2:299). A second reading still left Emerson cool: "His perceptions of particular facts are clear enough but his whole mind wants liquidity & expansion. He opens that Essay on poetry hardly & juvenile" (Rusk, *Letters of RWE*, 2:305).

16. Emerson acknowledged the receipt of her notes on Antoine Quatremère de Quincy's biography of Michelangelo and a letter by James Clarke (Rusk, *Letters of RWE*, 2:304).

17. Fuller wanted Caroline Sturgis to bring her copy of George Sand's *André*.

Fuller's letter to William H. Channing, 19 April 1840. By courtesy of the Trustees of the Boston Public Library.

on the laggards, and scold the lukewarm,
and act Helen MacGregor to those who
love compromise, by doing my little best to
sink them in the waters of Oblivion!!
Things go on pretty well, but I dare say people
will be disappointed, for they seem to be
looking for the gospel of transcendentalism.
It may prove as your Jouffroy says it
is with the French ministry; the public
wants something positive, and finding such
and such persons excellent at fault finding
raises them to be the rulers. when lo!
they have no noble and full yea, to
match their shrill and bold Nay, and
are hurled down again — Mr Emerson
knows best what he wants but he has
already said it in various ways. — yet
I deem the experiment is well worth
trying; hearts beat so high, they must
be full of something, and here is a
way to breathe it out quite freely. — It
is for dear New England that I wanted
this review; for myself, if I had wished
to write a few pages now and then. I had

140

ways and means of dispersing of them. But in truth I have not much to say, for since I have had leisure to look at myself I find that, so far from being a great original genius, I have not yet learned to think to any [light?] and that the utmost I have done in life has been to form my character to a certain consistency, cultivate my tastes, and [learn to] tell the truth with a little better grace than I did at first. For this the world will not care much, so I shall only hazard a few critical remarks, or an unpretending chalk sketch now and then, till I have learned to do something. There will be some beautiful poesies; about prose I know not yet so well. We shall be the means of publishing the little Charles Emerson left as mark of his noble course, and though it lies in payments you will think yourself a gainer by it I am sure.

[three lines crossed out and illegible]

141

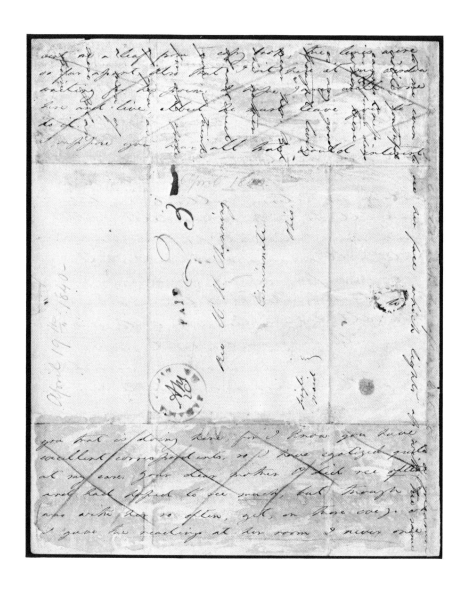

262.   To A. Bronson Alcott

June 1840

My friend, Mr Alcott,

You said the other day, that you and I looked at things in the same way, and that we had only a veil of words between us. I have desired my Brother to copy this leaf from my Journal which dates I think 1837 when I first knew you in Boston.[1] It was written one day after I had been talking with you, and trying to put myself into your state of mind. To me, it still records my impression. Does it say any thing to you?

M. F.

MsC (MH: 59m-306 [10, p. 84]; MB: Ms. Am. 1450 [1a]).

1. Fuller summarized Alcott's teaching philosophy by beginning with his lament: "O for the safe and natural way of Intuition. I cannot grope like a mole in the gloomy ways of Experience." Fuller concludes with Alcott's defense of his method: "I looked about for my mission. And, seeing that all other Redeemers had so imperfectly performed their tasks, I sought a new way. It seemed to me that they had all begun on the human being at too late a day and laid their plans too wide. And I said. They began with men, I will begin with babes. They began with the world and I will begin with the family. So I preached to them the gospel of the 19th century. I traced the thought of nature through all her disguises and permitted no act in my phenomenal or human self on an antagonistic character" (MH: Os 735 M.800[1]).

263.   To Richard F. Fuller

Jamaica Plain,
3d June, 1840

My dear Richard,

I have too long neglected my promise of writing to you. But I have had so much to occupy my mind that I cannot but hope you will excuse me, and indeed that you have been too agreeably engaged to think much about home.

We are all as well as usual. Mrs Grinnell has been staying with us and Miss Elizabeth Newcomb is here now.[1] We had planned an excursion to Mt Auburn for the afternoon of Election day when Arthur was at home to drive, but just as all were ready and one of the carriages at the door it began to rain. We were much disappointed, and so was Arthur; indeed, he observed, like Aunt Sarah "it always happens so to me.

I am sorry to say that mishaps have occurred to you also. One of your hens has proved an unnatural mother and pecked several of her children to death. Two turkies I understand are dead also. But as great care has been taken of them I hope you will behave like a man about it; perhaps these disappointments are meant to teach you that you are now too old to give so much time and thought to trifles.

Lloyd has behaved very well. He does much better when you are not at home to fret him, and contrary to your predictions *can* be influenced by kindness to do his duty. But Mother says she misses you extremely, and so do I.

There is not time for a long letter With best wishes for your present pleasure and future happiness I am, my dear Richard, yours affectionately

S. M. FULLER.

P.S. Our regards to Mr Lawrence and his family.[2]

ALS (MH: fMS Am 1086 [9:67]); MsC (MH: fMS Am 1086 [Works, 2:623–27]). *Addressed:* Richard F. Fuller. / Groton, / Mass. *Postmark:* Jamaica Plain Jun 3.

1. Possibly Abigail Barrell Grinnell of Providence, wife of William T. Grinnell.
2. Either the Amos Lawrence or the William Lawrence family of Groton.

264. To James F. Clarke

[ca. July 1840]
[Jamaica Plain?]

As to what you say of Shelley, it is true that the unhappy influences of early education prevented his ever attaining clear views of God, life, and the soul.[1] At thirty, he was still a seeker,—an experimentalist. But then his should not be compared with such a mind as ———'s, which, having no such exuberant fancy to tame, nor various faculties to develop, naturally comes to maturity sooner. Had Shelley lived twenty years longer, I have no doubt he would have become a fervent Christian, and thus have attained that mental harmony which was necessary to him. It is true, too, as you say, that we always feel a melancholy imperfection in what he writes. But I love to think of those other spheres in which so pure and rich a being shall be perfected; and I cannot allow his faults of opinion and sentiment to mar my enjoyment of the vast capabilities, and exquisite perception of beauty, displayed everywhere in his poems.

ELfr, from *Memoirs*, 1:165–66.

1. On 20 June, Clarke had commented on Shelley's *Essays and Letters* in a letter to Fuller: "I was grieved to find him to the last so beset and entangled in his theories, finding Christianity too 'stimulant,' and wishing Athenean culture to have been perpetuated instead thereof" (*Letters of JFC*, pp. 139–40).

265. To Almira P. Barlow[?]

Jamaica Plains. July 1840.

I am better this summer, but have had a most suffering winter. I cannot make much use of a life which once seemed so full of promise and power.— "Care is taken that the tree grow not up into the heavens."[1] I took pleasure in my "conversations," of which Ellen told me you had heard; they were worth having. I have the pleasure of sending you the first number of a Periodical some of us, your old friends, are going to scribble in. The introduction is by Mr Emerson; pieces on critics, and the Allston gallery, by me.[2] The next number will be better.

MsCfr (MH: fMS Am 1086 [Works, 1:23]).

Almira Penniman Barlow was one of Fuller's earliest friends. In 1830 Almira married David Hatch Barlow, a Unitarian minister, but the couple separated in 1840.

1. The motto begins the third part of Goethe's *Aus meinem Leben: Dichtung und Warheit*: "Es ist dafür gesorgt, dass die Bäume nicht in den Himmel wachsen."

2. Fuller wrote "A Short Essay on Critics" and "A Record of Impressions Produced by the Exhibition of Mr. Allston's Pictures in the Summer of 1839" for the first *Dial*.

266. To Ralph Waldo Emerson

Jamaica plain,
5th July, 1840.

My dear friend,

I wrote you a long letter on Friday after receiving yours, but on reading it over could not resolve to send it, so you will go to the letter box once again in vain.[1] I am very sorry to be inattentive, but I have felt entirely unlike writing. I have moods of sadness unknown I suppose to those of your temperament, when it seems a mockery and mummery to write of life and the affairs of my acquaintance.

Then I plunge into occupation, and this fortnight past have been no moment idle. I do hope that in the next stage of our existence whatever be[n] our pains and difficulties we may not have these terrible seasons of faintness and discouragement. I ought not to have them now for I will never yield to them or live in their spirit a moment. But when I do not write to you it is always either that I feel so, or am so busy I cannot.

Until I shall have seen Mr R. I cannot answer all your questions. Mais à present, you can have as many numbers as you want for yourself or your friends of this first no, but our contract with them was that twelve numbers should be given to Mr R. each quarter for the use of contributors. Of these I receive two.— Mr Thoreau will have it of course as we hope his frequent[n] aid. But I did not expect to furnish it to all who may give a piece occasionally. I have not sent it to E. H. or C. S. or W.— I sent a list to W. and J. of those to whom I wished this no. sent. I did not give Mr Stone's name, but doubtless Mr R. did. I will see about it, however. I presume Mr Cranch is a subscriber as is J. F. Clarke and others who will write, but I will look at the list when in town next Wednesday.[2]

I desired Mr Thoreau's Persius to be sent him, as I was going away to Cohasset at the time it came out and I understood from Mr R. that it was sent[n] and he did not correct it I do not know how this was, the errors are most unhappy. I will not go away again when it is in press.

I like the poetry better in small type myself and thought the title page neat and unpretending, but have no such positive feeling about such things that I would defer entirely to your taste. But now we have begun so I should think it undesirable to make changes this year, as the first vol should be uniform. I wish I had consulted you at first, but did not know you attached great[n] importance to externals in such matters, as you[n] do so little in others. The marks shall be made and the spaces left as you desire however after our respected poems!

I am glad you are not quite dissatisfied with the first no. I feel myself how far it is from that eaglet motion I wanted. I suffered in looking it over now. Did you observe the absurdity of the last two pages. These are things they had to fill up blanks and which thinking twas pity such beautiful thoughts should be lost put[n] in for climax.[3] Admire the winding up, the concluding sentence!! I agree Mr Alcott's sayings read well.

I thought to write about[n] the expostulation in your last letter, but finally I think I would rather talk with you.[4]

The next number we will do far better. I want to open it with your

Article. You said you might wish to make some alterations if we kept it— do you wish to have it sent you, the first part is left in type; they had printed a good deal before finding it would be too long. E. H's "poet," some of Cary's best, Ellery, and "the bard born out of time"! we must have for that[5]

I suppose you did not see Ellery at all or you would have mentioned it, and that you have heard news of W from[n] himself. I had a very good time at Cohasset with Cary, and when we meet will show you a few verses she wrote there. But I am reminded to say a few words apropos to her. C. told me you had spoken to her of my friends. This made me think you could not have fully understood the feeling which led A—[6] to trust you with a tale[n] which was not hers only. A—though frank is not communicative,[n] she has perfect power of keeping a secret. I do not think she would have spoken on this subject to any other than yourself. You gave her the feeling of the holy man, the confessor who should enlighten her at this moment to act in conformity with her purest and highest nature. She felt at once that she was spiritually in relation with you, and spoke as she would in the confessional. Do not think because persons are intimate with me that they know this or any of my other[n] friends' affairs. I know how to keep relations sacredly separate. I should never have let *you* know any thing about this if we had been intimate forever unless A. had. I never told C. till the other day as she knew so much I could not bear she should put the vulgar construction on the matter and told her enough to show how true and noble he had been.[7] But I shall speak to none other. And whatever people may surmise they do and should know nothing. The monument should be made of the purest marble alone.

When you see Mr E. G. Loring I wish he[n] may show you some letters from Jane he brought me the other day.[8] I think you would feel their beauty. That to him about the Carlyles is very good, but not so charming as one to Miss King which I fear you will not see.[9]

Charles Newcomb has been passing three or four days with me. He is wretchedly ill. I think he[n] may die, and perhaps it would be well, for I doubt if he has strength to rise above his doubts and fears. Oh how I thank Heaven that I am made of firmer fibre and more resolute mind. No sharp pain can debilitate like this vacillation of mind.

I hear Rakemann play frequently. I have regretted much that you do[n] not live nearer that I might have you at two or three musical entertainments. Especially one eveg when Knight was here and sang Beethoven's Rosalie.[10] Life ripples in in various ways, but I know that

that it brings any thing *positive* fit for the Concord mart George Simmons has been to see me.[11] S. Clarke has passed a night with me. I am going to pass next Wednesday morng with her at the Hall of Sculpture. I wish you were to be in town also. It is very pleasant to be there, the hall is full and not too full.

Affectionately yours,

S. M. FULLER.

Carlyle's letter shall go next time I send by stage.[12]

ALS (MH: bMS Am 1280 [2349]); MsCfr (MH: bMS Am 1280 [111, p. 139]; MB: Ms. Am. 1450 [73]). Published in part in Higginson, *MFO*, pp. 154–56; Rusk, *Letters of RWE*, 2:309–10; *JMN*, 11:483. *Addressed:* R. W. Emerson / Concord / Mass. *Postmark:* Jamaica Plain / July 6. *Endorsed:* Margaret Fuller / July 1840.

existence whatever be] existence whatever ⟨may⟩ be
we hope his frequent] we hope his ⟨permane⟩ frequent
that it was sent] that it was ⟨so⟩ ↑ sent ↓
you attached great] you attached ↑ great ↓
as you] as ↑ you ↓
should be lost put] should be lost ⟨they⟩ put
to write about] to write ⟨to you⟩ about
heard news of W from] heard ↑ news of ↓ W⟨'s news⟩ from
you with a tale] you with a ⟨?⟩ tale
though frank is not communicative] ↑ though frank ↓ is not ⟨no⟩ communicative
of my other] of my ↑ other ↓
I wish he] I wish ⟨m⟩he
I think he] I think ⟨perhaps⟩ he
that you do] that you ⟨did⟩ do

1. Fuller is answering Emerson's letter of 2 July, in which he gently reproached her for her silence and reported his reaction to the first issue of the *Dial*. He went on to make a number of queries that Fuller here addresses. Shall contributors be given free copies? Can the typography be changed so that the essays are physically distinguished from the poetry? Emerson concluded by saying, "Nevertheless it is a good book & the wise public ought to accept it as such" (Rusk, *Letters of RWE*, 2:309–11).
2. E. H. is Ellen Hooper, C. S. Caroline Sturgis, W. Sam Ward, and W. and J. Weeks and Jordan, publishers of the *Dial*. Mr. R. is George Ripley. Christopher Pearse Cranch (1813–92), later a close friend of Fuller's, graduated from the Divinity School in 1835. After several years of itinerant preaching, he turned to poetry and painting for a career. An early contributor to the *Western Messenger,* Cranch wrote frequently for the *Dial* (*DAB*).
3. To fill the final two pages, Fuller inserted a series of her own verses and one by Sarah Clarke, and concluded with a prose fragment whose last sentence was "Wise man, you never knew what it is to love."
4. On 21 June, Emerson wrote at length about his aspirations for the *Dial*. "Can we not," he asked, "explode in this enterprize of ours all the established rules of Grub Street or Washington Street? leave out all the ballast or Balaam and omit to count pages?" He tartly concluded, "Every dull sentence vulgarizes the book and when we have inserted our gems from the papers of love & friendship we shall feel that we have wronged our angels by thrusting them into unfit company" (Rusk, *Letters of RWE*, 2:305–6).
5. The next *Dial* opened with Emerson's "Thoughts on Modern Literature" and included Ellen Hooper's "The Poet," a number of Caroline Sturgis' poems, and Emer-

son's essay "New Poetry," which presented anonymously several of Ellery Channing's poems. Finally, Fuller did include Emerson's "Woodnotes," a poem whose opening lines proclaimed, "For this present, hard / Is the fortune of the bard / Born out of time."

6. Undoubtedly Anna Barker.

7. Emerson had told Sturgis something that Anna Barker and Fuller had told him in confidence about Sam Ward, the "he" Fuller mentions.

8. Ellis Gray Loring was a wealthy lawyer who was prominent in the abolition movement. Fuller often saw him, his wife, and his daughter, Anna.

9. Jane Tuckerman was then visiting England; Miss King is one of her future sisters-in-law, Augusta (1817–62) or Caroline (1820–1907), daughters of John Glen King of Salem (MVR 156:266; MVR 1909, 84:493).

10. Joseph Phillip Knight (1812–87), an English singer and composer, toured America from 1839 to 1841. "Rosalie" was a "cantata" adapted from Beethoven's "Adelaida" by Charles Edward Horn (1786–1849), a British singer, composer, and conductor who had immigrated to Boston (*Baker's Biographical Dictionary*).

11. George Frederick Simmons (see letter 200).

12. She did not, however, return Carlyle's letter of 1 April. On 19 July she told Emerson that she had given the letter to Ward to read and return.

267.   To Caroline Sturgis

Jamaica plain.
12th July 1840.

It is five o'clock, p. m.— I have just finished my day's work. The sweet South West is blowing most invitingly over the fields.— In my place Cary would not write a letter to me or any one. She would go walk in the fields—*with a book* like us others, I shall always say after Cohasset.

But such a long perspective of scribbling and fuss spreads out through the coming week! And am I not born to set an example of friendship and all the other virtues? Is not my superiority to be sustained as a thing of course? I will write!

My dear Cary, I thank you very much for the little writing case. I shall always value it— But do not be too quick to gratify my wishes lest you spoil me into wishing for Mount Ararat, perhaps.

I like your "*dream*" very much.[1] But why did you not finish it out. It was well worth it. And the Cohasset verses are none of them well written, nothing like as well as those at Nashon. Do not be too careless; the Muse also is an exact schoolmistress, there is danger that she may expel you, as Dolly Dix did.[2] Let the leaves from the blue-bell be true to the line of beauty and woven of finer tissue than these wild sea-weed.

Anna is coming the fifteenth this month, or after, but, as she will stay some time, I shall not send for you immediately. She is now giving all her time to her favorite brother, Tom.[3] She writes "We still hope to detain him a little longer— Life seems to me all adieus, this last will be a grief indeed— I love him very much; there is something so deep and stern about him. Once I wanted you should know each other, now I am careless about it, because his home is in a foreign land, and he is one you cannot know at once—could you be together as we are here—that would make me glad,— early and late— by sun and moon— walking and driving and looking on the solemn mountains that have become to me most beloved and blessed friends— so calm, so majestic, as if waiting God's word."

Just as I got here I was interrupted by a visit from your sister Ellen. She thinks somewhat of coming near as to board, but I am afraid she will not.

W. has been well enough to write to me some ten days but I have not seen him till this week.[4] I never saw any one so reduced in the same time. He is even emaciated, and seems scarce able to move He has lost all his beauty for the present, but was the more dear. I had a most happy hour with him. He was most happy, leaning on his own thoughts, gentle celestial, not hopeful, but faithful. He was delighted to find me in so quiescent a mood. He begged me to stay so, as long as he did. May our relation remain as sweet and untroubled as at present!

I believe I wrote you that the morng we wer to have gone to the Atheneum, he went to see Ellery and took him there to meet us. They staid a long time, and, as we did not come, parted and went home. Ellery never again went to see W. nor inquired after him; he went away without seeing any of those he had borne in mind in absence; he went suddenly as his father said "lest it should be impossible for him to return to his exile." I think he might as well be in one place as another, since he will not avail himself of the most precious friendships.[5]

Anna Shaw has passed an afternoon with me. She was interesting and droll, graceful and beautiful. Margaret Forbes has been ten days at Mr Emerson's and is perfectly happy. I have had two letters from Mr E. Soaring like an eagle, skimming like a swallow as usual, but never with me, nor in the depths.[6]

I have been reading a fine romance of Balzac's "Eugenie Grandet" I wish I could send it you, but it belongs to Mr Mottely.[7] I have also read a play of Ben Jonson's and Mr Brownson's review containing Frank Tuckerman's lecture.[8] It is boyish and all the materials taken from books, but better written than I had expected. Did you see Jane's lovely letters and did you see how she longed for the home from which you thought in her place you should escape? Is it that the worst built nest is better for a bird than the bleak strand? I have seen many people and done many things, but there is room for no more gossip now from your faithful friend

MARGARET F.

Which Italian poet did you want? Write whether you receive this letter.

ALS (MH: bMS Am 1221 [237]). *Addressed:* Miss Caroline Sturgis / Care Samuel Curson Esq / Newbury / Mass. *Postmark:* Jamaica Plain MS July 13. *Endorsed:* S. M. Fuller. 12th July 1840.

1. The reference is to Caroline Sturgis' poem "'The Dream,'" published in the second issue of the *Dial*.

2. Dorothea Dix, later known for her work as a reformer, taught school in Boston from 1831 to 1836.

3. Thomas Hazard Barker (1807–46) was the oldest surviving child of Jacob and Eliza Hazard Barker (*Barker Genealogy*, p. 180).

4. In June Emerson had reported that Sam Ward was ill with "fever & ague" (Rusk, *Letters of RWE*, 2:306).

5. Ward and Ellery Channing had been good friends since their schooldays at the Round Hill School in Northampton. Ward introduced Emerson to Channing's poems, and loyally financed several of Channing's subsequent volumes of verse. Channing was at this time on the way to Illinois, where he bought some land, built a cabin, and failed as a farmer (Hudspeth, *Ellery Channing*, pp. 20–22).

6. Margaret Perkins Forbes (1806–76), daughter of Ralph Bennett and Margaret Perkins Forbes, was an aunt of William Hathaway Forbes, who married Emerson's daughter Edith (Ralph E. Forbes, "The Forbes Family," NEHGS, p. 6). Emerson had written Fuller on 2 and 8 July (Rusk, *Letters of RWE*, 2:309, 313).

7. Honoré de Balzac's *Eugénie Grandet* was published in Paris in 1833. Thomas Motley (1812–95) was living with his wife, Eliza Bussey Davis (1814–94), on her father's estate in Roxbury (near Jamaica Plain). Benjamin Bussey founded Woodland Hill, an estate of over three hundred acres, later donated to Harvard as the Bussey Institute (*CVR*; MVR 447:347; *CC*, 15 November 1834; *Twentieth Century Biographical Dictionary of Notable Americans* [Boston, 1904]; Francis S. Drake, *The Town of Roxbury* [Roxbury, Mass., 1878], pp. 53, 440).

8. John Francis Tuckerman's essay-review of F. J. Fétis's *Biographie universelle des musiciens* appeared in Orestes Brownson's *Boston Quarterly Review* 3 (July 1840):332–57.

268. To Ralph Waldo Emerson

19th July 1840.

I suppose it is too warm for my dear friend to write at least[n] to so dull a correspondent, or perhaps it is that I have asked so many things. I am sorry you did not send the verses, for I wanted to take one or two for filling the gaps, and now have been obliged to take some not so good.[1] Have you not some distiches to bestow? I have two or three little things of yours which I wished very much to use but thought I must not without your leave.

When I wrote the first line of this letter I thought I should fill it up[n] with some notes I wished to make on the hall of sculpture. But I was obliged to stop by a violent attack of headach, and now I am not fit to write any thing good and will only scribble a few lines to send with your proof which Mr R. left with me.[2] He is much distressed at what he thinks a falling off in the end of your paragraph about the majestic Artist, and I think when you look again you will think you have not said what you meant to say. The "eloquence" and "wealth", thus grouped, have rather l'air bourgeoise— "Saddens and gladdens" is good. Mr R. hates prettinesses, as the mistress of a boarding house hates flower vases.

"Dreadful melody" does not suit me. The dreadful has become vulgarized since its natal day.

So much for impertinence! I am very glad I am to own these remarks about the Meister. As to the genius of Goethe the statement, though so much better than others, is too imperfect to be true. He requires to be minutely painted in his own style of hard finish. As he never gave his soul in a glance, so he cannot be painted at a glance. I wish this "Kosmos Beauty" was not here ever again, one does not like their friend to have any *way*, any thing peculiar, he must be too individual to be known by a cough or a phrase.— And is this *costly* true to the sense of kostiliche; that means worthy a high price, the other obtained at a high price, n'est ce pas? I cannot like that illustration of the humors of the eye.— I wish the word *whipped* was never used at all and here it is twice in nearest neighborhood[3]

At this place I was obliged to take to my bed,— my poor head reminding me that I was in no state for criticism. I have marked the parts I admire in the piece. It is really grand. I am sure you will be delighted with my approbation!

Are not you coming hither soon? I begin to want very much to know more about you. How is Lidian? that worthless Elizh I see is behaving just as I told her she would about her visit to me. What does Waldo say, and what has Ellen learnt? Be good to me, by and by I will be good so as to deserve it.

Meanwhile

> Accept a miracle instead of wit,
> All these dull lines by Spenser's pencil writ![4]

I let S. W. see Carlyle's letter, as I thought you would be willing and desired him to return it to you.

Cannot you send a distich to fit in here at the end of your piece.

AL (MH: bMS Am 1280 [2350]); MsC (MB: Ms. Am. 1450 [74]). Published in part in Higginson, *MFO*, pp. 157–58, and Rusk, *Letters of RWE*, 2:315. *Endorsed:* 1840.

to write at least] to write ↑ at least ↓

fill it up] fill it ⟨p⟩ up

1. Apparently several poems by Caroline Sturgis and Ellen Hooper.

2. Fuller wrote a three-page piece titled "The Atheneum Exhibition of Painting and Sculpture" for the second issue of the *Dial*.

3. Fuller is criticizing Emerson's draft of "Thoughts on Modern Literature." He replaced the "Kosmos Beauty," but "dreadful melody" stayed in his discussion of Goethe on pp. 156–57.

4. Fuller's modification of Hazlitt's quip in "On Wit and Humour" (in *Lectures on the English Comic Writers* [London, 1819], p. 23): "Wit may sometimes, indeed, be shown in compliments as well as satire; as in the common epigram—

> 'Accept a miracle, instead of wit:
> See two dull lines with Stanhope's pencil writ.'"

269. To Caroline Sturgis

Jamaica, 24th July. [1840]

My dear Cary,

I have put off writing to you from day today thinking I should be able to say that Anna has come, but she does not come, and I will not wait longer. I can send a line then.— Your letters delight me, write more. I must see the Blue bell myself, and this summer, I think, or autumn, I have not seen beauty enough; it is very tame to me here now.[1] I do not feel keenly at present. I feel like reading, and have read many books, but will not tell about them now. You shall have all the books you want when you come.

Marianne is gone to stay at Marblehead. Sophia Peabody wants you to send her a drawing you gave her once, and S. Clarke gave back to you with some others by mistake.[2] Do not fail to send it, if[n] you do you will plague her, and she does not deserve to be plagued.

Mr E. writes me that he has sent you all of your poems that he copied out. Please let me have them as soon as you can, that I may select the best. I want very much to make this no. of the Dial really good. I believe there is no secrecy about the *prose* pieces in the 1st no.

So much for business!

W. is staying at Nahant with his younger brothers. He says the air is doing him miraculous good and that he can be out in a boat the whole morng. I have not Ellery's address yet, but will get it, meanwhile write to him.

Do remember my telling you (I think at Cohasset) of a Mr Tracy staying with us when I was 15, and all that passed.[3] Well! I have not seen him since till yesterday he came here. I was pleased to find that even at so early an age I did not overrate those I valued. He was the same as in memory, the powerful eye, dignifying an otherwise ugly face, the calm wisdom and refined observation, the imposing maniere d'être which any where would give him an influence among men without his taking any trouble or making any sacrifice, and the great waves of feeling that seemed to rise at an attractive influence and overspread his being.— He said, nothing since his childhood had been marked like his visit to our house that it had dwelt in his thoughts unchanged amid all changes. I could have wished he had never returned to change the picture. He looked at me continually and said again and again he should have known me any where, but oh, how changed I must be since that epoch of pride and fulness! He had with him his son, a wild boy of five years old, all brilliant with health and energy and with the same powerful eye.[4] He said— "You know I am not one to confound acuteness and rapidity of intellect with real genius, but he is for those an extraordinary child. He would astonish you, but I look deep enough into the prodigy to see the work of an extremely nervous temperament.— And I shall make him as dull as I can. *Margaret*, (pronouncing the name in the same deliberate searching way he used to do) "I love him so well, I will try to teach him moderation. If I can help it he shall not feed on bitter ashes, nor try those paths of avarice and ambition."

It made me feel very strangely to hear him talk so to my old self. What a gulf between. There is scarce a fibre left of the haughty, passionate, ambitious child he remembered, and had loved.

I felt affection for him still for his character was formed then and had not altered except by ripening and expanding. But thus in other worlds we shall remember our present selves.

Writing at night I cannot help inking my letter you must excuse.

—I shall write again when Anna comes. I do hope she wont keep me waiting as she did last summer. Your friend

M. F.

ALS (MH: bMS Am 1221 [238]). Published in part in *Memoirs*, 1:76–77. *Addressed:* Miss Caroline Sturgis / care of S. Curson Esq. / Newbury / Mass. *Postmark:* Jamaica Plain MS Ju 25. *Endorsed:* S.M.F 24th July 1840.

to send it, if] to send it ⟨to her⟩, if

1. Bluebell was the Sturgis summer home in Newbury.

2. Sophia Peabody (1809–71), the youngest surviving daughter of Nathaniel and Elizabeth Palmer Peabody, was a neurasthenic artist. She was a devoted member of Fuller's conversations until her marriage in 1842 to Nathaniel Hawthorne (*Peabody Genealogy*, p. 85; *NAW*).

3. Albert Haller Tracy (1793–1859), a native of Connecticut, had moved to New York in 1811. After being educated in the classics and medicine, he turned to law and was admitted to the bar in 1815. He was elected to the U.S. Congress from Buffalo in 1819 and served till 1825. Like Timothy Fuller, Tracy was at this time a Jeffersonian. His career foundered when he declined a cabinet post offered by John Quincy Adams and a judgeship offered by DeWitt Clinton. In 1839 he ran for but lost a Senate seat and then declined another cabinet post, this one offered by John Tyler. In 1825 he married Harriet Foote Norton. Fuller again met Tracy as she returned in 1843 from her trip West (*Biographical Directory of the American Congress, 1774–1971* [Washington, D.C., 1971]; Evert E. Tracy, *Tracy Genealogy* [Albany, N.Y., 1898], p. 109).

4. Like his father, Albert Haller Tracy, Jr. (1834–74), was a lawyer, but thanks to a large legacy did not pursue his career (*Record and Statistics of the Academic Class of Fifty-Four, Yale University, 1854–1896* [Stamford, Conn., 1896], app., p. 21).

270. To John Neal

Jamaica Plain
28th July 1840

Dear Sir,

As my brother (a student in Harvard University) is to pass a few hours in Portland, I have desired him to deliver to you this first number of a periodical in which I am interested.ⁿ This will give him an oppory of seeing one of whom he has so often heard, and you, will perhaps have the kindness to tell him whether there is any thing he will have time to look at in your city.[1]

With respect yours

S. M. FULLER.

ALS (ViU). *Addressed:* John Neal Esq / Portland / Me. *Endorsed:* Miss Fuller / *Authoress.*

John Neal (1793–1876) was a novelist and essayist. He had lectured on temperance at the Greene-Street School in Providence when Fuller taught there (*DAB*; Henry L. Greene, "The Greene-St. School, of Providence, and Its Teachers," *Publications of the Rhode Island Historical Society*, n.s. 6 [January 1899]:199–219).

I am interested] I am ⟨?⟩ ↑interested↓

1. Arthur Fuller was delivering a copy of the *Dial* to Neal.

State Street, Boston, ca. 1840. From *American Scenery*, ed. N. P. Willis (London, 1840). Courtesy of the Pennsylvania State University Libraries.

271. To Caroline Sturgis

Sunday
16th August, [1840.]

My dearest Cary,

Anna has been here ten days and we have been even happier together than last year. We have now a fine plan. And that is for you to go with us to Concord next Saty Mr E. wishes me to write and invite you.[1] You must come to town on Friday. He will come on Saty morng and escort us all on Saty p.m. probably in the stage. We shall call for A. at Cambridge. You will thus see her all the way and at Concord in the way you wished, and the best, most various way. We shall stay till Monday p.m. perhaps longer. I will see you in town Saty morng or perhaps go from your house. I think you cannot fail to get this letter in time. I recd yours which I loved, but no time for words now. yours ever

M. F.

ALS (MH: bMS Am 1221 [239]). *Addressed:* Miss Caroline Sturgis / Care Samuel Curson Esq / Newbury, Mass. *Postmark:* Boston Mas Aug 17. *Endorsed:* S. M. Fuller / 16th Aug. 1840.

1. In a letter dated 16 August Emerson urged Fuller to visit him the following Saturday. He said he was writing to Caroline Sturgis to ask her to accompany Fuller to Concord, but he gave no indication here or in subsequent letters that he expected Anna Barker to join them. It was at this time that Fuller and Sturgis were pressing Emerson about his coldness as a friend. According to him, Fuller had two days earlier accused him of "a certain inhospitality of soul" (Rusk, *Letters of RWE*, 2:323, 325).

272. To Caroline Sturgis

Jamaica plain
Eveg of 8th Septr. [1840]

My dear Caroline,

Almost daily it comes into my mind that I should write to tell you how I fare,—yet it seems impossible. Rivers of life flow, seas surge between me and you I cannot look back, nor remember how I passed them.

I live, I am— *The carbuncle is found* And at present the mere sight of my talisman is enough.[1] The hour may come when I wish to charm with it, but not yet. I have no future, as no past. You also must be happy surely. There can be no "stern holding back" but all the pure in heart must be seeing God. Write to me, if you wish for I am not forgetting you.

AL (MH: bMS Am 1221 [240]). *Addressed:* Miss Caroline Sturgis / care S. Curson Esq. / Newbury, / Mass. *Postmark:* Jamaica Plain MS Sep 10. *Endorsed:* Sept 8th 1840. / S. M. Fuller.

1. Probably a reference to chap. 3 of Novalis' *Heinrich von Ofterdingen*. A beautiful young princess loses the talisman, a stone, that protects her from falling into the power of another person. A poor young man whose house she has visited finds the carbuncle, restores it to her, and becomes her lover.

273. To Caroline Sturgis

Jamaica plain,
26th Septr 1840.

My dear Caroline,

I received Jane's letter and your envelope with its enclosure of money. Ellen warmly thanks you; she is now feeling very forlorn at her approaching departure and is grateful for marks of kindness. She goes next week, with W. H. Channing. It is uncertain where she will stay,—in Cincinnati, if she can find employment there, otherwise in Louisville.[1]

All the girls leave me the 1st Octr. Mother and Eugene expect to sail the 10th My two friends are to be married the 3d Octr Rafaello's birthday.

I shall keep house here this winter alone with Lloyd.

I do not yet give up going to Newbury. I wish to see the beautiful place very much. Send often to the post office. If I can come I shall let you know a day or two beforehand. I will bring Jane's letter to you and that to me.

Of the mighty changes in my spiritual life I do not wish to speak, yet surely you cannot be ignorant of them.[2] All has been revealed, all foreshown yet I know it not. Experiment has given place to certainty, pride to obedience, thought to love, and truth is lost in beauty "I am no more below"— I have no words, nor can I now perceive that I shall be able to paint for any one the scenery, nor place in order the history of these great events Yet I have no wish to exclude any one, and of you I almost daily think with love. When we meet you may[n] probably perceive all in me. When we meet you will find me at home. Into that home cold winds may blow, keen lightnings dart their bolts, but I cannot be driven from it more. From that home I look forth and address you sweetly as my friend. Is it not enough?—

AL (MH: bMS Am 1221 [241]). *Addressed:* Miss Caroline Sturgis / Care S. Curson Esq. / Newbury / Mass. *Postmark:* Sept 29. *Endorsed:* S. M. Fuller / 25th Sept 1840.

you may] you ⟨may⟩ may

1. Ellen Fuller arrived in Louisville in October, hoping to establish herself as a schoolteacher. She lived with the George Keats family, often quarreling with them, until August 1841, when she moved to Cincinnati (Frederick T. McGill, Jr., *Channing of Concord* [New Brunswick, N.J., 1967], pp. 50–55).

2. The approaching marriage of Sam Ward and Anna Barker, together with Fuller's quarrel with Emerson about their friendship, prepared the way for a religious experience that profoundly moved Margaret Fuller. Emerson, who disliked what he saw, called it a "sort of ecstatic solitude" (*Memoirs*, 1:308).

274. To Ralph Waldo Emerson

29 Sept 1840

I have felt the impossibility of meeting far more than you; so much, that, if you ever know me well, you will feel that the fact of my abiding by you thus far, affords a strong proof that we are to be much to one another. How often have I left you despairing and forlorn. How often have I said, this light will never understand my fire; this clear eye will never discern the law by which I am filling my circle; this simple force will never interpret my need of manifold being.[1]

Dear friend on one point misunderstand me less.[n] I do not love power other than every vigorous nature delights to feel itself living. To violate the sanctity of relations, I am as far from it as you can be. I make no claim. I have no wish which is not dictated by a feeling of truth. Could I lead the highest Angel captive by a look, that look I would not give, unless prompted by true love. I am no usurper. I ask only mine own inheritance. If it be found that I have mistaken its boundaries, I will give up the choicest vineyard, the fairest flower-garden, to its lawful owner. [   ]

In me I did not think you saw the purity, the singleness, into which,[n] I have faith that all this darting motion, and restless flame shall yet be attempered and subdued. I felt that you did not for me the highest office of friendship, by offering me the clue of the labyrinth of my own being. Yet I thought you appreciated the fearlessness which shrinks from no truth in myself and others, and trusted me, believing that I knew the path for myself. O it must be that you have felt the worth of that truth which has never hesitated to infringe our relation, or aught else, rather than not vindicate itself. If you have not seen this stair on which God has been so untiringly leading me to himself, you have indeed been wholly ignorant of me. Then indeed, when my soul, in its childish agony of prayer, stretched out its arms to you as a father, did you not see what was meant by this crying for the moon; this sullen rejection of playthings which had become unmeaning? Did you then say^n 'I know not what this means; perhaps this will trouble me; the time will come when I shall hide my eyes from this mood;'—then you are^n not the friend I seek.

But did not you ask for a "foe" in your friend? Did not you ask for a "large formidable nature"? But a beautiful foe, I am not yet, to you. Shall I ever be? I know not. My life is now prayer. Through me sweetest harmonies are momently breathing. Shall they not make me beautiful,— Nay, beauty! Shall not all vehemence, all eccentricity, be purged by these streams of divine light? I have, in these hours, but one pain; the sense of the infinite exhausts and exalts: it cannot therefore possess me wholly; else, were I also one wave of gentlest force. Again I shall cease to melt and flow; again I shall seek and pierce and rend asunder.

But oh, I am now full of such sweet certainty, never never more can it be utterly shaken. All things have I given up to the central power, myself, you also; yet, I cannot forbear adding, dear friend. I am now so at home, I know not how again to wander and grope, seeking my place in another Soul. I need to be recognized. After this, I shall be claimed, rather than claim, yet if I speak of facts, it must be as I see them.

To L. my love. In her, I have always recognized the saintly element. *That,* better than a bible in my hand, shows that it cannot be to me wholly alien. Yet am I no saint, no anything, but a great soul born to know all, before it can return to the creative fount.

Yesterday, I saw Mr R. He had, on reflection, taken my frankness in the true way; we are much nearer, and, I think, shall go on better and better. Say no word of this or of aught personal to ———. His vanity makes him perfidious, without his intending it.

MsCfr, in Emerson's hand (MH: Os 735Laa 1840.9.29). Published in Rusk, *Letters of RWE,* 2:340–41; published in part in Miller, pp. 53–55, and Chevigny, pp. 124–25.
    misunderstand me less] misunderstand me ⟨not⟩ less
    singleness, into which,] singleness, ⟨which I myself do as yet but discern from afar, Yet,⟩ into which,

then say] then ⟨cry⟩ ↑ say ↓
then you are] ↑ then ↓ you are

1. For a possible answer to this letter, see Emerson's letter of October? 2? 1840?, in which he acknowledges, "You have a right to expect great activity great demonstration & large intellectual contributions from your friends, & tho' you do not say it you receive nothing. As well be related to mutes as to uncommunicating egoists" (Rusk, *Letters of RWE*, 2:342). The nature of their friendship had increasingly become a topic of conversation, for Fuller was finding it impossible to ignore his lofty reserve. In a journal fragment dated merely "22d Jany," probably written in 1840, she had poured our her frustration:

> Mr. E. scarce knows the instincts. And uses them rather for rejection than reception where he uses them at all. In friendship with R.W.E., I cannot hope to feel that I am his or he mine. He has nothing peculiar, nothing sacred for his friend. He is not to his friend a climate, an atmosphere, neither is his friend a being organized especially for him, born for his star. He speaks of a deed, of a thought to any commoner as much as to his peer. His creed is, show thyself, let them take as much as they can. . . . His friendship is only strong preference and he weighs and balances, buys and sells you and himself all the time. [MH: Os 735Z 1840.1.22]

275. To Albert G. Greene

Jamaica Plain
2d Octr 1840.

My dear Mr Greene

Where are the poems and essays and Pumpkin Monodies and Militia musters we were promised.[1] Send them, I beg, forthwith.

I shall not see you in P. this autumn, for the state of our affairs makes it impossible. Mother is going with my eldest brother[n] to N. Orleans, in consequence of the illness of my sister in law, leaving the care of all our affairs with me.[2] I trust those who gave their[n] names as wishing me to come clearly understand that I *always* made it conditional. I would not on any acct appear to treat with lightness persons for whom I have a sincere regard. And, as the misuse that I hear has been made of my name in P. by persons from whom I could not have expected such a course makes me a little anxious lest I should be thus misrepresented. I ask you, whom I believe to be sincerely my friend, to state the facts, if fault is found with me. That I never promised more than, that, if a class were offered me, *I would* come *if*[n] *I could.* And now I *cannot* with any convenience. In the spring perhaps I might, if it were wished.

I have heard with much regret of frequent illness in your family which is, I hope, now[n] at an end. Remember me to Mrs G. and your daughters[3] and believe me sincerely yours

S. M. FULLER.

ALS (RPB). Published in part in Higginson, *MFO,* p. 163. *Addressed:* Albert G. Greene, Esq / Providence / R.I.

Albert Gorton Greene was the most prominent writer of the literary circle in Providence when Fuller taught there.

going with my eldest brother] going ↑ with my eldest brother ↓
who gave their] who gave ⟨need⟩ their
would come *if*] *would* ↑ come ↓ *if*
I hope, now] I hope, ↑ now ↓

1. "Pumpkin Monodies" probably refers to Greene's unpublished 1839 poem "Pumpkin Pie," dedicated to Fuller, "whose heart is as big and as sound as a pumpkin and as worthy" ("Pumpkin Pie," 9 October 1839, Harris Collection, RPB). "Militia Musters" was another Greene poem (Rusk, *Letters of RWE,* 2:269).

2. Mrs. Fuller and Eugene arrived in New Orleans during the latter part of November. The ill sister-in-law was Eugene's wife, Anna (Margarett C. Fuller to Margaret Fuller, 22 November 1840, MH).

3. The Greenes had four daughters: Elizabeth Clifford (1825–57), who married, first, Cornelius Fenner and, second, Gardiner H. Clark; Arazelia Gray (1828–99), who married first Charles Potter and then Charles C. Van Zandt; Mary Clifford (1834–95), who married Samuel C. Eastman; and Sarah Margaret Fuller (b. 1839), who married the Reverend Samuel W. Duncan (Louise B. Clarke, *The Greenes of Rhode Island* [New York, 1903], pp. 587–88; *Boston Evening Transcript,* 13 March 1899; Guy S. Rix, *History and Genealogy of the Eastman Family of America* [Concord, N.H., 1901], 2:625).

276.   To William H. Channing[?]

10 October 1840

I felt singular pleasure in seeing you quote Hood's lines on "Melancholy." I thought nobody knew and loved his serious poems except myself, and two or three others, to whom I imparted them. Do you like, also, the ode to Autumn, and—

Sigh on, sad heart, for love's eclipse?[1]

It was a beautiful time when I first read these poems. I was staying at Hallowell, Maine, and could find no books that I liked, except Hood's poems. You know how the town is built, like a terraced garden on the river's bank; I used to go every afternoon to the granite quarry which crowns these terraces, and read till the sunset came casting its last glory on the opposite bank. They were such afternoons as those in September and October, clear, soft, and radiant. Nature held nothing back. 'T is many years since, and I have never again seen the Kennebec, but remember it as a stream of noble character. It was the first river I ever sailed up, realizing all which that emblem discloses of life. Greater still would the charm have been to sail downward along an unknown stream, seeking not a home, but a ship upon the ocean.

ELfr, from *Memoirs*, 2:44.

1. Thomas Hood (1799–1845), a friend of Charles Lamb, William Hazlitt, and Thomas De Quincy, published "Ode: Autumn" in 1823 and "Ode to Melancholy" in 1827. His "Ballad" opens with the line Fuller quotes (*DNB*).

277. To Caroline Sturgis

Jamaica plain
Sunday 18th Octr, [1840]

Your recognition, my Caroline, added to the happiness it could not deepen.— Rightly you say the past distrust was always forgiven by me as it is now by yourself. I knew it must come to an end and my truth at last be truly felt by one so true, but I did not hope we should meet so soon after waiting so long.

—I have returned to the world of dust a[nd] fuss and conflicting claims and bills and du[ties?] Yet through me flows the same sweet harmony and last[n] night in such full strains that it seemed as if that must be the last of[n] my human life. Yet here I am and willing to stay in a spot from which such infinite loveliness may be descried, such infinite holiness be known.

I have had other beautiful letters beside yours, one yesterday from Raphael and his Madonna.[1] They were at Franconia, and now in full flower. I knew it well, yet was it sweet to read the words as you shall sometime. Friday I went to Concord. Waldo had just received your letter; it seemed to have puzzled and disconcerted him.[2] I looked at him with great love, yet it seemed that he would be very slow in solving all these problems that are before him now. The Phalanx talk was useless, I should think to all present except myself. For me it brought out their different ways of thinking in strong relief, and helped me to a judgment.[3]

I do not feel inclined to write you a letter now, but if you stay as long as you thought (through Novr,) I shall, I know. Nearly the whole of the coming week I must give to setting mine house in order. With my class I shall begin the first Wednesday in Novr, a fort night from next Wednesday. It is as yet quite small. All the Jacksons have signed off, including probably Marianne. I heard a pretty anecedote of R. Lowell, but it would take too much space to write it now.[4] This day must be chiefly Mother's. Shall I not have the verses in a day or two. In love and deepest faith yours

MARGARET—

ALS (MH: bMS Am 1221 [226]). *Addressed:* Miss Caroline Sturgis / Care Saml Curzon Esq. / Newbury / Mass. *Postmark:* Jamaica Plain MS Oct 19.

sweet harmony and last] sweet harmony and ⟨through⟩ last
the last of] the last ⟨night⟩ of

1. Sam Ward and Anna Barker had been married on 3 October; they were now on their honeymoon (*Barker Genealogy*, p. 180).

2. As Fuller was writing this letter, Emerson was writing to Sturgis: "I am a slow scholar at magnetism, dear sister, & always read the newspaper whilst that subject is discussed. I do not pretend to understand anything in your last letter but its lyric measures wh. are always beautiful to me" (Rusk, *Letters of RWE*, 2:346).

3. On 17 October Emerson noted in his journal, "Yesterday George & Sophia Ripley, Margaret Fuller & Alcott discussed here the new social plans" for Brook Farm. He was no more impressed than Fuller: "I wished to be convinced, to be thawed, to be made nobly mad by the kindlings before my eye of a new dawn of human piety. But this scheme was arithmetic & comfort. . . . And not once could I be inflamed . . ." (*JMN*, 7:407–8).

4. James Russell Lowell was dividing his attention between his law studies with Charles Loring in Boston and his fiancée, Maria White, in Watertown.

278. To William H. Channing[?]

19 October 1840

[Dr. Eustis] was here.[1] Generally I go out of the room when he comes, for his great excitability makes me nervous, and his fondness for detail is wearisome. But to-night I was too much fatigued to do anything else, and did not like to leave mother; so I lay on the sofa while she talked with him.

My mind often wandered, yet ever and anon, as I listened again to him, I was struck with admiration at the compensations of Nature. Here is a man, isolated from his kind beyond any I know, of an ambitious temper and without an object, of tender affections and without a love or a friend. I don't suppose any mortal, unless it be his aged mother, cares more for him than we do,—scarce any value him so much. The disease, which has left him, in the eyes of men, a scathed and blighted tree, has driven him back to Nature, and she has not refused him sympathy. I was surprised by the refinement of his observations on the animals, his pets. He has carried his intercourse with them to a degree of perfection we rarely attain with our human friends. There is no misunderstanding between him and his dogs and birds; and how rich has been the acquaintance in suggestion! Then the flowers! I liked to hear him, for he recorded all their pretty ways,—not like a botanist, but a lover. His interview with the Magnolia of Lake Pontchartrain was most romantic. And what he said of the Yuca seems to me so pretty, that I will write it down, though somewhat more concisely than he told it:—

I had kept these plants of the Yuca Filamentosa six or seven years, though they had never bloomed. I knew nothing of them, and had no notion of what feelings they would excite. Last June I found in bud the one which had the most favorable exposure. A week or two after, another, which was more in the shade, put out flower-buds, and I thought I should be able to watch them, one after the other; but, no! the one which was most favored waited for the other, and both flowered together at the full of the moon. This struck me as very singular, but as soon as I saw the flower by moonlight I understood it. This flower is made for the moon, as the Heliotrope is for the sun, and refuses other influences or to display her beauty in any other light.

The first night I saw it in flower, I was conscious of a peculiar delight, I may even say rapture. Many white flowers are far more beautiful by day; the lily, for instance, with its firm, thick leaf, needs the broadest light to manifest its purity. But these transparent leaves of greenish white, which looked dull in the day, are melted by the moon to glistening silver. And not only does the plant not appear in its destined hue by day, but the flower, though, as bell-shaped, it cannot quite close again after having once expanded, yet presses its petals together as closely as it can, hangs down its little blossoms, and its tall stalk seems at noon to have reared itself only to betray a shabby insignificance. Thus, too, with the leaves, which have burst asunder suddenly like the fan-palm to make way for the stalk,—their edges in the day time look ragged and unfinished, as if nature had left them in a hurry for some more pleasing task. On the day after the evening when I had thought it so beautiful, I could not conceive how I had made such a mistake.

But the second evening I went out into the garden again. In clearest moonlight stood my flower, more beautiful than ever. The stalk pierced the air like a spear, all the little bells had erected themselves around it in most graceful array, with petals more transparent than silver, and of softer light than the diamond. Their edges were clearly, but not sharply defined. They seemed to have been made by the moon's rays. The leaves, which had looked ragged by day, now seemed fringed by most delicate gossamer, and the plant might claim with pride its distinctive epithet of Filamentosa. I looked at it till my feelings became so strong that I longed to share it. The thought which filled my mind was that here we saw the type of pure feminine beauty in the moon's own flower. I have since had further opportunity of watching the Yuca, and verified these observations, that she will not flower till the full moon, and chooses to hide her beauty from the eye of day.[2]

Might not this be made into a true poem, if written out merely as history of the plant, and no observer introduced? How finely it harmonizes with all legends of Isis, Diana, &c! It is what I tried to say in the sonnet,—

> Woman's heaven,
> Where palest lights a silvery sheen diffuse.[3]

In tracing these correspondences, one really does take hold of a Truth, of a Divine Thought.

ELfr, from *Memoirs*, 2:47–49.

1. Higginson identifies her source as "Dr. Eustis, in his garden at Brookline." William Eustis (1796–1843) was a nephew of Governor William Eustis. The son of Jacob (1755–1834) and Elizabeth Gray Eustis (d. 1847), the younger Eustis graduated from Harvard in 1830, took his M.D. degree in 1838, and practiced medicine until his death (Higginson, *MFO*, p. 96; Warner Eustis, *The Eustis Families in the United States* [n.p., 1968], 1:211).

2. Fuller later turned both the magnolia and the yucca into prose meditations: "The Magnolia of Lake Pontchartrain," *Dial* 1 (January 1841):299–305, and "Yuca Filamentosa," *Dial* 2 (January 1842):286–88.

3. Her "To Allston's Picture, 'The Bride,'" *Dial* 1 (July 1840):84.

279. To Caroline Sturgis

Thursday,
Oct 22d 1840.

dear Caroline,

Love goes forth towards you as I read your truest words. I would fain bless you for your recognition. I would sound a trumpet note clear as light now that you are ready for the Genesis. You will go forth, you will leave your heaven, you will not only make the lights, the night, the day, and the great sea but in the least creeping thing will harmonize love and express faith in the revolutions of being. Amen—now may be looked for the Sabbath when a divine consciousness shall proclaim *it is very good.* Life and peace bloom at once and the One divides itself to win the last divinest birth of Love.

But I can say very little now, scarce a word that is not absolutely drawn from me at the moment. I cannot plunge into myself enough. I cannot dedicate myself sufficiently. The life that flows in upon me from so many quarters is too beautiful to be checked. I would not check a single pulsation. It all ought to be;—if caused by any apparition of the Divine in me I could bless myself like the holy Mother. But like her I long to be virgin. I would fly from the land of my birth. I would hide myself in night and poverty. Does a star point out the spot. The gifts I must receive, yet for my child, not me. I have no words, wait till he is of age, then hear *him*

Oh Caroline, my soul swells with the future. The past, I know it not. I have just written a letter to our dear Waldo which gives me pain.[1] It was all into the past. His call bids me return, I know not how, yet full of tender renunciation, know not how to refuse. All the souls I ever loved are holy to me, their voices sound more and more sweet yet oh for an hour of absolute silence, dedicated, enshrined in the bosom of the One.

Yet the cross, the symbol you have chosen seems indeed the one. Daily, hourly it is laid upon me. Tremulously I feel that a wound is yet to be given. Separation! to be severed for ages from my rapture and the angel forms through which it shone, must not that be so? Oh, because I dread it, because my courage is not yet so perfect as my submission, because I might say, Father, if it be thy will let this cup pass, shall I not be forced to drink it? Oh the prophetic dread and hope and pain and joy. My Caroline, I am not yet purified. Let the lonely Vestal watch the fire till it draws her to itself and consumes this mortal part. Truly you say I have not been what I am now yet it is only transformation, not alteration. The leaf became a stem, a bud, is now in flower. Winds of heaven, dews of night, circles of time, already ye make haste to convert this flower into dead-seeming seed—yet Caroline far fairer shall it bloom again

Was it as you say that I wished too much to make a virtue bloom in my particular garden. If so I dare to say it was not for me, but for the Universe. I loved the realizing of ideas, and this was easiest in the nearness of mine own persons but it seems to me that they were always recognized with utmost joy elsewhere.

Still I perceive this love of realizing is here in the desire I feel for nun like dedication in these months to come. All that I have ever known comes up in my thoughts on the other side from what it did. I was stern and fearless. I am soft and of most delicate tenderness. I rushed into the melee an Amazon of breast undefended save by its inward glow. Shrouded in a white veil I would now kneel at the secretest shrines and pace the dimmest cloisters— I rushed out like the great sea, burst against all rocks, strewed with weeds and shells all matted and forlorn the loveliest shores, welcome alike the graceful nymph and the slimiest monster to a refuge or a death[.] in my deep mysterious grottoes I feared no rebuff, I shrunk from no publicity, I could not pause yet ever I sobbed and wailed over my endless motion and foamed angrily to meet the storm-winds which kept me pure— I would now steal away over golden sands, through silent flowery meadows farther still through darkest forests "full of heavenly vows" into the very heart of the untrodden mountain where the carbuncle has lit the way to veins of yet undreamed of diamond.

One day that I once lived at Groton rises on my thoughts with charm unspeakable. I had passed the night in the sick chamber of a wretched girl in the last stage of a consumption. It was said she had profaned her maiden state, and that the means she took to evade the consequences of her stain had destroyed her health and placed her on this bed of death. The room was full of poverty, base thoughts, and fragments of destiny. As I raised her dying head it rested against my bosom like a clod that should never have been taken from the valley. On my soul brooded a sadness of deepest calm. I looked ay I *gazed* into that abyss lowest in humanity of crime for the sake of sensual pleasure, my eye was steadfast, yet above me shone a star, pale, tearful, still it shone, it was mirrored from the very blackness of the yawning gulf. Through the shadows of that night ghost-like with step unlistened for, unheard assurance came to me. O, it has ever been thus, from the darkest comes my brightness, from Chaos depths my love. I returned with the morning star. No one was with me in the house. I unlocked the door went into the silent room where but late before my human father dwelt. It was the first winter of my suffering health the musings and vigils of the night had exhausted while exalting[n] me. The cold rosy winter dawn and then the sun. I had forgotten to wind up the clock[n] the day marked itself. I lay there, I could not resolve to give myself food The day was unintentionally a fast. Sacredest thoughts were upon it, and I comprehended the meaning of an ascetic life. The Angel that meets the pious monk

168

beside the bed of pestilence and low vice, that dwells with him in the ruined hut of his macerated body, hovered sweet though distant before me also. At times I read the Bible at times Wordsworth[n] I dwelt in the thoughtful solitudes of his Excursion I wandered like his white doe.[2] The change from my usual thoughts and feelings was as if a man should leave the perfumed, wildly grand oft times poisonous wildernesses of the tropics the crocodiles and lion hunts and haughty palms, for the snowy shroud, intent unpromising silence, and statuesque moons of the Northern winter from which Phenix like rises the soul into the tenderest Spring. The sunset of that day was the same which will shine on my last hour here below.— Winter is coming now. I rejoice in her bareness, her pure shroud, her judgment-announcing winds. These will help me to dedicate myself, all these Winter spirits will cradle my childhood with strange and mystic song. Oh Child who would'st deem thee mine canst thou read what I cannot write. No only one soul is there that can lead me up to womanhood and baptize me to gentlest May. Is it not ready? I have strength to wait as a smooth bare tree forever, but ask no more my friends for leaves and flowers or a bird haunted bower.

AL (MH: bMS Am 1221 [242]). *Addressed:* Miss Caroline Sturgis / Care Saml Curson Esq / Newbury / Mass. *Postmark:* Jamaica Plain MS Oct 23. *Endorsed:* Oct 22d 1840.

while exalting] while ⟨exh⟩ exalting
up the clock] up the ⟨winter⟩ clock
at times Wordsworth] at times Wordsworth⟨s⟩

1. Responding to her letter, which has not survived, Emerson wrote on 24 October, "I have your frank & noble & affecting letter, and yet I think I could wish it unwritten" (Rusk, *Letters of RWE*, 2:352).

2. "The Excursion" was published in 1814, and "The White Doe of Rylston" in 1815. In the latter poem, one of Wordsworth's favorites, Emily Norton, the last of her family, returns to her ancestral home at Rylston and is joined by a white doe, which becomes her companion and consolation. After her death, the doe watches over her grave.

280. To Caroline Sturgis

[ca. 25 October 1840]

I have read over[n] these letters twice.—[1] At Newbury I was disappointed in them, for then my soul, all bathed in rosy light, floated away from this cold blue.

But now I am in a less glowing atmosphere and looking this way see the rising stars. May thy voice call many forth. May I be pure of sight to discern the whole galaxy.

Yet Waldo is still only a small and secluded part of Nature, secluded by a doubt, secluded by a sneer. I am ashamed of him for the letter he wrote about our meeting.— It is equally unworthy of him and of what he professes for you. He calls you his sister and his saint yet cannot trust your sight. There are many beings who have reached a height of generosity and freedom far above him.

But none is truer, purer, and he is already profound.

What is all this talk about the positive degree? Still this same dull distrust of life! When the sun paints the cloud, when the tree clusters its leaves, when the bird dwells more sweetly and fully on a note than is necessary just to let his mate know he is wanted, the comparative and superlative degrees are used— The fact on which Waldo ever dwells in the world of thought, that whatever is excellent supersedes the whole world and commands us entirely for the moment, is expressed in the world of feeling by use of the superlative. Do we say dearest, wisest, virtuosest, best,—we make no vow, but express that the object is able to supersede all calculation

O these tedious, tedious attempts to learn the universe by thought alone. Love, Love, my Father, thou hast given me.— I thank thee for its pains.

I cannot read these letters without a great renewal of my desire to teach this sage all he wants to make him the full-formed Angel. But that task is not for me. The gulf which separates us is too wide. May thou be his friend, it would be a glorious office. But you are not so yet.

AL (MH: bMS Am 1221 [225]).

have read over] have read ⟨all⟩ over

1. At this time the continuing discussion about friendship among Emerson, Sturgis, and Fuller ended tensely. Fuller here specifically refers to Emerson's letter of 18 October to Sturgis, in which he said, "I have written you down in my book & in my heart for my sister because you are a user of the positive degree." Then he firmly brought the discussion to an end with Fuller on 24 October when he wrote, "I see very dimly in writing on this topic. It will not prosper with me. Perhaps all my words are wrong. Do not expect it of me again for a very long time" (Rusk, *Letters of RWE*, 2:347, 353). The result of his meditation on friendship appeared as the middle essay in *Essays: First Series* the following year.

281. To William H. Channing

25 and 28 October 1840
[Jamaica Plain?]

[I] This week I have not read any book, nor once walked in the woods and field.

I meant to give its days to setting outward things in order, and its evenings to writing. But, I know not how it is, I can never simplify my life; always so many ties, so many claims! However, soon the winter winds will chant matins and vespers, which may make my house a cell, and in a snowy veil enfold me for my prayer. If I cannot dedicate myself this time, I will not expect it again. Surely it should be! These Carnival masks have crowded on me long enough, and Lent must be at hand.[1] [   ]

———— and ———— have been writing me letters, to answer which required all the time and thought I could give for a day or two. ————'s were of joyful recognition, and so beautiful I would give much to show them to you. ————'s have singularly affected me. They are noble, wise, of most unfriendly friendliness. I don't know why it is, I always seem to myself to have gone so much further with a friend than I really have. Just as at Newport I thought ———— met me, when he did not, and sang a joyful song which found no echo, so here ———— asks me questions which I thought had been answered in the first days of our acquaintance, and coldly enumerates all the charming qualities which make it impossible for him to part with me! He scolds me though in the sweetest and solemnest way. I will not quote his words, though their beauty tempts me, for they do not apply, they do not touch me.[2]

Why is it that the religion of my nature is so much hidden from my peers? why do they question me, who never question them? why persist to regard as a meteor an orb of assured hope? Can no soul know me wholly? shall I never know the deep delight of gratitude to any but the All-Knowing? I shall wait for ———— very peaceably, in reverent love as ever; but I cannot see why he should not have the pleasure of knowing now a friend, who has been "so tender and true."[3]

———— was here, and spent twenty-four hours in telling me a tale of deepest tragedy. Its sad changes should be written out in Godwin's best manner: such are the themes he loved, as did also Rousseau.[4] Through all the dark shadows shone a pure white ray, one high, spiritual character, a man, too, and of advanced age. I begin to respect men more,—I mean actual men. What men may be, I know; but the men of today have seemed to me of such coarse fibre, or else such poor wan shadows?

———— had scarcely gone, when ———— came and wished to spend a few hours with me. I was totally exhausted, but I lay down, and she sat beside me, and poured out all her noble feelings and bright fancies. There was little light in the room, and she gleamed like a cloud

—— "of pearl and opal,"

and reminded me more than ever of

—— "the light-haired Lombardess
Singing a song of her own native land,

to the dying Correggio, beside the fountain.

I am astonished to see how much Bettine's book is to all these people.[5] This shows how little courage they have had to live out themselves. She really brings them a revelation. The men wish they had been loved by Bettine; the girls wish to write down the thoughts that come, and see if just such a book does not grow up. ——, however, was one of the few who do not over-estimate her; she truly thought Bettine only publishes what many burn. Would not genius be common as light, if men trusted their higher selves?

[II] I have let myself be cheated out of my Sunday, by going to hear Mr. [Dewey].[6] As he began by reading the first chapter of Isaiah, and the fourth of John's Epistle, I made mental comments with pure delight. "Bring no more vain oblations." "Every one that loveth is born of God, and knoweth God." "We know that we dwell in Him, and He in us, because he hath given us of the Spirit."[7] Then pealed the organ, full of solemn assurance. But straightway uprose the preacher to deny mysteries, to deny the second birth, to deny influx, and to renounce the sovereign gift of insight, for the sake of what he deemed a "*rational*" exercise of will. As he spoke I could not choose but deny him all through, and could scarce refrain from rising to expound, in the light of my own faith, the words of those wiser Jews which had been read. Was it not a sin to exchange friendly greeting as we parted, and yet tell him no word of what was in my mind?

Still I saw why he looked at things as he did. The old religionists did talk about "grace, conversion," and the like, technically, without striving to enter into the idea, till they quite lost sight of it. Under-valuing the intellect, they became slaves of a sect, instead of organs of the Spirit. This Unitarianism has had its place. There was a time for asserting "the dignity of human nature," and for explaining total depravity into temporary inadequacy, [III] a time to say that the truths of Essence, if simplified at all in statement from their infinite variety of existence, should be spoken of as One rather than Three. (Though that number, if they would only let it reproduce itself is of highest significance) yet the time seems now to have come for reinterpreting the old dogmas. I would now preach the Holy Ghost as zealously as they have been preaching Man, and faith instead of the understanding and mysticism instead &c

It is by no means useless to preach.[8] In my experience of the divine gifts of solitude I had forgotten what might be done in this other way. O that crowd of upturned faces with their look of unintelligent complacency. Give me tears and groans rather if there be a mixture of physical excitement and bigotry. Mr Dewey is heard because, though he has not entered into the secret of piety, he wishes to be heard and with a good purpose; can make a forcible statement and kindle himself[n] with his own thought. How many persons must there be who cannot worship alone since they are content with so little. Can we not wake the spark that will melt them, till they take beautiful forms and can exist each alone? Were one to come now who could purge as with fire, how would these masses glow and be clarified— Today, dear friend, I hoped you would not leave but ennoble the profession. Mr. Dewey made a good suggestion *"Such things could not be said in the open air"* You will preach for the open air. Speak thunder and lightning and dew and rustling leaves, and palest stars.— Yet must the preacher have the *thought* of today before he can be its voice. None of us have it yet but you and I are nearer than others because not so ready to dogmatize as if we had got it, neither content to stop short with mere impressions and presumptuous hopes. I feel it is coming, sometimes I think I shall have it in a day, many steps have I counted steps of purest alabaster of shining jasper, also of rough brick and slippery mossgrown stone. We shall reach what we will, since we neither fear lest these steps shall lose us in the deepest vault of earth, nor vague of upper air, for our God knows not fear only reverence, and his plan is All.

Were you here and the words could be spoken as they rise perhaps this thought would be found sooner, perhaps not, you will not spare trouble to write me your glimpses, will you. You will not regard inadequacy of expression, that *must* exist till the whole be known. I shall understand your leadings. Come what may I do not expect to be the[n] voice of this epoch. Perhaps you may; that would make me glad. But all my tendency at present is to the deepest privacy.— Where can I hide till I am given to myself? Yet I love the others more and more, and when they are with me must give them the best from my scrap.

When I see their infirmities I would fain heal them, forgetful of my own! But am[n] I left one moment alone, then a poor wandering pilgrim, yet no saint, I would seek the shrine, would therein die to the world and then if from the poor reliques some miracle might be wrought, that is for them!—

Yet some of these saints were able to work in their generation, for they had renounced all!

Well farewell, Sunday, scanty day.— This is Anna's birthday too.[9] Last year on this day she sent me a book; was not that like her, to give at a time when all others receive. Just so at her marriage she now gave me the gift I delight to think of this.

Wednesday eveg 28th

This is my first day of loneliness. I went into town on Monday and staid with mother till she sailed yesterday They have been expecting to sail ever since the 15th and the days of waiting have been forlorn and of late to Mother so oppressive that I was very anxious to have her go yet the last look at her sweet face, and the last goodbye to Eugene now that he has finally parted from his anchorage made me very sad. As a family we are finally broken apart now; it is well; for some months I have been preparing, indeed I feel no longer equal to my own part yet the last moment was sad. I feel by no means secure that Mother will reap the benefits I wish from this step, but it was the best I knew.

In town I saw the Ripleys.— Mr R. more and more wrapt in his new project. He is too sanguine, and does not take time to let things ripen in his mind, yet his aim is worthy, and with his courage and clear mind his experiment will not, I think, to him at least be a failure. I will not throw any cold water, yet I could wish him the aid of some equal and faithful friend in the beginning, the rather that his own mind, though that of a captain is not that of a conqueror. I feel more hopeful as he builds less wide, but cannot feel that I have any thing to do at present except to look on and see the coral insects at work.

Ballou was with him to night, he seems a downright person, clear as to his own purposes and not unwilling to permit others the pursuit of theirs.[10]

Sophia R. read me her letter to you. I told her the truth that I cannot understand her mental processes, and that what she says sounds to me factitious at first, though my confidence in her always prevents my indulging such a thought. I understand her husband much better, though we are so utterly dissimilar, and she usually goes higher and sees clearer than he does. I can talk with him endlessly though not deeply, with her I can go only a step though she loves me and I her, she seldom misunderstands me, he often. About this letter I could not follow her at all. How can one be indifferent to seeing the thought verified by the act, if they care for life at all. How be destitute of moral enthusiasm in a world so full of imperfection! She read me a late letter of Mrs Noblers to illustrate what she said, and to be sure I disliked *that*, and saw the danger of people's constantly lauding one another for trifling acts of truth and goodness, till they visit each other only on stilts. Your letter I read again and with new approval. I understand that scripture well.

S[am] and A[nna] returned Monday night, but I had not courage to see them, so fatigued was I. I left a note desiring them to come out, and found the sweetest little one from them awaiting my return.

Lloyd's joy at seeing me was quite pathetic. He had a message from the Shaws about taking me to night to see the marbles by torchlight, and was, I saw, much afraid I should accept it.[11] He was quite chivalrous, running about doing the honors and telling the news. I thought myself quite a heroine to take the task[n] of civilizing him this winter, and lo! here it is half done to my hand merely by the situation.

Well here I am— It is the first day for a year that I have passed entire at my own good pleasure, always excepting Cohasset and Newbury.[n] I have written no letter, I have looked at no account. I have given no task, my thoughts have ranged at will and this at home.[12]

Have I been happy? Yes,— Shall I be six months of such days? I shall not have them! There is some magic about me which draws other spirits into my circle whether I will or they will or no. It would be the same if I planted my staff in a desert.— So be it, I have not been impatient nor will be, if only for dread of the bard's saying.

> Wer sich der Einsamkeit ergibt,
> Ach! der ist bald allein,
> Ein jeder lebt, ein jeder liebt,
> Und lässt ihn seiner Pein[13]

Last night in visiting each solitary chamber I missed my children with their loving looks. The love was shallow, but it was pure.

This reminds me of what I heard in town that James is a Father and has gone to see his child.[14] This news made me more grave even than such[n] usually does. I suppose because I have known the growth of James's character so intimately. I called to mind a letter he had written me of what we had expected of our Fathers. The ideal Father, the profoundly wise, provident, divinely tender and benign, he is indeed the God of the human heart. How solemn this moment of being called to prepare the way, to *make way* for another generation. What fulfilment does it claim in the character of a man that he should be worthy to be a Father, what purity of motive, what dignity, what knowledge! When I recollect how deep the anguish, how deeper still the want, with which I walked alone in hours of childish passion, and called for a Father often saying the Word a hundred times till it was stifled by sobs, how great seems the duty that name imposes.[15] Were but the harmony preserved throughout, Could the child keep learning his earthly as he does his heavenly father from all best experience of life till at last it were the climax ["]I am the Father. Have ye seen me, ye have seen the father,"[16] but how many sons have we to make one father. Surely to spirits not only purified but perfected this is the climax of their being, a wise and worthy parentage.

Here I always sympathize with Mr Alcott, He views the relation truly. [   ]

The last leaves of October, dull, faded, drenched with black rain, yet scorn them not, for on the bank where they are strewed forlorn, the violet shall peep forth in a more genial season![n]

I: ELr, from *Memoirs*, 2:50–52. II: ELfr, from *Memoirs*, 2:84–85. III: ALfr (MB: Ms. Am. 1450 [40]). III published in part in *Memoirs*, 2:85–86, and Higginson, *MFO*, pp. 183–84.

kindle himself] kindle ⟨kindle⟩ himself
to be the] *This phrase and the three preceding sentences are canceled by a later hand.*
But am] But ↑am↓
take the task] take ⟨on myself⟩ the task
always excepting Cohasset and Newbury] ↑always excepting Cohasset and Newbury↓
than such] than ⟨it⟩ ↑such↓
season!] *The last paragraph is a postscript on the outside of the letter.*

1. This was a time of extreme emotional tension for Fuller. Not only had she the *Dial* to edit and her conversations to open on 4 November, but she was trying to compose herself after the marriage of the Wards and the emotional struggle with Emerson.
2. The identity of Fuller's correspondents is unclear, but one may have been Charles Newcomb; the meeting at Newport may have been with Sam Ward.
3. "O Douglas, O Douglas! tindir and trewe," from stanza 31 of Sir Richard Holland's *Buke of the Howlat* (ca. 1450). Though not the Douglas motto, this phrase was associated with the clan.
4. William Godwin (1756–1836) published *The Adventures of Caleb Williams* in 1794 and *St. Leon* in 1799.
5. Probably Bettina von Arnim's *Günderode.*
6. Though Channing left a blank in the *Memoirs* and blotted the name on the surviving holograph, enough can be read to identify Orville Dewey. Dewey graduated from Williams College and from Andover Theological Seminary, but became a Unitarian. After two years as Dr. Channing's assistant, Dewey became the minister of the Unitarian Church in New Bedford from 1823 to 1833. From 1835 to 1848 he was the minister at the Church of the Messiah in New York. He was a popular, accomplished preacher, one greatly admired by Fuller's friends Mary Rotch and Eliza Farrar (*Heralds*, 3:84–89).
7. Isa. 1:13, 1 John 4:7, and 1 John 4:13.
8. Behind her comments here lies Fuller's knowledge that Channing was not an

Albert Gorton Greene. Courtesy of the Rhode Island Historical Society.

accomplished preacher. She is deliberately building his confidence at the expense of Dewey.

9. Anna Barker Ward was born on 25 October 1813 (*Barker Genealogy*, p. 180).

10. Adin Ballou (1803–90), a reformer of even more enthusiasm than George Ripley, was instrumental in founding the Hopedale Community. The son of a Rhode Island farmer, Ballou had no formal education, but he became an inspired preacher after he had a vision. He was ordained in 1821 by the Connecticut Christian Conference and again in 1823 as a Universalist. Ballou held Universalist and Unitarian pulpits in Milford, Massachusetts, New York City, and Mendon, Massachusetts. In 1822 he married Abigail Sayles (1800–1829); his second wife, whom he married in 1830, was Lucy Hunt (b. 1810) (*Heralds*, 2:297–300; Adin Ballou, *An Elaborate History and Genealogy of the Ballous in America* [Providence, 1888], pp. 363–65; MVR 420:553).

11. Both Francis George Shaw (1809–82) and his wife, Sarah Blake Sturgis Shaw (1815–1902), were Fuller's close friends. The son of Robert Gould and Elizabeth Willard Parkman Shaw, Francis went into his father's highly lucrative business, retired in 1840 with an ample fortune, and spent his time on Fourierism and literary study. He translated George Sand's *Consuelo* and *La Comtesse de Rudolstadt* (*NEHGR* 37:116; *Memorial Biographies*, 2:38–61; Hodgman, "Elias Parkman," p. 60). Sarah was the daughter of Nathaniel Russell (1799–1856) and Susan Parkman Sturgis (1780–1827). Fuller had known Sarah and her brothers and sisters since their childhood (*Sturgis of Yarmouth*, pp. 50–51). The Frank Shaws were a prominent antislavery family whose son, Robert Gould Shaw (1837–63), died a hero in the Civil War at the head of a black regiment. He is immortalized in Augustus Saint-Gaudens' monument facing the Massachusetts State House. The "marbles" are probably the sculptures on exhibit at the Boston Athenaeum. Fuller described the collection (with marbles and casts of works by Hiram Powers, Shobal Clevenger, and Bertil Thorvaldsen) in *Dial* 1 (October 1840):-260–63 (Swan, *Athenaeum Gallery*, pp. 153–54).

12. Fuller is being disingenuous with Channing, for she had just written Emerson yet another letter about friendship (see letter 280).

13. Fuller accurately quotes the first four lines of one of the "Harfenspieler" poems in Goethe's *Wilhelm Meisters Lehrjahre*. Sung by a wandering, half-mad Harper, this poem appears in bk. 2, chap. 13. Carlyle translates the lines (*Wilhelm Meister's Apprenticeship and Travels*, 23:167–68):

> Who never ate his bread in sorrow,
> Who never spent the darksome hours
> Weeping and watching for the morrow,
> He knows ye not, ye heavenly Powers.

14. Herman Huidekoper Clarke (1840–49) (William W. Johnson, *Clarke-Clark Genealogy: Records of the Descendants of Thomas Clarke, Plymouth, 1623–1697* [North Greenfield, Wis., 1884], p. 85).

15. Fuller's own evaluation of her father can be found in *Memoirs*, 1:14: "He had no conception of the subtle and indirect motions of imagination and feeling."

16. John 8:19.

282. To William H. Channing[?]

[ca. 31 October 1840]

[I] It rained, and the day was pale and sorrowful, the thick-fallen leaves [II] ever shrouded the river. We went out in the boat and sat under the bridge. To me the pallid silence, the constant fall of the rain and leaves were most soothing, life had been for many weeks so crowded with thought and feeling, pain and pleasure," rapture and care. Nature seemed gently to fold us in her matron's mantle. On such days the fall of the leaf is not sad as on that you described, only meditative. She seemed to loose the record of past summer hours from her permanent life" as lightly as spontaneously as the great genius casts behind him a literature, the Odyssey he has outgrown.

—In the evening the rain ceased about nine o clock the west wind came, and we went out in the boat for some hours; indeed we staid till the last clouds passed from the moon. Then we climbed the hill to see the full light in solemn sweetness on the fields and trees and river. I will send you some verses I found in Caroline's little book which seem to express that evening.— I never enjoyed any thing more in its way than the three days alone with her in her boat upon the little river. Not without reason was it that Goethe limits the days of intercourse to *three* in the Wanderjahre. If you have lived so long in uninterrupted communion with any noble being and with nature, a remembrance of man's limitations seems to call on Polycrates to cast forth his ring—[1] She seemed the very genius of the place so calm and lofty and so secluded.— I could not make out whether you had ever been there, though Mrs Curson talked of you a great deal, yet I think you must and tell me, if so, did you not long to be the miller.[2] I never saw any place that seemed to me so much like home. The beauty," though so great is so perfectly unobtrusive. As we glided along the river I could frame my community far more naturally and rationally than your Mr Brisbane.[3] A few friends should wander along a little stream like this, seeking the homesteads. Some should be farmers, some woodmen, others bakers, millers &c By land they should carry to one another the commoditie[s] on the river they should meet solely for society. At sunset many of course would be out in their boats, but they would love the hour too much ever to disturb one another. I saw the spot where we should meet to discuss the high mysteries that Milton speaks of. Also I saw the spot where I invite" you to meet Anna and Raphael and myself and live [III] through the noon of night, in silent communion. When we wished to have merely playful chat, or talk on politics or social reform, we would gather in the mill, and arrange those affairs while grinding the corn. What a happy place for children to grow up in! Would it not suit little ——— to go to school to the cardinal flowers in her boat, beneath the great oak-tree?[4] I think she would learn more than in a phalanx of juvenile florists. But, truly, why has such a thing never been? One of these valleys so immediately suggests an image of the fair company that might fill it, and live so easily, so naturally, so wisely. Can we not people the banks of some such affectionate little stream? I distrust ambitious plans, such as Phalansterian organizations!

[Mr. Ripley] is quite bent on trying his experiment.[5] I hope he may succeed; but as they were talking the other evening, I thought of the river, and all the pretty symbols the tide-mill presents, and felt if I could at all adjust the economics to the more simple procedure, I would far rather be the miller, hoping to attract by natural affinity some congenial baker, "und so weiter."[6] However, one thing seems sure, that many persons will soon, somehow, somewhere, throw off a part, at least, of these terrible weights of the social contract, and see if they cannot lie more at ease in the lap of Nature. I do not feel the same interest in these plans, as if I had a firmer hold on life, but I listen with much pleasure to the good suggestions.

I: ELfr, from *Memoirs*, 2:44. II: ALfr (MB: Ms. Am. 1450 [163]). III: ELfr, from *Memoirs*, 2:47. II published in part in *Memoirs*, 2:44–47.

pain and pleasure] pain ↑ and ↓ pleasure
her permanent life] her permanent ⟨live⟩ life
The beauty] ⟨y⟩ The beauty
the spot where I invite] the spot ⟨to which⟩ ↑ where ↓ I invite

1. Polycrates, tyrant of Samos, who was famous for his good fortune, tempered his prosperity by throwing his most valuable jewel into the sea. A few days later, however, he received as a present a large fish in which the lost jewel was found (*Lempriere's Classical Dictionary* [London, 1848], p. 549). Schiller wrote a ballad, "Der Ring des Polykrates," in 1797. Fuller probably had the story from him (Gero von Wilpert, *Schiller-Chronik* [Stuttgart, 1958], pp. 211, 213).

2. Samuel Curzon (1781–1847) was a miller whose family Fuller visited in Newburyport. His father, also named Samuel, who eloped with Elizabeth Burling of Baltimore, was challenged and killed by her brother William Burling. William took Elizabeth and her child to the West Indies, where young Samuel was raised as a Burling. Shortly after the turn of the century he learned his father's identity, changed his name to Curzon, and emigrated to New England. In 1816 he married Margaret Searle (1787–1877), daughter of George and Mary Atkins Searle (*Cleveland and Cleaveland*, pp. 1755–56, 1067–68; Briggs, *Cabot Family*, pp. 468–69).

3. Albert Brisbane (1809–90) was an American disciple of Charles Fourier, the French reformer who advocated that society be organized in cooperative groups large enough to provide for the industrial and social needs of its members.

4. Probably Frances Maria Adelaide, Channing's eldest child.

5. George Ripley, who was organizing Brook Farm. At the close of the previous paragraph, Fuller clearly deprecates Ripley's plans. A phalanstery was the large building designed as the living quarters for a phalanx, the basic Fourierite social unit of 1,600 men, women, and children. In Fourier's system, the building was elaborately planned with wings, a tower, a grand entrance, and postal pigeons (Nicholas V. Riasanovsky, *The Teaching of Charles Fourier* [Berkeley, 1969], pp. 42–46).

6. "And so forth."

283.   To Ralph Waldo Emerson

Jamaica Plain: November 1840

This day I write you from my own hired house, and am full of the dignity of citizenship. Really, it is almost happiness. I retain, indeed, some cares and responsibilities; but these will sit light as feathers, for I can take my own time for them. Can it be that this peace will be mine for five whole months? At any rate, five days have already been enjoyed.

ELfr, from *Memoirs*, 1:301.

284.   To Ralph Waldo Emerson

Jamaica plain
7th Novr 1840.

Arrived safe 5th inst. the beautiful poem and the letter. About the former I think it shall be published, but have as yet thought chiefly of my own pleasure in reading it. But will not Mr. A. give, also, some pages of his own.[1] It is my sincere desire that he should. I prithee woo him thereto, as you know how.

I rejoice to hear you will give some prose, for I thought you had threatened not. Will you arrange the Ellery poems and prefix the fitting word?[2] I should like the other papers you speak of, if it suits your leisure. We must make haste to print all the good things we have, lest both editor and publishers tire of their bargain at the end of the year. The Violet, omitted through some blunder last time, shall put forth its sweet flower even amid the frosts of January.[3]

I begin to be more interested in the Dial, finding it brings meat and drink to to sundry famishing men and women at a distance from these tables.

Meseems you ought to know with what delight the "Woodnotes" have been heard!

My days flow sweetly on, their only fault is being too long for my strength. . The most important event of the week is that I have written to Bettine. Anna Shaw's brother takes the letter and I hope she may be induced to answer it. I will tell you what it said when we meet.

I sent "Nature," (and lamented I had not your book proper for the occasion) John Dwight's volume and "the Dial."[4] But I told her we did not print any thing here for her and that she must consider the dispatch only as a token of respect.

My first meeting with my class seemed to me very sweet, and I suppose if there had been a chill in the atmosphere I should have felt it. Some have left me, among whom I regret the loss of Marianne Jackson, but those who remain seem truly interested, and I think we shall have a much more satisfactory communication than before.

Will you send to me at Miss Peabody's the remaining volumes of Pietro della Valle which she is to have in her Foreign Library, and foreign they will surely be.—[5] The other day I was sitting there and two young ladies coming in asked first for Bettina and then for Les Sept Chordes &c— I suppose next time they will ask for Pietro and Munchausen.[6]

Affectionately yours

MARGARET F.

Where is George Bradfords promised essay?—[7] With last year's snow? &c

---

ALS (MH: bMS Am 1280 [2351]). Published in Rusk, *Letters of RWE*, 2:354. Addressed: R. W. Emerson, / Concord / Mass. *Postmark:* Jamaica Plain MS Nov 9. *Endorsed:* Margaret Fuller / Nov. 1840.

1. On 4 November Emerson sent Fuller Henry More's "Cupid's Conflict," a poem Alcott contributed in place of an original composition (Rusk, *Letters of RWE*, 2:354–55). Fuller published the poem in *Dial* 2 (October 1841):137–48.

2. Ellery Channing's poem "The Guardian the Lover & the Maid," which Emerson had mentioned in his 4 November letter, was published as "Theme for a World-Drama," *Dial* 1 (April 1841):520–22.

3. Ellen Louisa Tucker Emerson, "The Violet," *Dial* 1 (January 1841):314.

4. Fuller was translating Bettina von Arnim's *Günderode*. Dwight's volume was his *Select Minor Poems, Translated from the German of Goethe and Schiller*, vol. 2 of *Specimens of Foreign Standard Literature*, ed. George Ripley (Boston, 1838). Fuller's letter to Bettina is now lost. Joseph Coolidge Shaw (1821–51), who had just graduated from Harvard, was going to Rome to study theology. In 1847 he was ordained a Roman Catholic priest, and in 1850 he joined the Society of Jesus ("Harvard Class of 1840: Class Records," Harvard archives, pp. 197–200).

5. Pietro della Valle (1586–1652) was an Italian traveler in the Orient. His *Viaggi di Pietro della Valle il Pellegrino . . . descritti da lui medesimo in 54 lettere familiari* was published at Rome in three volumes (1650–73).

6. Karl Friedrich Hieronymus, Baron Münchhausen (1720–97), told imaginative stories about his army service. These tales were collected by Rudolf Raspe and published in 1786 as *Baron Munchhausen's Narrative of His Marvellous Travels and Campaigns in Russia* (Oxford, 1786) (OCGL).

7. Emerson had earlier told Fuller that Bradford would write an essay on the "Abolition question," but nothing came of the offer (Rusk, *Letters of RWE*, 2:318).

285.   To William H. Channing

Sunday 8th Novr [1840]

It has been a great disappointment not to hear from you this week. Your mother let me know of your safe arrival, but I had expected you would write to me almost immediately, so hard is it to cure some people of vanity![1]

Most beautiful was my meeting with our friends the first day of this month, the first of our new alliance.[2] The moon came in so stilly. We sat together all the evening, with but few words, all three meeting in one joy.

I cannot think about it or write about it except of

> "a fair luminous cloud
> Enveloping the earth"

and

"When the little halcyon builds her nest the waters wait and the storms too till she be ready to leave it, even if they wait fourteen days."[3]

Yet, strange to tell, my first thought when they had gone was 'I would not be so happy.'

Is it that whatever seems complete sinks at once into the finite?

Anna's strongest expression of pleasure and which she repeated again and again was "I feel as if I had been married twenty years." Tuesday Cary spent with me, and we read all Mr. E's letters to both of us this summer. They make a volume, and passages are finer than any thing he has published.[n]

Wednesday I opened with my class. It was a noble meeting. I told them the great changes in my mind, and that I could not be sure they would be satisfied with me now, as they were when I was in deliberate possession of myself. I tried to convey the truth, and though I did not arrive at any full expression of it, they all with glistening eyes seemed melted into one love.— Our relation is now perfectly true and I do not think they will ever interrupt me.

Anna[n] sat beside me, all glowing, and the moment I had finished she began to speak. She told me afterwards she was all kindled, and none there could be strangers to her more.

I was really delighted by the enthusiasm of Mrs Farrar.[4] I did not expect it; all her[n] best self seemed called up, and she feels that these meetings will be her highest pleasure.

Ellen Hooper too was most beautiful. I went home with Mrs Farrar

183

and had a long attack of nervous headach. She attended anxiously on me, and asked would it be so all winter. I said if it were I did not care, and truly I feel now such an entire separation from pain and illness, such a calm consciousness of another life while suffering most in the body, that pain has no effect except to steal some of my time. And I believe it compensates by purifying me. I do not regret it in the least.

Mrs F. told me some very interesting traits from her visit to Butternuts, if I have time I shall write them out for you.[5] The first story of Melissa will remind you of[n] a beautiful passage in De Maistre's Soirees de St Petersbourg if you have ever read them.[6]

The second of *Edith* the schoolmistress I am not sure I can do justice to. Did you not choose the name of Edith because it gives an idea of such purity.[7] Sometimes the stars drop a name on the person to whom it belongs as in the case of the Edith of Butternuts.

I have been writing the companion to the Yuca, the Magnolia, for the Dial. I hope you will like it. All the suggestion was that he said its odour was so exquisite and unlike that of any other Magnolia. If you like it, I will draw the soul also from the Yuca and put it into words.

Sophia Ripley has been here all day. Mr R. this eveg, and since they went our landlord to whom I have been preaching that the life is better than meat, for the things he said grieved me for his soul. He seemed moved, and even if he did not hear me, the boys did and were struck with the contrast betwixt Living and "getting a living."
[   ]

ALfr (MB: Ms. Am. 1450 [41]); MsCfr (MH: bMS Am 1280 [111, pp. 104–6]). Published in part in *Memoirs*, 1:339–40, and *JMN*, 11:477.

published] *This sentence and the two preceding it have been canceled by a later hand.*
Anna] *The name has been canceled by a later hand.*
it; all her] it; ⟨it⟩ all her
remind you of] remind you ⟨in⟩ of

1. Channing left New York the first week in October and arrived in Cincinnati the third week of that month (Channing to William Greene, 1 October 1840, OCHP).

2. Sam and Anna Ward.

3. The first quotation is from Coleridge's "Dejection: An Ode"; the second is unidentified.

4. Eliza Rotch Farrar, wife of Professor John Farrar of Harvard, was one of Fuller's closest friends.

5. Mrs. Farrar had been visiting her brother Francis Rotch at Butternuts, his home in Morris, New York. Fuller was a good friend of his daughter, Maria (1826–54), who in 1849 married Colonel Radcliff Hudson (1819–1904) (Bullard, *Rotches*, p. 443).

6. Joseph de Maistre (1753–1821), a philosopher and moralist, fled from France to Switzerland in 1793. *Les soirées de Saint-Pétersbourg* (Paris, 1821) takes the form of a dialogue between a count, a Russian senator, and a young French émigré. Their

topics include evil, suffering, and the efficacy of prayer. The story of Melissa is told in letter 292.

7. Channing used the name Edith in "Ernest the Seeker." The story of Edith told by Mrs. Farrar may be found in letter 292.

286. To Henry D. Thoreau

1st Decr. [1840]

I am to blame for so long detaining your manuscript.[1] But my thoughts have been so engaged that I have not found a suitable hour to reread it as I wished till last night. This second reading only confirms my impression from the first. The essay is rich in thoughts, and I should be *pained* not to meet it again. But then[n] the thoughts seem to me so out of their natural order, that I cannot read it through without *pain*. I never once feel myself in a stream of thought, but seem to hear the grating of tools on the mosaic. It is true as Mr E. says, that essays not to be compared with this have found their way into the Dial. But then those are more unassuming in their tone, and have an air of quiet good-breeding which induces us to permit their presence. Yours is so rugged that it ought to be commanding. Yet I hope you will give it me again, and if you see no force in my objections disregard them.

S. M. FULLER.

ALS (NNPM). Published in Sanborn, *Thoreau*, pp. 172–73, where it is misdated, and in *Thoreau Correspondence*, pp. 41–42; published in part in Hanscom, *Friendly Craft*, p. 196. *Addressed:* H. D. Thoreau. *Endorsed:* S. M. Fuller.

But then] But ↑ then ↓

1. Exactly when Fuller met Henry Thoreau (1817–62) is not clear, but the fact that she describes him to her brother Richard in May 1841 suggests that she did not know him well earlier. Though he was the sort of writer for whom the *Dial* was planned, Fuller was unenthusiastic about Thoreau's prose. She did, finally, publish five of his poems. Their friendship seems to have been sure though not overly warm. For his part, Thoreau was probably referring to Fuller when he wrote, "I know a woman who possesses a restless and intelligent mind, interested in her own culture, and earnest to enjoy the highest possible advantages, and I meet her with pleasure as a natural person who not a little provokes me, and I suppose is stimulated in turn by myself. Yet our acquaintance plainly does not attain to that degree of confidence and sentiment which women, which all, in fact, covet. I am glad to help her, as I am helped by her; I like very well to know her with a sort of stranger's privilege" (Thoreau, *Week*, p. 279). With this letter Fuller returned Thoreau's essay "The Service," which was not published until 1902.

Henry D. Thoreau. Crayon drawing by Samuel Worcester Rowse. Courtesy of the Concord Free Public Library.

287.   To William H. Channing[?]

3 December 1840

—— bids me regard her "as a sick child;" and the words recall some of the sweetest hours of existence. My brother Edward was born on my birth-day, and they said he should be my child.[1] But he sickened and died just as the bud of his existence showed its first bright hues. He was some weeks wasting away, and I took care of him always half the night. He was a beautiful child, and became very dear to me then. Still in lonely woods the upturned violets show me the pleading softness of his large blue eyes, in those hours when I would have given worlds to prevent his suffering, and could not. I used to carry him about in my arms for hours; it soothed him, and I loved to feel his gentle weight of helpless purity upon my heart, while night listened around. At last, when death came, and the soul took wing like an overtasked bird from his sweet form, I felt what I feel now. Might I free ——, as that angel freed him!

In daily life I could never hope to be an unfailing fountain of energy and bounteous love. My health is frail; my earthly life is shrunk to a scanty rill; I am little better than an aspiration, which the ages will reward, by empowering me to incessant acts of vigorous beauty. But now it is well with me to be with those who do not suffer overmuch to have me suffer. It is best for me to serve where I can better bear to fall short. I could visit —— more nobly than in daily life, through the soul of our souls. When she named me her Priestess, that name made me perfectly happy. Long has been my consecration; may I not meet those I hold dear at the altar? How would I pile up the votive offerings, and crowd the fires with incense! Life might be full and fair; for, in my own way, I could live for my friends.

ELfr, from *Memoirs*, 2:53–54.

1. Edward Breck Fuller, born on his sister's eighteenth birthday, 23 May 1828, died on 15 September 1829 (*CVR*).

288.   To Ralph Waldo Emerson

Tuesday eveg.
[ca. 4 December 1840][n]

I wrote to you last night, and today the lines about your Essay seem so dull, so cold, and so impertinent withal that I have a mind to burn the paper—[1] Yet let them go— I should have *said* the same, and the office of our best sentiments is to make us altogether better not to induce us to suppress the worst or select the best of ourselves.

Yet here is something obviously wrong in this attempt to measure one another, or one another's act. It seems as if we could not help it in this our present stage, as if we should jostle and bruise one another, if we had not some idea of our respective paths and places. But surely there will come a purer mode of being even in the world of Form. We shall move with an unerring gentleness, we shall read in an eye beam whether other beings have any thing for us; on those who have not our only criticism will be to turn our eyes another way. Then there will be no more negations, we shall learn to be ourselves by the achievements of other natures and not by their failures. Then our actions will not be hieroglyphics any more but perfect symbols. Then parting and meeting will both be equally beautiful, for both will be in faith. Then there will be no more explanations but with every instant revelations Then will be no more intercourse, but perfect communion with full-eyed love.— But then—we shall write essays" on Art, more than cavils at them.

Adieu— *en* Dieu

AL (MH: bMS Am 1280 [2342]); MsC (MB: Ms. Am. 1450 [70]). Published in Rusk, *Letters of RWE*, 2:366, and Miller, p. 56. *Endorsed:* M. Fuller / 1839.

[ca. 4 December 1840]] *Despite the endorsement, Fuller's mention of* your Essay *dates the letter in late 1840, for on 4 November of that year Emerson promised an essay on art for the* Dial. *On 1 December he was still working on it, and her letter to him of 6 December suggests she may not yet have seen it. On 8 December Emerson mentioned that Fuller had read it; thus she could have seen a preliminary draft any time between 7 November and 8 December 1840* (Rusk, Letters of RWE, 2:355, 362–63, 365–66).

shall write essays] shall write ⟨no more⟩ essays

1. Fuller had probably read a draft of "Thoughts on Art," *Dial* 1 (January 1841): 367–78, though she may have seen a version of "Art," the final essay of Emerson's *Essays: First Series.* See letter 289.

289. To Ralph Waldo Emerson

Jamaica plain
6th Decr 1840.

Dear Waldo,

W. Story's piece cannot be admitted into this number of the Dial, if only on account of its length.—[1] Even if you did not give your essay on Art there would not be room for this," as the number is nearly full with what I have promised to receive, and this would occupy at least thirty pages of print.

I am well pleased by the remarks on works of art. And like the spirit of the whole, though it does not enable to form a sure estimate of the author's mind, as I seem to hear Page talking all through it.[2]

If these are your pencil-marks you did not, I think, read it through, the latter part is so full of bad faults in style and imagery" which you have not marked. I mention this because if W. S. is inclined to take the pains (which would do him a world of good) to sift and write it over I would insert it in the April number.

He might take some other subject than the Gallery (the Night and Day[3] for instance)" and yet interweave what he has said of all the statues" as illustrations of his opinions." I wish too he would compress his article; it is too long for us, and would also be improved there by. And take heed of such expressions as "hung for hours on the head" (of Augustus) &c

If he will do this he must let us know by the 1st Jany, for I have already a good deal on hand for the April number.

I shall depend on your Essay and hope to receive it certainly on Wednesday, for we are harried now. Shall have" the proofs of "Orphic sayings" sent to Mr A. but wish him to be sure and return them next day. He will not get them for a week or more.[4]

Will you forgive me if I do not publish Ellery's verses now? I have others which I prefer for this no. and there are reasons not worth stating here, but which I can tell when we meet.

These sonnets have the fault of seeming imitated from Tennyson, and, though they have some merit, it is not *poetical* merit. If I publish them, I cannot all together. I will take the last for this no, if he is willing it should go alone, and lets me know in time.[5] Though I have many short poems in my drawer I like better, yet I do not wish to discourage these volunteers who are much wanted to vary the manoeuvres of the regular platoon.

As to the Mythological evegs, let that pass for the present, for my life is as yet all too crowded, and I do not want any new call quite yet. But I will bear your promise in mind, supposing I feel ready for such meetings presently.

Nothing but business letters till this Dial be out. And then my family, all absent, compel me to over much letter writing. So bear with dulness from your affte

M.

ALS (MH: bMS Am 1280 [2352]). Published in Rusk, *Letters of RWE*, 2:362–63. *Endorsed:* Margaret Fuller / Dec. 1839 ↑ 40 ↓

be room for this,] be room for ⟨it⟩ ↑ this ↓,

bad faults in style and imagery] bad faults ⟨as a piece of wri⟩ ↑ in style and imagery ↓

the Gallery (the Night and Day for instance)] the Gallery ↑ (the Night and Day for instance) ↓

said of all the statues] said of ↑ all ↓ the statu⟨t⟩es

illustration of his opinions] illustration ↑ of his opinions ↓

Shall have] Shall ⟨po⟩ have

1. William Wetmore Story had written Emerson on 15 November 1840 offering the essay, but it was never published (Rusk, *Letters of RWE*, 2:363n).

2. William Page (1811–85) was a friend of Story and James Russell Lowell, both of whom were keeping their distance from Fuller at this time. Page studied with Samuel F. B. Morse and became a successful portrait painter, numbering among his patrons many of the most influential politicians of the day. He lived in Italy for eleven years and later became president of the National Academy of Art. Fuller had praised his artistic promise in her review of the Athenaeum exhibit (*DAB*; Joshua C. Taylor, *William Page: The American Titian* [Chicago, 1957]).

3. Horatio Greenough made casts of "Day" and "Night," monuments on Michelangelo's tomb of Giuliano de' Medici in Florence. Greenough gave the casts to Thomas H. Perkins, a wealthy Boston merchant and a prominent patron of the arts. Perkins deposited the casts in the Boston Athenaeum in 1834 (Swan, *Athenaeum Gallery*, pp. 139–43).

4. The second group of Alcott's "Orphic Sayings" appeared in *Dial* 1 (January 1841):351–61.

5. The first of Channing's sonnets did not appear in the *Dial* until April 1841.

290. To William H. Channing

[8? December 1840]

[I] [   ] I went with the Shaws to see Mrs Wood[n] in the Sonnambula.[1] Generally it was sad to hear the beloved Bellini so murdered. Neither of the Woods have a spark of genius to enter into this most sweet and tender nature. And the most beautiful of all the melodies While I view etc. was given to Brough, which was the same as if Tennyson's Elegiacs[2] had been given to Morse (of the Cambridge omnibus)[n] to recite in public.

But nothing could spoil the opera, which expresses an extacy, a trance of feeling better than any thing I ever knew. I have loved every melody in it for years, yet it was happiness to hear the exquisite modulations as they flowed out of one another, endless ripples on a river, deep, wide, and strewed with blossoms. The flower scene would overpower, if Bellini's Amina could sing it. "Oh dont mingle one human feeling" burst out as from the lyres of heaven. I never have known any one more to be loved than Bellini; no wonder the Italians make pilgrimages to his grave. In him thought and feeling flow always in one tide, he never divides himself from your soul. He is as melancholy as he as sweet, but his melancholy is not impassioned, but purely tender, that of a soul dreaming of its star.

There was a young man with us with a most poetic face. I met him again next day at dinner, his name is Heath. He talked of the Lady of Shalot and looked as if he might have lived as she did.[n3] [   ]

[II] My book of amusement has been the Evenings of St. Petersburg. I do not find the praises bestowed on it all exaggerated. Yet De Maistre is too logical for me. I only catch a thought here and there along the page. There is a grandeur even in the subtlety of his mind. He walks with a step so still, that, but for his dignity, it would be stealthy, yet with brow erect and wide, eye grave and deep. He is a man such as I have never known before.

I: AMsfr (MB: Ms. Am. 1450 [42]). II: ELfr, from *Memoirs*, 2:54.

May be a journal entry rather than a letter. The holograph is numbered 23 in the upper right corner of the first side of the manuscript. Possibly this and letters 291 and 292 are parts of the same "letter journal," a form of writing Fuller often did for her friends.

the Shaws to see Mrs Wood] *The names have been heavily canceled by a later hand.*

(of the Cambridge omnibus)] (↑ of ↓ the Cambridge omnibus)

as she did.] *This paragraph has been canceled by a later hand.*

1. Vincenzo Bellini's opera *La sonnambula* was performed in Boston on 7 December, with Joseph Wood (b. 1801) and Mary Paton Wood (1802–64) in leading roles. Joseph Wood, an Englishman, made his debut in Dublin and then at Covent Garden in 1826. In 1831 he caused a scandal by luring Mary Paton away from her first husband and marrying her himself. She had appeared in the premier of Weber's *Oberon* (*Boston Daily Advertiser*, 7 December 1840; *The Memoir of Mr. and Mrs. Wood* [Philadelphia, 1840], pp. 5–21; *Baker's Biographical Dictionary*). Vincenzo Bellini (1801–35) wrote *La sonnambula* in 1831; the very popular opera was first produced in America in New York on 13 November 1835 (*Grove's Dictionary of Music and Musicians*, 5th ed., 10 vols. [New York, 1966], 7:965).

2. Tennyson's "Leonine Elegiacs" was published in his *Poems, Chiefly Lyrical* (London, 1830).

3. John Francis Heath (1811–62), a Virginian, graduated from Harvard in 1840 and studied at Heidelberg, Göttingen, and Berlin before becoming a doctor (*Harvard College University at Cambridge, New England: Class of 1840*, p. 29). Tennyson's "Lady of Shallot" was first published in *Poems* (London, 1833).

291. To William H. Channing

10 December 1840

Two days in Boston; how the time flies there and bears no perfume on its wings,— I am always most happy to return to my solitude, yet willing to bear the contact of society, with all its low views and rash blame, for I see how the purest ideal natures need it to temper them and keep them large and sure. I will never do as Waldo does, though I marvel not at him.

How, when I hear such things, I bless God for awakening my inward life. In me, my Father, thou wouldst not, I feel, permit such blindness. Free them also, help me to free them, from this conventional standard, by means of which their eyes are holden that they see not. Let me, by purity and freedom, teach them justice, not only to my individual self,—of that small part of myself I am utterly careless,—but to this everflowing Spirit. Oh, must its pure breath pass them by?

ELfr, from Higginson, *MFO*, pp. 120–21.

292. To William H. Channing

13th Decr. [1840]

I have not time to write out as I should this sweet story of Melissa, but here is the outline.[1]

More than four years ago she[n] received an injury which caused her great pain in the spine and went to the next country town to get medical advice. She stopped at the house of a poor blacksmith, only an acquaintance, and has never since been able to be moved. Her mother and sister come by turns to take care of her. She cannot help herself in any way, but is completely dependent as an infant. The blacksmith and his wife gave her the best room in their house, have ever since ministered to her as to a child of their own, and when people pity them, for[n] having to bear such a burthen they say "It is none, but a blessing."

Melissa suffers all the time and great pain. She cannot amuse or employ herself in any way, and all these years has been as dependent on others for new thoughts, as for daily cares. Yet her mind has deepened, and her character refined under those stern teachers Pain and *Gratitude*, till she has become the patron saint of the village, and the Muse of the village schoolmistress. She has a peculiar aversion to egotism, and could not bear to have her mother enlarge upon her sufferings to Mrs F.

"Perhaps it will pain the lady to *hear* that!" said the mild religious sufferer who had borne it without a complaint.

Whom the Lord loveth he chasteneth. The poor are the generous, the injured the patient and loving.

All Mrs F. said of this girl was in perfect harmony with what De Maistre says of the saint of St Petersburg who, almost devoured by cancer, when asked, "Quelle est la premiére grace que vous demanderez à Dieu, ma chère enfant, lorsque vous serez devant lui?" she replied Je lui demandeari pour mes bien faiteurs la grace de l'aimer autant que je l'aime"

When they were lamenting for her "je ne suis pas, dit elle, aussi malheureuse que vous le coryez; Dieu me fait la grace de ne penser qu'a lui."[2]

Of Edith. Tall, gaunt, hard-favored was this candidate for the American Calendar, but Bonifacia might be her name." From her earliest years she had valued" all she knew, only as she was to teach it again. Her highest ambition was to be the schoolmistress, her recreation to dress the little ragged things, and take care of them out of school hours. She had some taste for nursing the grown up, but this was quite subordinate to her care of the buds of the forest. Pure, perfectly beneficent, lived Edith, and never thought of any thing or person, but for its own sake. When she had attained midway the hill of life, she happened to be boarding in the house" with a young farmer who was lost in admiration of her love. How he wished he too could read.— What, cant you read, oh, let me teach you. You never can; I was too thick-skulled to learn even at school. I am sure I never could now.— But Edith was not to be daunted by any fancies of incapacity, and set to work with utmost zeal to teach this great grown man the primer. She succeeded and won his heart thereby. He wished to requite the raising him from the night of ignorance as Howard and Nicholas Poussin did the kind ones who raised them from the night of the tomb by the gift of his hand.[3] Edith consented on condition that she might still keep school. So he had his sister come to "keep things straight." Edith and he go out in the morning, he to his field, she to her school, and meet again at night, to talk, to plan, I hope, to read also.

The first use Edith made of her accession of property through her wedded estate was to give away all she thought superfluous to a poor family she had long pitied, and invite a poor sick woman to her "spare chamber." Notwithstanding a course like this her husband has grown rich and proves that the pattern of the widows cruise was not lost in Jewery.

Edith has become the Natalia of the village, as is Melissa its "Schöne Seele"[4]

Are not these pretty stories? Do such things happen in your parish?—

I will not write to you of these Conventions[n] and Communities unless they bear better fruit than yet.[5] The Convention was a total failure as might be expected from a movement so forced. A great fuss they have made here about your name being used, indeed it was not in its place signed to their call. But I suppose you thought of it only as a ripple of the great stream.[n] We will take heed, and walk in less muddy paths to the gaol, even if they be beset with thorns, and wolves bark in the circling night.

Edmund Quincy and Mr Adam seemed the morning I was there like bewildered sheep amid apes, and mastiffs, and wild boars.[6]

"Community" seems dwindling to a point, and I doubt the best use of the plans as projected thus far will prove the good talks it has given us here upon principles. I feel and find great want of wisdom in myself and the others; we are not ripe to reconstruct society yet. Mr E. knows deepest what he wants, but not well how to get it. Mr R. has a better perception of means, less insight as to principles, but this plan has done him a world of good. He will not say, however, that he considers his plan as a mere experiment, and is willing to fail, or can well bear to fail. I tell him that he is not ready till he can say that. He says he can bear to be treated unjustly by all concerned. There is something fine and gentlemanly in his nature which comes up now and then, and at the time makes one pardon quite his want of poesy and patience!

Today Mr E. has been here and we have had a sunshiny talk. He has finally decided not to join Mr R. and, instead, wishes to take Mr Alcott and his family into his house, a plan most unpromising, but for the nobleness of motive, in my friend.—[7] If it takes effect, you shall hear about it.[n]

Oh Christopher Columbus, how art thou admired when we see how other men go to work with their lesser enterprizes! [   ]

Amsfr (MB: Ms. Am. 1450 [43]). Published in part, and misdated, in *Memoirs*, 2:54–57, and Higginson, *MFO*, p. 180.

May be a journal entry rather than a letter. The two manuscript sheets are folded and numbered (33–38) in Fuller's hand in the top right corners. The document may be a copy she made for herself.

years ago she] years ago ⟨messa⟩ she
pity them, for] pity them, ⟨they⟩ for
might be her name] might be her ⟨?⟩ ↑ name ↓
she had valued] she had ⟨fo⟩ valued
be boarding in the house] be boarding ↑ in the house ↓
of these Conventions] of these ⟨Convenients⟩ Conventions
stream.] *The preceding two sentences have been canceled by a later hand.*
about it.] *This paragraph has been canceled by a later hand.*

1. This is the story Eliza Farrar told Fuller. See letter 285.

2. From "Troisième entretien," *Les soirées de Saint-Pétersbourg*: "What is the first favor you will ask of God, my dear child, when you are before him? She replied, I will ask him to grant my benefactors the favor of loving him as much as I love him. . . . I am not, she said, so unfortunate as you think; God gives me the grace to think only of him" (trans. Robert D. Habich).

3. Which Howard Fuller means is unclear. The seventeenth-century painter Nicolas Poussin fell ill in Rome and was befriended by Jacques Dughet. In gratitude, Poussin married one of the Dughet daughters and then adopted his brothers-in-law, Jean and Gaspard, and trained them as artists (*Bryan's Dictionary of Painters and Engravers* [London, 1926], 4:152).

4. The reference is to bk. 6 of Goethe's *Wilhelm Meisters Lehrjahre*. "Schöne Seele": beautiful soul.

5. "Communities" here refers to Brook Farm; "Conventions" refers to the convention of the Friends of Universal Reform, held at the Chardon Street Chapel, 17–19 November (*Boston Daily Advertiser*, 20 November 1840). It was a tumultuous meeting, at which the sabbath as a divine institution was discussed. Emerson later wrote, "A great variety of dialect and of costume was noticed; a great deal of confusion, eccentricity and freak appeared, as well as of zeal and enthusiasm" (*Complete Works of Emerson*, 10:374). The convention attracted such reformers as Dr. Channing, William Lloyd Garrison, Theodore Parker, and Maria Chapman.

6. The reformer Edmund Quincy (1808–77), second son of Josiah Quincy, Sr., was elected chairman of the convention. William Adam, an abolitionist, had taught Oriental literature at Harvard (*DAB; Boston Daily Advertiser*, 18 November 1840; Harvard archives).

7. Ripley's plan was much discussed by Emerson, Fuller, and their friends. On 2 December, Emerson outlined for his brother William the plan to raise $30,000 to buy the farm at Roxbury. But on 15 December, Emerson wrote Ripley stating his reasons for not joining the community. He closed by saying, "Whilst I refuse to be an active member of your company I must yet declare that of all philanthropic projects of which I have heard yours is the most pleasing to me" (Rusk, *Letters of RWE*, 2:365, 371). The scheme to help Alcott failed.

293. To Arthur B. Fuller

Jamaica Plain,
20th Decr 1840.

It is not, my dear Arthur, because I "have so little to say to you" that my letters are short, but because bad health and many engagements oblige me to such economy of time. You know, too, that writing is of all occupations, the very worst for my malady, and as I *must* do a great deal at any rate I abstain always when I can. Bear this in mind, and dont measure my interest in your pursuits, or affection for yourself by the number or length of my letters.

I continue to manage very well. The fatted pig is killed, and was found in good order, not-withstanding your and Richard's evil omens from the character of our prodigal son here. We banquet on pork rather more constantly than is agreeable to a "true believer" like my self.

My other life continues its usual course. I have been to hear the Sonnambula, but with scarce more satisfaction than our fastidious Richard derived from his concert, of which, I suppose, he has given you an account.

The news of Ellen's illness was sad to me both on her own account and Mother's over whose visit a cloud is cast at once. Mr Keats's letter to me was kind and clear. She will have, I am sure, all the attention and wise counsel she needs. The fever was gone and only a rheumatic affection remained of which the physician thought she would soon be free. I shall hope very soon to hear again.

About your school I do not think I can give you much advice which would be of value unless I knew your position more in detail.[1] The important rule is, as[n] in all relations with our fellow creatures, Never forget that, if they are imperfect persons, they are immortal souls, and treat them as you would wish to be treated by the light of that thought.

As to the application of means— Abstain from punishment as much as possible and use encouragement as far as you can *without flattery*. But be even more careful as to strict truth in this regard towards children than to persons of your own age. For to the child the parent or teacher is the representative of Justice, and as that of life is severe, an education which in any degree, excites vanity is the very worst preparation for that general and crowded school.

I doubt not you will teach grammar well, as I saw you aimed at principles in your practise,— In geography, try to make pictures of the scenes, that they may be present to their imagination, and the nobler faculties be brought into action as well as memory— In history study and try to paint the characters of great men; they best interpret the leadings of events amid the nations.

I am pleased with your way of speaking of both people and pupils your view seems from the right point, yet beware of over great pleasure in being popular or even beloved. As far as an amiable disposition and powers of entertainment make you so, it is a happiness, but is there one grain of plausibility, it is poison.— But I will not play Mentor much, lest I make you averse to write to your very affte sister

MARGARET.

ALS (MH: fMS Am 1086 [9:69]); MsC (MH: fMS Am 1086 [Works, 1:641–45]). Published in part in Higginson, *MFO*, pp. 83–84. *Addressed:* Arthur B. Fuller / Westford / Mass.

rule is, as] rule is, 〈?〉 as

1. Arthur Fulier taught school at Westford (and later at Duxbury) while a student at Harvard (Richard F. Fuller, *Chaplain Fuller* [Boston, 1863], p. 52).

294. To Maria Weston Chapman

Jamaica plain,
26th Decr 1840.

My dear Mrs Chapman,

I received your note but a short time before I went to the conversation party. There was no time for me to think what I should do or even ascertain the objects of the Fair.[1] Had I known them I could not by any slight suggestion have conveyed my view of such movements. And a conversation on the subject would interrupt the course adopted by my class. I therefore, merely requested Miss Peabody to show the papers and your note to me before I began on the subject before us.

The Abolition cause commands my respect as do all efforts to relieve and raise suffering human nature. The faults of the party are such as, it seems to me, must always be incident to the partizan spirit. All that was noble and pure in their zeal has helped us all. For the disinterestedness and constancy of many individuals among you I have a high respect. Yet my own path leads a different course and often leaves me quite ignorant what you are doing, as in the present instance of your Fair.

Very probably to one whose heart is so engaged as yours in particular measures this indifference will seem incredible or even culpable. But if[n] indifferent I have not been intolerant; I have wronged none of you by a a hasty judgment or careless words, and, where I have not investigated a case so as to be sure of my own opinion, have, at least, never chimed in with the popular hue and cry. I have always wished that efforts[n] originating in a generous sympathy, or a sense of right should have fair play, have had firm faith that they must, in some way, produce eventual good.

The late movements in your party have interested me more than those which had for their object the enfranchisement of the African only. Yet I presume I should still feel sympathy with your aims only not with your measures. Yet I should like to be more fully acquainted with both.[n] The late Convention I attended hoping to hear some clear account of your wishes as to religious institutions and the social position of woman. But not only I heard nothing that pleased me, but no clear statement from any one. Have you in print what you consider an able exposition of the views of yourself and friends?— Or if not, should you like yourself to give me some account of how these subjects stand in your mind? As far as I know you seem to me quite wrong as to what is to be done for woman! She needs new helps I think, but not such as you propose. But I should like to know your view and your grounds more clearly than I do.

With respect

S. M. FULLER.

ALS (MB: Ms. A. 9.2, vol. 14, no. 82). Published in Wade, pp. 556–57, and Chevigny, pp. 238–39. *Addressed:* Mrs Chapman / West St. *Endorsed:* Margaret Fuller to / Mrs Chapman 1840.

Maria Weston (1806–85), daughter of Warren and Anne Bates Weston of Weymouth, became an abolitionist in 1834 and was thenceforth the leading member of the Boston Female Anti-Slavery Society; in 1840 she was serving on the executive committee of the New England Anti-Slavery Society. She was one of the editors of the *Non-Resistant* and at various times edited the *Liberator* for William Lloyd Garrison. In 1830 she married Henry Grafton Chapman (*DAB*; *NAW*).

But if] but ⟨though⟩ ↑if↓
wished that efforts] wished that effor⟨?⟩ts
acquainted with both.] acquainted with ⟨your views⟩ ↑both.↓

1. The annual Massachusetts Anti-Slavery Fair opened on 22 December. It offered for sale clothing, toys, china, books, and drawings (*Boston Daily Advertiser*, 21 December 1840).

295. To Caroline Sturgis

Sunday eveg
Jany 24th 1841.

dear Caroline, Can you do any thing about tickets to Mr E's lecture in case he[n] should not send us any.[1] I shall come to your house tomorrow aftn as I said I would. If you have prepared your mother I intend talking with her[n] about Spring St.

I have read no Dante, nor thought about any lesson to you, but hope the inspiration will come with the hour— truly—I have had no appetite for his banquet.[n]

Hercules I fancy when *in* the fire which so pleased his father Jove, could not have touched the cup, though filled with nectar by Hebe his bride.

198

Dante,— thou didst not describe in all thy apartments of Inferno, this tremendous repression of an existence half unfolded, this swoon as the soul was ready to be born. Thy Lucifer upholds the earth, but bears not on his heart the weight of future heavens *known not felt*, pressing, yet still of incalculable dimensions.

Poets of the lesser orders suffer not thus To them "some God gives to tell what they suffer"

"Still day and Night alternate in their bosoms"

But in the intervals of life they write what they have lived, saying what they have felt.

But they who are but the hieroglyphics of their future being. Souls which must be all before they can speak one word, Destinies strangely mismatched with the ungrateful Hermes, travel to the mount of life through fields of graves, and nothing is heard but the slow tread of their footsteps.

My wings were just budded; they are pushed back upon my heart, but they are no longer tender with the plumage of the nest, they will not fold back over it and keep it warm again. So the breast must ache.

Silent lies the pool, all nature crowded around in the prayer of conscious mutilation. Yet will it move no more till the true Angel descend.

The ruined city lies beneath the moon, cold and barren falls her light, on palaces, richly sculptured, but without a roof or a hearth stone, on temples of purest marble, but bereft of their gods. The lion and the dragon have gone forth into the desert, the owl hoots her dull comment, the young Eagles are not yet strong enough to cry till they are heard by their far distant sire!

Oh I could write it into endless images, all, all of lead. But hoard thy life, faithful Aloes! Shroud thy[n] love, unwearied snow, yield not a single violet, to this warm but black rain. There is no spring to pierce to thy heart, say nothing if thou canst not tell thy heart. Yet even to day a bird sang.

To *stand* and wait, I cannot.[2] I will lie down on the earth and look up at the sky. My Star has hid its beam, but many others are there, cold to me yet bright. I cannot love them, yet will bless Eternity that gives them their turn. Probably they were lost in night while mine was in the ascendant. Pray for me, radiant friends, I bless, I do not envy ye. I bide my time God's time.

AL (MH: bMS Am 1221 [243]). *Addressed:* Miss Caroline Sturgis / 50 Summer St / Boston.

in case he] in case ⟨yo⟩ he
talking with her] talking with⟨out⟩ her

Maria Weston Chapman. By courtesy of the Trustees of the Boston Public Library.

200

had no appetite for his banquet.] had no ↑ appetite for his ↓ banquet. ⟨f⟩
Shroud thy] Shroud⟨,⟩ thy

1. Emerson delivered his lecture "Man the Reformer" before the Mechanics' Apprentices' Library Association at the Masonic Temple on Monday, 25 January. He published the lecture in *Dial* 1 (April 1841):523–38 (William Charvat, "A Chronological List of Emerson's American Lecture Engagements," *Bulletin of the New York Public Library* 64 [September 1960]:503).

2. Fuller's modification of the concluding line of Milton's Sonnet 19, "They also serve who only stand and waite."

296.   To William H. Channing

[2 February 1841]
[Jamaica Plain]

[   ] come true!
Write to me what ever you think about the Dial. I wish very much to get interested in it, and I can only do so by finding that those I love and prize are so. It is very difficult to me to resolve on publishing any of my own writing; it never seems worth it, but the topmost bubble on my life; and the world, the Public alas!—give me to realize that there are *individuals* to whom I can speak.—

[   ] went last week to hear Mr E. lecture on Reform. I had made an extract from this for you, but he has now resolved to publish it in the Dial. His book, also, is in press.[1] You say there is somewhat in Evil deeper than he sees, write to me of this. I have written and thought much on the [   ] *not* give up Ernes[t] [   ] [why?] should you? [   ] all in your nic[   ] me something [   ] [a]t any rate. I cl[   ] our aid. [   ] all my [   ] two early [   ]
   Decr a[   ] one whi[ch] [   ] you an[   ] now. There are
[   ] books
   fr[   ] which wish to [   ] extracts [   ] you. "Fest[us]"[2]
[   ] "Die Gun[derode] [   ] do you [   ] them. [   ]

ALfr (MB: Ms. Am. 1450 [45]). Published in part in Higginson, *MFO*, p. 162. *Addressed:* Rev [   ]. *Postmark:* Jamaica Plain Feby 3. *Endorsed:* 2 February 1841.
   Dated from endorsement; letter is badly torn.

1. Emerson sent the manuscript for *Essays* to his publisher on the first of the year; on 12 January he told Fuller that the proofs were beginning to come. James Munroe published the volume on 20 March (Rusk, *Letters of RWE*, 2:376, 387).

2. Fuller was enthusiastic about Philip Bailey's poem *Festus* (London, 1839), which she reviewed in *Dial* 2 (October 1841):231–61, and again in the *New-York Daily Tribune* for 8 September 1845. Bailey (1816–1902) expanded the poem in several revisions,

until it contained some forty thousand lines by 1889. He is now remembered as the father of the "Spasmodic School" of English poetry (*Oxford Companion to English Literature*, ed. Paul Harvey, 3d ed. [Oxford, 1946]).

297. To William H. Channing

19 February 1841

[I] Have I never yet seen so much as *one* of my spiritual family? The other night they sat round me, so many who have thought they loved, or who begin to love me. I felt myself kindling the same fire in all their souls. I looked on each, and no eye repelled me. Yet there was no warmth for me on all those altars. Their natures seemed deep, yet there was not one from which I could draw the living fountain. I could only cheat the hour with them, prize, admire, and pity. It was sad; yet who would have seen sadness in me? [   ]

Once I was almost all intellect; now I am almost all feeling. Nature vindicates her rights, and I feel all Italy glowing beneath the Saxon crust. This cannot last long; I shall burn to ashes if all this smoulders here much longer. I must die if I do not burst forth in genius or heroism.

[II] [   ] I am sorry to perceive that there is in these leaves absolutely nothing that I have done or seen all these days. I wish I had given you both sides, for it has not been the mere sobbing of the night wind that is on these leaves. I have served and looked about me with a placid brow and a keen eye. I was not seen of men to fast, neither when with[n] them did I waste the hours. But in truth I was not interested in all that, and my true life was only dropping the lead ever deeper into the depths, as I have written it to thee. Now I have drawn it up, and may cast the net into the bright waters, perhaps send the prey to thee.

And yet there have been outward things this winter that if I could record them with one stroke of the pen! I meant to have translated for you the best passages of "Die Gunderode" (which I prefer to the correspondence with Goethe. The two girls are equal natures, and *both* in earnest. Goethe made a puppet show for his private entertainment of Bettina's life, and we wonder she did not feel he was not worthy of her homage) But I have not been well enough to write much and these pages are only what I have dictated; they are not the best, yet will interest you. The exquisite little poem by Gunderode read aloud two or three times that you may catch the music; it is of most sweet mystery. She is to me dear and admirable. Bettine only interesting She is of religious grace. Bettine the fulness of nature.

I shall not write again, perhaps for two or three weeks. Write to me often at least of books and facts *that* will not violate the silence.

25th Eveg
  to day looking over the books I found a number of the W. Messenger in which you write of Evil and cast out those same suggestions as in your letter to me.[1] I read it with profound interest. To be at once an *aged saint* and the last born, phenix, born of *genius*, that would be returning to God, would it not?
  [   ] most populous city, yet I wish you might have it. The busiest knight errant was sometimes left alone to sleep on the greensward in the dim forest. And you should have been a knight, with your true sword and steed your one friend noble as yourself, and the offer of daily deeds in which to tell your soul without the aid of all this chattering. But alas! you are neither knight nor prince, but a preacher! And how can you preach your life who were[n] [   ]
  Read these side by side with Waldo's paragraphs, and say is it not deeper and true to live than to think. Sometimes I seem quite distant and bright as if with central knowledge. I do to night, and then it seems to me that these childish stammerings of imperfect feeling intimate all, while these chasings up and down the blind alleys of thought neither show the centre nor the circumference. Yet is his a noble speech. I love to reprove myself by it. [   ] for you! nor for them![n]
  William you will not freeze me again, and then will come summer breezes, instead of this monotonous sobbing in the dry leaves. [   ]

I: ELfr, from *Memoirs*, 2:57–58. II: ALfr (MB: Ms. Am. 1450 [27]). Published in part in Higginson, *MFO*, pp. 191–92.
  neither when with] neither ↑ when ↓ with
  were] *This paragraph has been canceled by a later hand.*
  for you! nor for them!] *These words and the remainder of the letter are written across the first page of the surviving manuscript.*
  1. "Moral Evil," *Western Messenger* 6 (March 1839):333–38.

298.   To Elizabeth Hoar

20 Feb 1841
It is proposed that I have an evening class in Boston and a few gen-

tlemen my friends are to be members.[1] There are to be only 5 or 6 meetings.

MsCfr (MH: bMS Am 1280 [111, p. 107]). Published in *JMN*, 11:478.

1. Fuller's only unsuccessful series of conversations was the one devoted to mythology, in which men joined the group. Emerson, who apparently was a chief offender, remembered that Fuller "seemed encumbered, or interrupted, by the headiness or incapacity of the men, whom she had not had the advantage of training, and who fancied, no doubt, that on such a question, they, too, must assert and dogmatize" (*Memoirs*, 1:347–48).

299. To William H. Channing[?]

Sunday, 21 February 1841

I have been reading, most of the day, the "Farbenlehre."[1] The facts interest me only in their mystical significance. As of the colors demanding one another in the chromatic circle, each demanding its opposite, and the eye making the opposite of that it once possessed. And of nature only giving the tints pure in the inferior natures, subduing and breaking them as she ascends. Of the cochineal making mordants to fix its dye on the vegetables where it nestles. Of the plants which, though they grow in the dark, only make long shoots, and refuse to seek their flower.

There was a time when one such fact would have made my day brilliant with thought. But now I seek the divine rather in Love than law.

ELfr, from Higginson, *MFO*, pp. 101–2.

1. Goethe's *Zur Farbenlehre* (Tübingen, 1810) developed a theory of light and color contrary to Newton's.

300. To Charles K. Newcomb

Thursday morng
[25 February 1841?]

Thou wilt find thyself deceived dear Charles, in expectation of a letter from me, though truly I should like to write it, but thou knowest

I belong to the bread-winning tribe who serve the clock and it will only give me these two minutes to say to thee that the Symphony is to be performed *next Saty eveg,* to urge thy coming, and promise us a walk beneath the stern blue skies of Sunday morng.[1] A friend

M. F.

Will you go with me?

ALS (MH: fMS Am 1086 [10:133]). *Addressed:* Charles King Newcomb / Providence / R.I. *Postmark:* Boston Feb 25 MS.

1. The postmark clearly dates this letter, but which symphony Fuller is referring to is unclear. The Boston Academy of Music did perform Beethoven's Fifth Symphony during this season, but that performance was probably on Saturday, 3 April (see letter 302). The *Boston Daily Advertiser* announced Henry Russell's "farewell concert" for Saturday, 27 February.

301. To William H. Channing[?]

29 March 1841

Others have looked at society with far deeper consideration than I. I have felt so unrelated to this sphere, that it has not been hard for me to be true. Also, I do not believe in Society. I feel that every man must struggle with these enormous ills in some way, in every age; in that of Moses, or Plato, or Angelo, as in our own. So it has not moved me much to see my time so corrupt, but it would if I were in a false position.

[George Ripley] went out to his farm yesterday, full of cheer, as one who doeth a deed with sincere good will. He has shown a steadfastness and earnestness of purpose most grateful to behold. I do not know what their scheme will ripen to; at present it does not deeply engage my hopes. It is thus far only a little better way than others. I doubt if they will get free from all they deprecate in society.

ELfr, from *Memoirs,* 2:58–59.

302. To William H. Channing

[5 April 1841]

[   ] it is to be that I shall have something positive to do for you, before I depart. If so, it will[n] compensate for past obstructions.

I hope you will go to the Ripleys for a time and that you will be in perfect peace there to work and to think."

Mr Parker preached a grand sermon yesterday at Purchase St. It was on Idolatries. He wound up with the Idolatry of Jesus.—[1] As they thought of giving him a call he wished to let them know all his thoughts as explicitly as they lay before himself. When he came down, he was in a fine glow; *you* would have said he looked *manly*. I quite loved him.

Saturday evening I heard one of Beethoven's great symphonies.[2] Oh William, what majesty what depth, what tearful sweetness of the human heart, what triumphs of the Angel mind! Into his hands he drew all the forces of sound, then poured them forth in tides such as ocean knows not, then the pause which said It is very good and the tender touch which woke again the springs of life. When I read his life I said I will never repine. When I heard this symphony I said I will triumph more and more above the deepenin[g] abysses. The life is large which can receive a Beethoven. I lived that hour.— There are many true men. I have you to be my friend.— I begin to revive, though I have had too much fatigue lately and my head still aches and aches. You are right to suppose I have been ill, in the month of January I lost too much blood in one of my nervous attacks and have been somewhat too ethereal and too pensive ever since. [   ]

ALfr (MB: Ms. Am. 1450 [46]). *Addressed:* Rev W. H. Channing / Cincinnati, / Ohio. *Postmark:* Boston MS Apr 5. *Endorsed:* April 5th 1841—

so, it will] so, ⟨if⟩ it will

think.] *Everything to this point has been canceled by a later hand.*

1. According to his sermon record book, Theodore Parker preached twice at Ripley's church on 4 April. His first sermon was "Influence of Religion on Thought"; his second, "Idolatry" (Theodore Parker sermon record book, p. 30, MB).

2. This may have been the first performance in America of Beethoven's Fifth Symphony. Henry Schmidt, the first violinist, conducted the Boston Academy of Music's orchestra on 3 April (Kinkeldey, "Beginnings of Beethoven," p. 243; *Boston Daily Advertiser*, 31 March 1841).

303. To Richard F. Fuller

Cambridge 6th April
1841.

My dear Richard,

On examining Mr Curtis's butcher's account I find still due him

$9 = 81—$ which I wish you to get paid him.[1] If you can be sure that it is faithfully done there is no need of a receipt as I have one in full.

This note I want you to give Mr Weld and see what he says about his rose-bushes.[2]

I enclose two keys which Lloyd brought me just as I was going away. I do not know which is the key of the storage room. The other probably belongs to Mr Weld's house. I intrust both to your care. Look into the room and see if all is right and tight, and see if in my little writing desk I have left my velvet, pen-wiper. (N.B. do all this Fast day p.m. as you return.)[3]

Let Lloyd return with you to Jamaica plain and go once more to Mr Charles Greene for his bill. Get it and pay it if you can and have Lloyd thank Mr G. with due respect.

On Mr Henry's bill should be an item for smoking the hams 50 cnt. beside jobs at our house and carrying me to Boston.

You know you are to settle with Mr Ripley about the cow.

See that all Lloyd's things are in good order, and, if you find he wants a coarse frock to work in, get his measure to have it made.— If you can carry them I wish you would buy him a couple of pounds figs and a bag of little crackers. Do" not give him *too much* good advice but a small dose, such as he can bear at one time. I shall expect to learn all about him from you.

As he returns with you Fast day he is to get his clothes from Mary. And there are some of Mother's things left with her to wash which I want you to put away in the store room. See why she did not bring mine to town as I expected on Saturday p. m. and if they have not yet been sent, have them sent on Friday to Dr Randall's. I think she must have sent them, but I will depend on you to ascertain all about it before you pay her *twenty dollars* still due her on her wages. As she does not write let her acknowledge the receipt of all her dues in the presence of witnesses.

Having transacted all my out of town affairs I request you as my man of business to call on A. W. Fuller Esq. and ask for a memorandum of his account of money I have recd since Mother went away and names of the persons in whose behalf the orders are. I will compare it with mine and square up when I am in town next.

I enclose fifty dollars which will be enough and more for all unless Mr Greene offers a bill in full which he has never yet done. If he does, take it, and I will pay through Miss Tilden.

I will expect you out here with your accounts next Saturday eveg you can come here and ask for me and I can, probably, see you alone. Then you can sleep with Arthur and, if it is fine, I will walk with you next day to Mt Auburn. Bring a memorandum of what is to pay for making Lloyd's vest.

Farewell, dear Richard, I consider you as one of my best friends, and I believe this would give you true pleasure. I have no more letters from the family yet, but enclose Mother's last which you did not see. I am very agreeably situated with my kind friends here; had an attack of headach the first night but begin to feel much better now— I have not yet seen Arthur

Very afftely yr sister

MARGARET.

Mr Henry bought me two feet wood from Eben Weld see that paid too.

ALS (MH: fMS Am 1086 [9:68]); MsC (MH: fMS Am 1086 [*Works*, 2:627–35]). *Addressed:* Richard F. Fuller.

Do] ⟨You⟩ Do

1. Possibly either Joseph Herman Curtis (1806–90) or his brother, George Scarbrough Curtis (1809–97), both Roxbury residents (Samuel C. Clarke, *Records of Some of the Descendants of William Curtis* [Boston, 1869], p. 21; *Boston Evening Transcript,* 3 March 1890, 6 November 1897).

2. Ebenezer Weld, Jr. (1817–87), a Roxbury handyman (Charles F. Robinson, *Weld Collections* [Ann Arbor, 1938], p. 152).

3. Thursday, 8 April, had been appointed the annual day of fasting, an occasion that prompted the editors of the *Christian Register* to say, "We cannot but hope that the approaching Fast will witness less dissipation and disorder, and be more decently and religiously observed than heretofore" (*Christian Register,* 3 April 1841).

304. To Ralph Waldo Emerson

[ca. 25] April 1841

I am glad Henry T[horeau] is coming to you; *that* seems feasible.[1] No, I have not heard the result of your projects, but I thought you were not sufficiently in light as to what you wanted, to succeed.[2] Cela n' est pas votre metier, je crois.[3] All you could hope would be some instructive blunder. Let others cook the *potage,* and you examine the recipe.

MsCfr (MH: bMS Am 1280 [111, p. 190]). Published in *JMN,* 11:490.

1. On 22 April Emerson wrote Fuller: "Henry Thoreau is coming to live with me & work with me in the garden & teach me to graft apples." Thoreau moved into the Emerson home on 26 April 1841 and stayed until May 1843, when he went to Staten Island (Rusk, *Letters of RWE,* 2:394; Walter Harding, *The Days of Henry Thoreau* [New York, 1965], pp. 127, 147).

2. The other plans involved Emerson's wish to help the Alcotts, whom he had proposed to take into his home; to have the servants and his family eat at a common table; and, finally, to take responsibility for a young Irish boy, Alexander McCaffery. The Alcotts did not move in, however, the servants rebelled at the idea of sitting with the family, and Alexander returned to New Jersey (Rusk, *Letters of RWE*, 2:371, 382, 389).

3. "That is not your forte, I believe."

305. To Ralph Waldo Emerson

Cambridge 10th May
1841

Your letter, my dear friend, was received just as I was on the wing to pass a few days with the fledglings of Community; and I have only this evening returned to answer it.[1] I will come on Saturday afternoon next if no crass accident mar the horizon of my hopes, and the visible heavens drop not down Niagaras. All that I have to say may best be reserved till I come; it is necessary that I should be economical, for I have of late been as gentle, as dull and as silent as the most fussy old bachelor could desire his housekeeper to be. You said, however, I could come and *live* there, if I had not a mind to talk, so I am not afraid but will come, hoping there may be a flow after this ebb, which has almost restored the health of your affectionate

Margaret.

I have put Rev on the cover contrary to my usual want, but of late I write so many letters to the soi-disant Divines that the prefix drops from the pen before I heed.

ALS (MH: bMS Am 1280 [2353]); MsC (MB: Ms. Am. 1450 [164]). Published in part in Higginson, *MFO*, pp. 181–82; the postscript appears in Rusk, *Letters of RWE*, 2:398. *Addressed:* Rev. R. W. Emerson / Concord / Mass. *Postmark:* Cambridge MS May 11. *Endorsed:* Margaret Fuller / May, 1841.

1. Emerson wrote on 6 May, urging Fuller to visit Concord, and railed against his poor health and "our national hurry" (Rusk, *Letters of RWE*, 2:398).

306. To Richard F. Fuller

Concord,
25th May, 1841.

My dear Richard,
I enclose this letter from Mother, probably the last I can receive

from her. I took away the last leaf by Eugene as it contained something I thought he might not like to have me send about. It is written with sweetness and self-possession; he seems to feel as if he knew very well what he is about.[1] Let us give him the most affectionate reception. You will see what Mother wishes to have done about her plants. I need not, I know, commend them to your care.— I want you Saturday eveg or Sunday to go to C. Port to Mrs Gannett's and tell her I think they may arrive next week, yet I cannot be sure as they may stay longer either in Louisville or Cincin than I now suppose.[2] If they receive my letter on their way they will probably all three, Mother, F. and W.H. go out directly to Mrs Gannett's and if she has not two rooms vacant then, Mother can go to Aunt K's till Mr Brodhead's family leave Mrs G.— You had better read aloud what I say that Mrs G. may distinctly understand. And give her my best respects.

I am living here the quiet country life you would enjoy. Here are hens, cows, pigs! and what I like better wildflowers and a host of singing birds. By the way, I dont think you could gratify Mrs Ward more than on the Sunday you go to Jamaica to get her a bouquet of wild flowers.[3] Borrow a tin pail or box and wet them when you put them in; they may thus be brought to town perfectly fresh. Mr. Emerson works five or six hours a day in his[n] garden and his health which was in a very low state this spring improves day by day.[4] He has a friend with him of the name of Henry Thoreau who has come to live with him and be his working-man this year. H. T. is three and twenty, has been through college and kept a school, is very fond of classic studies, and an earnest thinker yet[n] intends being a farmer. He has a great deal of practical sense, and as he has bodily strength to boot, he may look to be a successful and happy man. He has a boat which he made himself, and rows me out on the pond. Last night I went out quite late and staid til the moon was almost gone, heard the whip-poor-will for the first time this year. There was a sweet breeze full of appleblossom fragrance which made the pond swell almost into waves. I had great pleasure. I think of you in these scenes, because I know you love them too. By and by when the duties are done, we may expect to pass summer days together

I have had a letter from Lloyd, stating that "he did not like the Community as he expected, for he has to work when he does not wish to"!![5]

My love to Arthur. I wrote to him before I recd his letter. Probably I may not write again as I expect to be in Cambridge by[n] Monday eveg next. very affectionately your sister

M.

ALS (MH: fMS Am 1086 [9:71]); MsC (MH: fMS Am 1086 [Works, 2:635–41]). Published in part in Miller, pp. 74–75, and Chevigny, p. 121. *Addressed:* R. F. Fuller. / Care Curtis & Merriam / 40 Kilby St. Boston / Mass. *Postmark:* Concord Mas May 26.

a day in his] a day in ⟨his⟩ his
thinker yet] thinker ⟨but⟩ yet
Cambridge by] Cambridge ⟨on⟩ by

1. In a letter of 20 April, Eugene took exception to a letter (now lost) that she had sent, saying, "You have hardly ever spoken so reproachfully to me" (postscript to Margarett C. Fuller to Margaret Fuller, 20 April 1841, MH).

2. Sarah White Gannett, wife of the Reverend Thomas Brattle Gannett of Cambridgeport.

3. In his reply of 30 May, Richard reported on his visit to the Wards, praising Anna and saying that "it must be hard, I should think for one bro't up in one of the aristocratic families of a slaveholding state" to have Christian charity (MH).

4. To his brother William, Emerson remarked on his visitors—Fuller, Thoreau, and Mary Russell—and observed that he himself had been "a skeleton all the spring until I am ashamed" (Rusk, *Letters of RWE*, 2:402).

5. Lloyd was staying at Brook Farm.

307. To Caroline Sturgis

Saturday Morng
[June 1841?]

Dearest Caroline,

I have reaped nothing but disappointment all this week, and I do not feel as if I could come to see you or go to Spring St.[1] Although I suppose I shall only pass one of these wearisome days here, I had rather than to go away. Perhaps I will come next Saturday and go to Spring St. At any rate I think I shall ride over to see you in the course of the week. Come here, if you can. I begin to be really depressed and feel as I would not have my foe feel. The price of our grains of ambrosia is here so painfully coined, so slowly doled out. And how much, how much of this sort of pain I must look forward to in the future. I cannot look with delight just now even on the perfumed and leafy June. Love me and wish me good,

MARGARET.

ALS (MH: bMS Am 1221 [228]). *Addressed:* Miss Caroline Sturgis / Brookline. *Endorsed:* June.

1. Fuller probably visited Brook Farm in West Roxbury, but she may have stayed with the Frank Shaws, who also lived on Spring Street.

308.   To Charles K. Newcomb

Sunday
[June 1841]

My dear Charles,

Will you tomorrow write to me by post exactly how Lloyd is and whether it is necessary or even desirable that I should come over to see him? I do not wish to, unless he really needs me, as I do not think I have ever had the measles. But I had rather come than run the least risk about him. I suppose from what Mr Odiorne tell me, that he has had them lightly and is getting well.[1] But be very particular in your letter and ask Mrs Ripley and Mrs Barker both that I may know just what to do.

Direct Cambridge—Mass. Care Prof Farrar, and I will come on Tuesday p. m. if wanted.

I shall come very soon at any rate, both because I want to see Lloyd, and want to know that you are not uncomfortable in the room with him. I want too a good walk with you, though perhaps it may be a silent one. *My* mind, at least, lies very still at present and yields up all the talk to this luxuriant June.

Affectionately yours

MARGARET F.

My love to Mrs Ripley: I hear with sorrow she is ill.

ALS (MH: fMS Am 1086 [10:138]). *Addressed:* Mr. / C. K. Newcomb.

1. Probably William Henry Odiorne (1804?–97) of Cambridgeport (*CVR*; Mt. Auburn).

309.   To Ralph Waldo Emerson

Brookline.
Monday evening 21st June. [1841]

Dearest Waldo,

By the light of this new moon I see very clearly that you were quite in the right and I[n] in the wrong.[1] I dont know how I could persist so in my own way of viewing the matter in the face of your assuring me that myself had fixed a later day and of your exertions to keep your engagement and bring your poesies. I think I was very ill-natured, perverse, and unreasonable, but I am punished when I think of you riding home alone and thinking it all over as I know you must for I have been able to get into your way of viewing it now. Whatever I may have said in my pet this afternoon be sure I can never be long ignorant what is due to you and that I am more happy to find you right than to be so myself because in many respects I value you more than I do myself. In truth today there was a background to my thoughts which you could not see, and I might have known you could not but which altered the color and position of every object. Now will you not as soon as you sincerely can write to say that you will bear no thought of this unless I behave again in this ungracious way and then you must tell me what I said this time and check my impetuous ways. I wanted this afternoon as soon as you were really out of the house to run after you and call as little children do kiss and be friends; that would not be decorous *really* for two Editors, but it shall be so in thought shall it not? If you dont answer me well I will not be vexed to make up for so much crossness today.

Your affectionate

MAGDALEN"

I have changed my name for tonight because Cary says this is such a Magdalen letter.

ALS (MH: bMS Am 1280 [2554]). Published in Rusk, *Letters of RWE*, 2:408–9. *Addressed:* Mr R. W. Emerson / Concord / Mass. *Postmark:* Brookline Mass June 22. *Endorsed:* Margaret Fuller / June 1841.

right and I] right and ⟨you⟩ I
affectionate Magdalen] affectionate ⟨Margaret.⟩ Magdalen

1. Apparently on this day Emerson and Fuller had had words over the second part of "Woodnotes," which he had just completed and which he thought was to be published in the July *Dial*. Fuller, however, had already sent the entire manuscript to the printer, so the poem had to wait for the October issue (pp. 207–14). In response to her apology, Emerson wrote, "I shall never dare quarrel with you, if you are so just, mitigable, & bounteous. I see not how I can avoid sending you my verses to read, whilst the white wand is extended" (Rusk, *Letters of RWE*, 2:408–9; Myerson, *New England Transcendentalists*, pp. 65–66).

310. To William H. Channing

[July? 1841?]

[   ] and it is sweet to be with her and her fair children in that bright and peaceful home."

The more I think of it, the more deeply do I feel the imperfection of your view of friendship which is the same Waldo E. takes in that letter on Charles's death.[1] It is very noble but not enough for our manifold nature. Our friends should be our incentives to Right, but not only our guiding but our prophetic stars. To love by sight is much, to love by faith is more; both are the entire love without which heart, mind, and soul cannot be alike satisfied. We love and ought to love one another not merely for the absolute worth of each but on account of a mutual fitness of temporary character. We are not merely one another's priests or gods, but ministering angels, exercising in the past the same function as the Great Soul in the whole of seeing the perfect through the imperfect nay, making it come there. Why am I to love my friend the less for any obstruction in his life? is not the very time for me to love most tenderly when I must see his life in despite of seeming; when he *shows it* me I can only admire; I do not *give* myself. I am *taken captive*. How shall I express my meaning? Perhaps I can do so from the tales of chivalry where I find what corresponds far more thoroughly with my nature than in these stoical statements. The friend of Amadis expects to hear prodigies of valor of the absent preux, but if he be mutilated in one of his first battles shall he be mistrusted by the brother of his soul more than if he had been tested in a hundred. If Britomart finds Artegall bound in the enchanter's spell, can she doubt therefore him whom she has seen *in the magic glass*. A *Britomart* does battle in his cause and frees him from the evil power, a dame of less nobleness, sits and watches the enchanted sleep, weeping night and day, or spurs away on her white palfrey to find some one" more helpfull than herself.[2] But they are always faithful through the dark hours to the bright. The Douglas motto "Tender and trew" seems to me the worthiest of the strongest breast. To borrow again from your Spenser, I am entirely suited with the fate of the three brothers Diamond and the rest.[3] I could not die while there was yet life in my brother's breast. I would return from the shades and nerve him for the fight. I could do it for our hearts beat with one blood. Do you not see the truth and happiness of this waiting tenderness. The verse

> Have I a lover
> Who is noble and free
> I would he were nobler
> Than to love me.[4]

does not come home to me though *this* does,

I could not love thee, sweet, so much
Loved I not honor more.[5]

I sympathized with you when you said you felt deep compassion for
me. I often feel it for myself. Tieck who has embodied so many Runic
secrets explained to me what I have often felt when he tells of the
poor changeling child when turned from the door of her adopted
home she sat down on a stone and felt such a pity for herself that
she wept.[6] Yet me also the wonderful bird singing in the wild forest
shall again tempt on and not in vain! Yet pity me not where I love,
but where I do not. The soul pines to know the All well enough to
love all,[n] happy where there is any outlet for the tide of thought and
love. The tragedy is deep in proportion to the character, but it is only
in time. Do not think of making me calculate about my powers or concentrate on them on work. I have no powers except so far as inspired
by high sentiment, if I economized, I should be naught. Do not, I im-
plore you, whether from pride or affection, wish to exile me from the
dark hour. The manly mind might love best in the triumphant hour,
but the woman could no more stay from the foot of the cross, than
from the Transfiguration. And I am fit to be the friend of an immortal mortal because I know both these sympathies. You know I was prepared with you. I drew your lot myself: "Except ye drink his blood ye
are none of his."[7] At the foot of the cross, at the door of the sepulchre
I must await the prince my youthful thought elected.[n] You often say
still I must exaggerate. *I do not.* You do not yet understand me. I
promise I will not wed myself to a fancy or a resolve. I have written
all this letter in praise of fidelity yet I will resign the thought of you
the moment it no longer inspires me. But that will only be when the
divining sense is quenched.
Eveg. I felt some pain this afternoon in seeing you[n] [   ]

ALfr (MB: Ms. Am. 1450 [165]). Published in part in *Memoirs*, 2:42–44, and Higginson, *MFO*, pp. 72–74.
  home.] *The opening has been canceled by a later hand.*
  find some one] find some ↑ one ↓
  to love all] to love ⟨it⟩ ↑ all ↓
  the prince my youthful thought elected] *Canceled by a later hand.*
  I felt some pain this afternoon in seeing you] *Canceled by a later hand.*
  1. Probably the letter of 12 May 1836 to Lidian Emerson on the death of his brother
Charles, in which Emerson wrote, "And so, Lidian, I can never bring you back my
noble friend who was my ornament my wisdom & my pride" (Rusk, *Letters of RWE*,
2:20).
  2. Fuller's allusions are to Edmund Spenser's *Faerie Queene*. In bk. 5, Amidas fights
with his brother Bracidas over two islands inherited from their father. Artegall medi-

ates between the two. In bk. 3, Britomart, daughter of King Ryence, falls in love with Artegall, disguises herself as a knight, and goes in search of her beloved.

3. Priamond, Diamond, Triamond, sons of Agape in bk. 4 of *Faerie Queene*. Agape bargains with the Fates that whichever son dies first, his soul shall pass into the next; when the next dies, both their lives pass into the third son.

4. Emerson, "The Sphinx," first published in *Dial* 1 (January 1841):348–50.

5. Richard Lovelace, "To Lucasta, Going to the Warres."

6. Fuller refers to Ludwig Tieck's "Blonde Eckbert," one of the first *Novellen*, a genre that became prominent in German literature. First published in *Ritter Blaubart* (Berlin and Leipzig, 1797), the story recounts the life of Eckbert's wife, Bertha, who as a child was given up to a poor couple by her unmarried mother. Not knowing her parentage, she flees her adoptive home, is taken in by a kindly sorceress, again runs away, and marries Eckbert, her brother. In her last flight, Bertha steals a magic bird from the sorceress (*OCGL*; J. G. Robertson, *A History of German Literature*, 5th ed. [Edinburgh, 1966], p. 356).

7. Probably a version of John 6:53: "Except ye eat the flesh of the Son of man, and drink his blood, ye have no life in you."

311. To Charles K. Newcomb

Sunday
18th July. [1841]

I was truly sorry, my dear Charles, that I could not see you more in these last Spring St days, but there are ever many conflicting claims in this brief life. Possibly I may see your fields again before going to Newport, yet is it not probable. I send the wine as your Mother desired, and I charge you to take it whenever you feel the need. On return you must send me the ballad, The Cave Myths which is a" grand conception and of which I often think, and the little poem of which you spoke.[1] In these most calm and holy starlit" nights think always that I am affectionately your friend

MARGARET F.

ALS (MH: fMS Am 1086 [10:145]). *Addressed:* Charles K. Newcomb, / Brook Farm.
which is a] which is ↑a↓
holy starlit] holy starlit(e)

1. Fuller asks for Newcomb's poetry. Apparently he sent it (see letter 325).

312. To Margarett C. Fuller

Cambridge
20th July, 1841

Dearest Mother,

I today recd a letter from Mrs D'Wolf, expressing a warm desire that you should visit her.[1] I know it will give her daily pleasure for you to stay as long as you can feel inclined. She wants me to let you know how very retired they live lest you should find it dull, but says if you can enjoy it she shall much, and thinks you will love her little Willie, of whom she seems very fond.[2] Mr D.W. has been very ill, and the children have had the whooping cough severely, but they are all recovering now. When you are ready to go write three[n] days beforehand and direct Mrs M. D. Wolf Care W.B D Wolf, Esq. Bristol R. I. and say just when you will come that they may meet you with the carriage at the landing. The best way is for you to go to Providence in the morng cars, go to Mrs Newcomb's or Mr Grinnell's and take the boat for Bristol in the afternoon. I hope you have made arrangements with Mrs G. so that you will not be paying for your room all this time, for I know M[ary] would delight to have you stay there as long as you choose and you could not be more agreeably situated. There is nothing that I know of to bring you back here at present, for both Arthur and I are going away in a few days, so dont waste your money for want of clear plan.

I have a letter from dear Eugene who seems quite confident that Wm will help him, and therefore did not expect to return. Also one from Ellen in a much more cheerful strain and still expecting to set out in August. She had not recd yours. Also one from Richard whose heart seems fixed on going to College. W.H. has been to see me: he is much depressed, by not getting more business while at N. Bedford. I confess I feel very weary of them all; there is not one except Arthur on which my mind can rest, and I long to fix it on my own plans where I am clear and sure and strong, and might find repose if not happiness. But we must both be patient. Although I am not in favor at all so far as I see yet of your going to Canton, yet now you are on the spot. I wish you to look steadily and fully at that also. See how it would suit you and whom else of your family it could avail. My friend W. is as much at sea as ourselves.[3] I have talked with him of the plan we mentioned and his heart inclined towards it, but new circumstances have come up in his lot the past week, and I cannot tell at all how he will incline at last. Beside here is Richard steering in an opposite direction.[4]

I had a very happy time at Spring St, health and spirits and sunshine were ours. Now I am very busy preparing the next Dial and have so much writing to do that it is very fatiguing to write this or any letter in addition.[5] I want you to write me this week, direct care Prof. Farrar Cambridge.

I went to see Grandmother on Saty; she was pretty well. Remember me with affection to my Aunts and please mention in your letter how Aunt A[bigail] is— very afftly yours

MARGARET F.

Write neatly and elegantly I pray to the elegant M[ary].

ALS (MH: fMS Am 1086 [9:58]); MsC (MH: fMS Am 1086 [Works, 2:525–31]). *Addressed:* Mrs Margaret Fuller / Care Frederic Lincoln Esq / Canton / Mass. *Postmark:* Cambridge / MS / Jul 21.

write three] write ⟨two⟩ three

1. Mary Soley DeWolfe, Fuller's friend from her school days in Groton, who lived with her husband, William Bradford DeWolfe, in Bristol.

2. Willie is William Bradford DeWolfe, Jr. (1840–1902), third of Mary's five children (Calbraith B. Perry, *Charles D'Wolf of Guadaloupe* [New York, 1902], p. 137).

3. William Henry Channing had recently left Cincinnati. He was thinking of leaving the ministry.

4. Richard was working in a dry-goods store in Boston, but he had written his sister on 17 July (MH), saying abruptly, "Boston is a Dungeon, in which I cannot live," and announcing his plans to enter Harvard.

5. In the next issue of the *Dial*, Fuller published two long essays, "Lives of the Great Composers" and a review of Philip Bailey's poem *Festus*.

313. To Caroline Sturgis

Cambridge,
22d July. 1841.

Dearest Cary,

I have not written earlier, not only[n] because I have been so very much engaged, but because I have been waiting to hear from M. Channing, and thinking every day that I should hear. This day the letter came. She has engaged us lodgings near the beach and *opposite the gate of Paradise* for the first fort night. And Mrs Wilcox will receive us afterwards to stay at the Glen as long as we choose; I think at present I shall wish to stay a fort night.[1] When we return I want to go to Newbury. M. C. told these people we should be there the 29th or 30th. I want to go on *Friday the 30th* which will give us three evegs to the full moon. I cannot get ready earlier.

Will you come to Boston Thursday of next week and we will go in the 7 o clock train next morng as that is the way M. has arranged. If convenient, I will stay Thursday night at your house with you, if not at Anna's or the Randalls.

Write me directly about this. I cannot get your letter at any rate before Tuesday.

I had your other. God bless you! I *am* very "happy these few moments" and so deeply that it seems some balm must linger ever in the
heart.[2] My affte regards to Mrs Curson. Yours ever, as ever

MARGARET.

ALS (MH: bMS Am 1221 [244]). *Addressed:* Miss Caroline Sturgis / Care Saml.
Curson Esq / Newburyport. / Mass. *Postmark:* Boston Mas. Jul 23. *Endorsed:* July.

not only] not ↑ only ↓

1. M. Channing is Mary Channing, Dr. Channing's daughter; Mrs. Wilcox is unidentified; The Glen is Mary Rotch's Newport summer home; Paradise was "a long and
beautiful grove of sycamore trees, that skirts the foot of a rocky hill" along Sachuset
beach at Newport (Bullard, *Rotches*, p. 94; John Dix, *A Hand-book of Newport* [Newport,
1852], p. 79).

2. Fuller's letter answers Sturgis' of 10 July (MH), in which she urges Fuller to come
to Newburyport and "be happy a few moments if you can."

314. To Margarett C. Fuller

Cambridge,
29th July. [1841]

Dearest Mother,

I have read this letter of Ellen's. I am still against your going to
housekeeping, as far as I know. But, if you can form plans as *you are
sure* to advantage in Canton, form them without reference to me. I
could do well enough if free from anxiety about the family. But as far
as I see at present I am in favor of Mrs Gannett's. I will write again
at Newport. At present I am perfectly crowded and almost crazy with
work. I cannot come to Canton. Dont mind what Ellen says she is no
judge at that distance what had best be done. Go to Bristol without
deciding any thing yet. I am going to B. to get you a dress and some
other little things which please accept from me. I am perfectly able to
give, having just recd thirty[n] dollars quite unexpectedly through a tale
given to the Token, so have no scruple.[1] Arthur looked at J. P. but
did not happen to find your dress and it would not do for Bristol,
if he had. I am going to get you a Mousseline. Yr ever affte

M.

Have had no time to see Frances this week past.[2]

ALS (MH: fMS Am 1086 [9:104]); MsC (MH: fMS Am 1086 [Works, 2:255–57]).
Addressed: Mrs Margaret Fuller / Canton / Mass.

Written on the outside, in another hand, is this note: Miss Fuller will send by stage tomorrow (Tuesday) ⟨?⟩ A Dress, which if not delivered—please enquire for at Stage office—

recd thirty] recd ⟨three⟩ thirty

1. No trace of a story by Fuller in *The Token*, a Boston annual gift book (1827–42), has appeared.

2. Frances Hastings Fuller, wife of Fuller's brother William Henry.

315.   To William H. Channing

[31 July 1841]

[   ] the merest trifle precipitated the whole mass; all became clear as crystal, and I saw of what use the tedious preparation had been by the deep content I felt in the result. It will be so with thee, if thou dost not hasten into action.

Today in the exquisite calm of this scene I felt as poor Bettine did to Gunderode. "Oh could I bear thee in my arms through the world to a soft mossy place."[1] There I well know it would not be *ages* of repose the Soul would crave; she only needs to take her own time to rest upon the friendly bough and sleep in the embosoming Night, secure that she will not be rudely waked by the glare of factitious demands.— Here are no deep forests, nor ster[n] mountains, nor narrow, sacred valleys, but the little white farm-house looks down from its gentle slope on the boundless sea, and beneath the moon beyond the glistening cornfields is heard the endless surge. All around the house is most gentle and friendly, with many common flowers that seem to have planted themselves, and the domestic honeysuckle carefully trained over the little window. Around are all the common farmhouse sounds the poultry making a pleasant recitative between the carols of singing birds; even geese and turkies are not inharmonious when regulated by the diapasons of the beach. The orchard of very old apple trees, whose twisted forms tell of the glorious winds that have here held revelry, protects a little homely garden such as gives to me an indescribable refreshment, where the undivided vegetable plots, and flourishing young fruit trees mingling carelessly[n] seem as if man had dropt the seed just where he wanted the plants, and they had sprung up at once. The family too seem at first glance well suited to the place, homely, kindly, unoppressed, of honest pride and mutual love, not unworthy to look out upon the far-shining sea! Yesterday afternoon we went with the last rosy light to the beach and passed all the evening. It was a most melting mood; this beach, far more beautiful than the other, seems in its curve to clasp the ocean to its breast whereat [   ]

ALfr (MB: Ms. Am. 1450 [47]). Published in part in *Memoirs*, 2:59–60. *Addressed:* William H. Channing / Cambridge / Mass. *Postmark:* Newport R.I Aug. *Endorsed:* July 31st 1841 Newport—

mingling carelessly] mingling ⟨cease⟩carelessly

1. Fuller again quoted this excerpt from *Die Günderode* in *Dial* 2 (January 1842): 329: "Oh, as I went home I loved thee so! In thought I wound my arms about thee so close; I thought I would bear thee in my arms to the end of the world, and set thee down on a fair mossy place; there would I serve thee" ("O ich hatte Dich im Heimgehen so lieb, ich schlang meine Arme um Dich so fest in Gedanken, ich dacht, ich wollte Dich tragen auf meinen Armen ans End der Welt und dort Dich an einen schönen moosreichen Platz niedersetzen, da wollt ich Dir dienen") (Bettina von Arnim, *Werke und Briefe*, ed. Gustav Konrad [Cologne, 1959], 1:351).

316.   To Margarett C. Fuller

Paradise Farm!
5th August, 1841.

Dear Mother,

I don't remember whether the agreement was for you to write to me, or I to you first, but, as I receive no letter, suppose it must be I who am to begin. My last days at Cambridge were very crowded and yet, after all, I did not finish my writing, but had to bring it here. Today I put the last touch and feel at leisure to enjoy the beauty around me. I am perfectly happy in being here, as you may judge I ought from the date. We are about a mile and a half from Newport, on the second beach, which is far more beautiful in its curve and longer than the first beach, is bounded by noble rocks and little frequented by the fashionables, a circumstance to me most agreeable as I love to indulge now and then in a somewhat savage dishabille. We are close to the high peak of Paradise which overlooks the ocean and adjacent country with much boldness. This dear little white farm house is on the slope of the hill, rather more than a quarter of a mile from the great ocean. Lying on my bed I can see the wide blue waters glittering, the surf breaking on the shore. I bathe every morning;[n] the kind farmer, (unlike those in Mass. who seem to have a vulgar dislike to see others have tastes in which they do not share,) as soon as he saw we liked bathing spent nearly a day in preparing a bathing house for us. I like him and his family. There is an aged Mother who reminds me of Grandmother, but is in more full possession of her faculties; a house full of good-humored, busy young men and women and gay, docile[n] children. They love flowers, like you; have a scarlet honeysuckle trained over the door and little window stands with greenhouse plants. I shall stay here the greater part of the time while on the Island: it is much more beautiful than at the Glen. I please myself thinking you will have the same delicious temperature at Bristol, and a beautiful waterview too, though not like this. Remember me with much affection to Mary.

I hope you got your dress safe and that it pleased you: they are colors I like very much but not those mentioned in your letter to Aunt K. (which I did not see till I had bought it) and our tastes are so different I am always afraid of not pleasing you. However it will make a nice[n] dress, and I think you will find it none too warm for Bristol. Here is no muslin, or calico weather, and I presume it is quite *as* cool at Bristol.

Dear Arthur went off in very good spirits. From Eugene I did not hear again, but hope you have. From Ellen I had a letter the day before I came away; she was well; still expected to set off on her return early[n] in August. She was again very urgent to have a house taken, but I think her being in such a hurry is a great mistake. She brings no pupils, and, if she thinks of getting day-scholars, is much mistaken if she talks of getting them "any-where." She would have to know *where* to have a chance I am still decidedly in favor of Mrs Gannett's for the winter; by spring we will see clear. But, Mother, do not entangle yourself by any promises to (*my brother*) *William H.* I cannot enlarge on this subject, but do not. If you and Ellen would prefer passing the winter at Canton, and Fanny to be confined there, I have no objection, but do not compromise the future *yet.*

I was not able to see Fanny for some days before I left. I did not go out at all, I was so very busy. I want to know her plans and how she is, please mention when you write. I was very sorry I could not go to see Grandmother more, but it was impossible: if I had spent my strength on walking I could not have got ready to come here at all. I am already much stronger for the bathing and sea air.

My love to Aunt A. I will endeavor to go see her in the course of the autumn, but probably not on my way home. I hope she is better for your tender care; it seems to me any one must. Write to me as soon as you can after receiving this—direct Miss S. M. Fuller, Care, Rev Dr Channing Newport, Rhode Island and pay postage, as it is inconvenient for me to pay it to the Dr. He has made me a pleasant little visit since I came and Mary has been here today, but we are distant from them: at the Glen I shall see them often. I saw my friend you wot of almost daily and had a most happy time: he came to go with me to see you, but you had flown. Caroline desires her love to you Very affey yours

M.

ALS (MH: fMS Am 1086 [9:73]); MsC (MH: fMS Am 1086 [Works, 2:531–39]). *Addressed:* Mrs Margaret Fuller / Care of Frederic Lincoln Esq / Canton Mass. *Postmark:* Newport R.I. Aug 9.

every morning] every ⟨⟩ morning
gay, docile] gay, ⟨busy⟩ docile
make a nice] make a ⟨warm⟩ nice
her return early] her return⟨,⟩ early

317. To William H. Channing

Paradise *Farm!*ⁿ
6th August [1841] Eveg.

My dear friend,

No letter from you yet; do not flatter yourself that I am not anxious to hear how you are. The proof-sheet came today, and I send by Mrs Rogers the rest of the copy. Here, at my ease, I have written of my hero, and have, at least, covered much paper.[1] Indeed it canot fail to be good; the facts speak for themselves.

Many, many sweet little things would I tell you; only they are so very little. I feel just now as if I could live and die here. I am out in the open air all the time, except about two hours in the early morning, and, now the moon is fairly gone, late in the evening. While she was here we staid out then too. Every thing seems sweet here, so homely, so kindly; the old people chatting so contentedly the young men and girls laughing together in the fields, not vulgarly but in the true kins-folk way, little children singing in the house and beneath the berry bushes. The never ceasing break of the surf is a continual symphony calming the spirits which this delicious air might else exalt too much. Every thing on the beach becomes a picture: the casting the seine, the ploughing the deep for sea weed, (this when they do it with horses is prettiest of all, but when you see the oxen in the surf, you lose all faith in the story of Europa,ⁿ as the gay waves tumble in on their lazy sides.[2] The bull would be a fine object on the shore, but not, not in the water. Nothing short of a dolphin will do! Late tonight from the highest Paradise rocks, seeing Cary wandering, and the horsemen careening on the beach, so spectrally passing into nature amid the pale brooding twilight, I almost thought myself in the *land of souls!* (Hibernia!ⁿ But in the morning it is life, all cordial and common. This half fisherman, half farmer life seems very favorable to manliness. I like to talk with the fishermen, they are not boorish, nor limited, but keen-eyed and of a certain rude gentleness Two or three days ago I saw the sweetest picture. There is a very tall rock, one of those natural pulpits at one end of the beach, as I approached I saw a young fisherman with his little girl, he had nestled her into a hollow of the rock and was standing before her with his arms round her and looking up in her face. I never saw any thing so pretty; I stood and stared, country fashion, and presently he scrambled up to the very top with her in his arms. She screamed a little as they went, but when they were fairly up on the crest of the rock she chuckled and stretched her tiny hand over his neck to go still farther. But when she found he did not wish it, she leaned against his shoulder, and he sat, feeling himself in the child like that exquisite Madonna, and looking out over the great sea. Surely the "kindred points of Heaven and Home"³ were known in his breast, whatever guise they might assume." I thought of you, William, that your home might but be on this gentle shore, and that you might plough the waves instead of your own overtasked life, and that you might sit so on the high rock with your little Fanny in your arms, and by the music of the waves teach her to worship the declining Sun, and the holy uprise of the stars. How truly she would then be yours! I would look at you from the peaks of Paradise; but I should not like you to wear a red flannel jacket as this Father did;— though tis the true picturesque color.

But the sea is not always lovely and bounteous. Generally since I have been here she has beamed her bluest. The night of the full moon we staid out on the far rocks The afternoon was fair, the sun set nobly with many violet mantles, but he left them to the moon and she not only rose red, lowering, and of impatient attitude but kept hiding her head all the evening with an angry struggling gesture. C. said "This is not Dian" and I replied "No, now we see the Hecate, and we exchanged no other word. But the damp, cold wind came sobbing, and the waves began sobbing and wailing, too, and I was seized with a sort of terrible feeling such as I never had before, even in the darkest, most treacherous rustling wood. The moon seemed sternly to give me up to the demons of the rock, and the waves coldly to mourn, a tragic chorus, and I felt a cold grasp. I suffered so much I said nothing, but it seemed to me we should never get home without some fatal catastrophe. I never felt more relieved than when, as we came up the hill the moon suddenly shone forth. It was ten oclock and here every human sound is hushed, and lamp put out at that hour. How tenderly the grapes and tall corn ears glistened and nodded and the trees stretched out their friendly arms, and the scent of every humblest herb, was like a word of love, after the sullen brine. But the waves also at that moment put on the silvery gleam, and looked most soft and regretful That was a real voice from Nature; what did it say?— I have so many thoughts and most of the "*conscious and unconscious,*" but now I cannot.

Next week, if you are good and write to me well, or if you are not good, and[n] I am as much of a spend thrift as I usually am you will have another letter. But you will feel how much I wish to hear and write. Is there hope you will be able to write as you thought for the Dial? Let me know, when you can because else I must plan. Goodnight dear friend.

If you could only bathe in the open sea daily for a month, you would find yourself *well* and a *creative Genius.*

Have I spoiled my story by[n] calling my rock *a pulpit*! Cary drew them, but the sketches[n] are not good enough to send. She made the fishermen look too young and sentimental and the child not rustic enough.

AL (MB: Ms. Am. 1450 [48]). Published in part in *Memoirs,* 2:60–62.

Paradise *Farm*!] *Fuller wrote in the margin:* So they date here!
in the story of Europa] in ↑ the story of Europa ↓
land of souls! (Hibernia!]) *land of souls*! ↑ (Hibernia!) ↓
assume.] *Here six lines of manuscript have been canceled by a later hand.*
and] *The beginning of the paragraph has been canceled by a later hand.*
my story by] my story ↑ by ↓
but the sketches] but ⟨they⟩ the sketches

1. Probably Beethoven, about whom Fuller wrote in her essay "The Great Composers" for the October 1841 issue of the *Dial.* Which Mrs. Rogers Fuller means is not clear; perhaps Maria DeWolfe Rogers (1795–1890), wife of Robert Rogers, a Bristol banker. Fuller had met them in 1839 (George Howe, *Mount Hope* [New York, 1959]).
2. Zeus, having fallen in love with Europa, daughter of Agenor, king of Tyre, took the form of a white bull. Europa thought him so gentle that she climbed onto his back, only to be carried away as the bull swam to Crete.
3. Wordsworth, "To a Skylark," l. 12.

318. To Margarett C. Fuller

The Glen, R. I.
22d August, 1841

Dearest Mother,

The reason you have not heard from me sooner is that the glare from the rocks and water affected my eyes so much that I have been afraid to use them. I have suffered, too, in my head considerably from too much exposure to the sun. That cool elastic air from the sea is very delusive: I used to get all scorched and not know it till I came into the house.— I left the Paradise farm house about a week ago and came here to my ancient haunt; the soft green of the Glen and the thick gloom of Dr Channing's beautiful shrubberies are most soothing after the bright blue sea. This is my last day here; tomorrow we return to Cambridge.

Dr C's family are kind as ever. I go there every day. William C. is staying there now, and will remain till Thursday. He asks after you with much affection. His lot seems finally decided. He will not go back to the West, but take a farm next spring, and his Mother will accompany him. He is going next week to look at one in Stockbridge, which, if large enough, they would like, as many of their friends live there. These prospects make him happy at last. From him I learn that Ellen is in Cincinnati, and they are trying to get a school for her there, though without much prospect of success, so she changed her intentions after writing to Richard. Have you letters from her, or from Eugene? I have none now for near a month, and am very desirous to hear. But place children, and goods and a' steadily in the Divine guard, dear Mother. Do not poison your benign spirit with anxiety. The time is come when the younger members of the family must run those risks which are to form their characters, and develope their powers; Mother and sister must now "stand and wait" rather than counsel or cherish.

From Frances I have a letter, dated Nantucket written apparently in excellent spirits. She says she returns to Cambridge 1st Septr but does not say what arrangements she has made for her confinement, nor where she expects to be at that time.

From Richard I have a very manly and considerate letter about the Wilson place. It certainly seems a chance of securing a home where we *might* live if we wished that is a pity to let slip. But I can get no clear light to buy it. I agree with you that I do not see how we could live there just at present without more expense and difficulty than is wise to encounter. Yet it might prove a better investment of part of the money than the present mortgage, even if we bought it to let. Dare you trust me, if time should press, and I could get the advice of friends learned in the law (of purchase) to take[n] any step I may think best on returning to C I do not think I should think best [to] buy it, yet if it could be got for 18-00 it might be a real bargain. Write to me immedy on this subject, as also, when you expect to be in Cambridge.

I shall not remain there long. Yet do not hurry your present visit. But when you are ready to come, Aunt K. for a day or two when you and I can meet, or the Randalls for *the* visit where I can see you equally well, would be very glad to have you.

My best love to Mary. I wish it had been in my power to see her and hers But I feel now that I have had play enough and want to return to work, and to plan the future. Keep up your courage dearest Mother. This is a trying time in your life, but none better than yourself can feel there is a justice which cannot fail those who are innocent and strive to be just

Most affectionately your daughter

M.

Mrs Brown has a son three weeks, Mrs Harrison one ten days old.

ALS (MH: fMS Am 1086 [9:74]); MsC (MH: fMS Am 1086 [Works, 2:539–45]). *Addressed:* Margaret Fuller / Care W. B. D'Wolf Esq. Bristol—R.I. *Postmark:* Fall River Mass Aug 26.

to take] to ⟨pr⟩ take

319. To William H. Channing

[29 August 1841]

[   ] and the words were struck out like sparks of fire.[1] I heard as I went in that he said he should do, what I supposed he would, *define his position*, and he did so in a manner that satisfied me as to his character. He was bold, calm, wide, truly dignified If he has had moments of weakness, they are over; he has again that decision and (a little cold and haughty) self-reliance I have been[n] used to prize in him. But then he gave us too the gauge of his intellect, and I understood him far better than ever before. Idealism is with him only a matter of taste; he is a man of the world and a scholar but neither poet nor philosopher. The subject was "what part shall the scholar take in the contest between Conservatism and Reform?" And Waldo said he never saw the root of every thing cut away with such sweetness nor any thing to surpass the easy elegance with which he poised himself in the air after taking away all possible foot hold.

Mr Stetson said it was amusing to see the alternations of applause;[2] first Conservative, then Reformer, but neither daring to be ardent, lest he should be smartly tapped on the head next minute. The oration[n] will be printed, I hope, and you will read, but I wish you might have heard it.

I went with the Ripleys to Waltham, where was [a] party for H. H. of all his friends, and I had a good hour with Waldo. H. staid there, as did G. Bradford, and Russell, the naturalist, with whom I had an interesting meeting, but there is [no] room to tell you about it.[3] Mere letters are su[ch] paltry things. I never have more than begun when I get to this place. I returned yesterday weary with overmuch prattling and with so many. But this liebe, liebste Sonntag[4] I ha[ve] been at rest and so happy. The F's are at N. Bedford.[5] I have been absolutely alone a[ll] day, except the affectionate Nancy to attend me when I wanted her. I have not left my ro[om] [   ] on the tops of [   ] and only the crickets voice fills the gentle gloom. It is a [   ]

ALfr (MB: Ms. Am. 1450 [49]). *Addressed:* William H. Channing / Rondout, / Ulster Co. New York. *Postmark:* Cambridge MS Aug 30. *Endorsed:* Aug 29. 1841. Cambridge—
I have been] I ↑ have been ↓
The oration] ⟨It⟩ ↑ The oration ↓

1. Fuller is describing Frederic Henry Hedge's "Conservatism and Reform," the Phi Beta Kappa address he gave on 26 August. Hedge published the oration in Boston in 1843 and later in *Martin Luther and Other Essays* (Boston, 1888, pp. 129–65) (David T. W. McCord, *Catalogue of the Harvard Chapter of Phi Beta Kappa* [Lunenberg, Vt., 1970], p. 166).

2. Caleb Stetson (1793–1870), an original member of the Transcendental Club, graduated from Harvard in 1822 and from the Divinity School in 1827. In that year he married Julia Merriam (1804–89) and was ordained at Medford (Harvard archives; Charles Hudson, *History of the Town of Lexington* [Boston, 1913], 2:431, 670).

3. John Lewis Russell (1808–73), a man with a very erratic temper, graduated from Harvard in 1824 and from the Divinity School in 1831. From 1831 to 1854 he held various pulpits, but he was best known for his work in botany. He was librarian and cabinet keeper of the Essex County Natural Historical Society as well as professor of botany in the Massachusetts Horticultural Society from 1833 till his death (Edmund B. Willson, "Memoir of John Lewis Russell," *Essex Institute Historical Collections* 12 [1874]: 163–78).

4. "Dear, most dear Sunday."

5. The Farrars.

320.   To Margarett C. Fuller

Cambridge
31st August, 1841.

Dearest Mother,

I write a few lines hoping they may reach you, before you leave Bristol, but must be as brief as possible, since I have a great deal of other writing to do. Your letter did not reach me till this morng— I see more day light than I did. I entirely agree with you now that it is not best[n] to buy the Wilson place. I have a letter from Ellen, the best I have ever recd. I shall show it you as soon as you[n] come. She has a prospect of being able to stay in Cincini this winter where she will make friends and get that experience that may make it worth while for her to have gone out. She seems reconciled in the way of true wisdom. She says "tell Mother that, if it could have been right I should have so loved to see her, but still we shall sometime meet and it is all for the best" Our friends will now be hers; they are most kind she says; write to her dear Mother, perhaps she will not to you, till she is less excited and hurried, but she needs encouragement and soothing.

From Eugene the boys have a paper on which is written, "you will not hear from me again till October" I do not know what to infer from this unless that he has left N.O.

I shall now remain with Mrs F. through the winter, in compliance with an urgent and affectionate invitation both from her and Mr F. I shall have a fire in my room all the time, so that I can study and write to my heart's content, and every comfort and kindness, so you may well be at ease about me.

If, after F's recovery, you go back to Canton, I want you to have a room in Aunt Betsy's house, and some one to make your fire every morng and that excellent stove I had in mine last winter. I depend on your being settled comfortably. But we will talk of this and of the future when you come. Do not hurry for me. I am going to Newton on Saty for two or three days, then come back here to finish the Dial. I shall not leave here certainly before Tuesday or Wednesday 14th or 15th, so you will have time to stay two or three days at P. and as much at Canton, if so inclined. Write me how soon you will be here, on Saty the 11th if I may decide.

Love to Mary and the sweet children I knew you would be struck with the beauty of M's conduct at home. I thought perhaps you would both ride over by the ferry to see me. I wish you had,— The boy[s] are well your most afftely

MARGARET.

Wm and F. will be back tomorrow, I suppose.

ALS (MH: fMS Am 1086 [9:75]). MsC (MH: fMS Am 1086 [Works, 2:545–51]). *Addressed:* Mrs Margaret Fuller / Care W. B. D'Wolf Esq / Bristol—R.I. *Postmark:* Boston MS Aug 31.

is not best] is not ⟨better⟩ best
as soon as you] as soon as ⟨she⟩ you

321.   To Ralph Waldo Emerson

Cambridge
8th Septr 1841.

I was very sorry, dear friend, to miss your visit. I had supposed you would write when you were likely to come that I might be sure and be here.

I shall certainly not go to Newbury before the middle of next week, and perhaps not then. An event has occurred which disturbs my plans and disturbs my mind, so that I do not yet know what I shall do. This is my sister Ellen's engagement to—Ellery Channing!!!![1]

The thought of this is not new to me. His poems have several times suggested her[n] to my mind, and the possibility flitted across my mind both when she went to the West and now when she stopped at Cincinnati. Still in its suddenness it comes like a blow— And from the letters I have yet recd matters seem going on so rapidly and there is so much that makes me anxious and uncertain that it seems at moments I must go to Cincinnati. I think I certainly should but for the expense which I must not incur unless necessary.

No more about this now; when we meet I can speak more fully and more composedly. I shall then know my ground. But I do not suppose I can know any thing about Ellery's feelings unless I could see him. Sam is pleased; he thinks it is an auspicious connection.

About our poor little Dial, as often before, it irks me to think. Let me try to write precisely. My article on Festus lies half-finished.[2] I hope to finish it, and if so, could do without your aid this time. But there is so much to interrupt, and (if Serenissimo will allow the words) to distress and perplex me just now, that I am not sure of being able to concentrate my thoughts upon it. You showed me in June a prosa that you said you could modify so as to be willing to print it. Now if I could have this on Monday or Tuesday of next week with discretionary power either to use it *this* number if I do *not* finish the Festus, or *the next* if I *do*; it would give me peace.[3] Can this be? please answer at once.

Oh how much I should like to see you! if there is any chance of your being here again within a week, mention the day in your letter.

My love to E. H. Tell her of the engagement and that she is like to hear of another quite as surprizing ere another moon has waxed and waned.

Your affectionate

Margaret

ALS (MH: bMS Am 1280 [2355]). Published in Rusk, *Letters of RWE*, 2:446. *Addressed:* R. W. Emerson / Concord / Mass. *Postmark:* Cambridge MS Sep 8. *Endorsed:* Margaret Fuller / Sept. 1841.

suggested her] suggested ⟨the thought of⟩ her

1. Exactly how and when Fuller learned of the engagement is not clear. Channing wrote Mrs. Fuller on 5 September (MH), saying, "You have probably heard that Ellen is engaged to me." This letter obviously had not been received when Margaret wrote to Emerson. Channing and Ellen Fuller were married on 24 September 1841.

2. The review appeared in the October issue.

3. Emerson replied on 13 September and sent an almost-finished essay on Landor, which was published in the October issue (Rusk, *Letters of RWE*, 2:446–47).

322.   To Ralph Waldo Emerson

Cambridge,
16th Septr 1841.

My dear friend,

I will beg you, if it be possible, to come to town next *Wednesday.* I must go to town early that day to meet a person on business, which will prevent my seeing you in the morng but in the aftn and evening I shall be disengaged, and will come to Mr Adams's at four p m. if that suits you. If in the eveg, please call on me at Dr Randalls.[1]

If you prefer Monday, you will find me *here* at any hour you please to appoint, and we can talk undisturbed.

Mr Ripley is coming here to see me on Saturday," and if you can be in town by the Wednesday morning stage, I probably can make an appointment for him to be there and you see him and Jordan at the same time.[2] But if you can stay Wednesday night, and talk with me *first* I should prefer it and could make an appointment for him to meet you *Thursday morng.*

I hope to get away from town Thursday or Friday of next week.

Now you have this tangled mesh before you, you can choose your thread.—

I send you on this day

1st, my brother Richard, who, having utterly reluctured from commerce and the city, is now bent on entering college as Sophomore next February. He wants to be with some one capable of fitting him, to board with some farmer the while at a low rate, and chop wood &c for exercise! He has not been able to make such arrangements as he wished at Lancaster and other places to which he is recommended, and I have thought that Henry Thoreau, might be willing to constitute himself his teacher, (for I suppose even those who can live on board nails may sometimes wish to earn a little money) and that some farmer in Concord might afford the desired hospitium. I should like to have Richard[n] in the Concord air; he is a fine, manly youth, and my chief hope. Let him talk with Henry T. if there is any chance of his taking him, but do not trouble yourself with hospitality or care. He can pass the night at the tavern and, (if he can come to C.) look out quarters for himself.[3]

2d. Henry T's verses.— I have kept "The fisher boy"; that copy was for myself; was it not?[4]

3d That part of your article which contains the paragraph on Character.[5] Richard will bring it back to me, after you have put in the wedge. I cannot spare it for this number, and, though you think you could so much improve it surely it is very excellent now.

4th Some Dialese which you, perhaps, may care to glance at.

5th A Martineau letter containing her raptures about your book. But do not show it to *any one*, for you see she expresses reliance on my discretion as to what she says about Miss Sedg-wick and, as she will write the same to several others, I do not wish to take the credit of being the one to[n] tell it about.[6]

6th Three letters from Cary, also for yourself only. Perhaps she has written to you about Ellery's engagement, but I do not wish any other to see what so few can comprehend.[7] I see why he loves my sister; she is, in some respects, very beautiful, and has, as Sam used to say "what is rarest, an expression of unbroken purity." It is no less natural and honorable to her that she loves him as she does, and I sympathize with her childlike raptures. But in what I know of either party I see such perils to the happiness[n] and good of the other, and the connexion has been so precipitately formed that I feel overshadowed by it as by a deep tragedy that I foresee, but, as if in a dream, cannot lift my hand to prevent.[8] Yet I know there is a brighter side and the evils may not come. If they must, they also will find their explanation and their compensation in Heaven's long year.

MARGARET.

I recd your letter this morng perhaps you will not perceive that I have so.

ALS (MH: bMS Am 1280 [2356]). Published in Rusk, *Letters of RWE*, 2:449–50. *Addressed:* R. W. Emeron / Concord / Mass. *Endorsed:* Margaret Fuller / Sept. 1841.

on Saturday] on ⟨Th⟩ Saturday
to have Richard] to have ⟨him⟩ ↑ Richard ↓
credit of being the one to] credit of ↑ being the one ↓ ⟨allow⟩ to
perils to the happiness] perils to ↑ the ↓ happiness

1. Emerson replied that he would meet her "at 2 Winthrop Place at 4 P.M." (Rusk, *Letters of RWE*, 2:448).

2. The *Dial* was entering a crisis with its publisher, William Hamilton Stewart Jordan (1814?–98). The magazine had been published by Weeks, Jordan and Company from its first issue through the April 1841 issue (MVR 482:510; Rusk, *Letters of RWE*, 2:457; Myerson, *New England Transcendentalists*, pp. 71–72).

3. Richard moved to Concord in November to prepare himself for Harvard (Richard Fuller to Margaret Fuller, 14 November 1841, MH).

4. Thoreau's poem "The Fisher's Son," apparently written in late 1839 or early 1840, did not appear in the *Dial*. In July Emerson had asked Fuller to return some sheets of Thoreau's verse but then in August sent her new poems, including "The Fisher's Son." She seems to be responding to the earlier request (*Collected Poems of Thoreau*, pp. 121–23, 358; Rusk, *Letters of RWE*, 2:434–36, 442–43).

5. Emerson's "Walter Savage Landor," *Dial* 2 (October 1841):262–71. He responded to Fuller, "I have inserted in the Landor piece the copulative sentence & have added an extract from the Dialogue Richard I. & Abbot of Boxley" (Rusk, *Letters of RWE*, 2:450). The changes appear on pp. 265–66 and 268–71.

6. In her letter to Fuller of 9 August (MH), Harriet Martineau called Emerson's *Essays* "a gem set in the brow of your nation" but condemned Catherine Sedgwick for betraying the Italian liberals: "[I] wonder how one so timid could be so rash, how so noble a soul could put away its common sense for the time, and one so loving, with such an *instinct* of kindness, so unconsciously do mischief."

7. Sturgis did not easily accept Channing's engagement. In a letter of 9 September (MH), she wrote, "Perhaps, dear Margaret, you may think Ellery's engagement pains me for myself, but it does not. For a little time I thought I could love him, but it has past. . . . I saw from Ellery's last letter that he was withdrawing himself from me. It was very sweet, but nothing for me." She tactlessly closed the discussion, "Give my love to Ellen when you write to her, for I feel affectionately towards her, although I cannot think she is noble enough to be his wife."

8. Fuller thought Channing was charming but irresponsible. He had no means of supporting a wife, and Fuller knew her sister could be quick-tempered and was in poor health. Unfortunately, Margaret's assessment was correct: the Channings had a troubled marriage; Ellery was moody and overbearing, and the family was quite poor. In 1853 they separated for several months.

323. To Ralph Waldo Emerson

[October, 1841?]

How true and majestical it reads; Surely you must have said it this time. The page flows too, and we have no remembrance of "Mosaic or Medal."

Dear Waldo, I know you do not regard our foolish critiques, except in the true way to see whether you have yet got the best *form* of expression. What do we know of when you should stop writing or how you should live? In these pages I seem to hear the music rising I so long have wished to hear, and am made sensible to the truth of the passage in one of your letters "Life, like the nimble Tartar &c[1]

I like to be in your library when you are out of it. It seems a sacred place. I came here to find a book, that I might feel more life and be worthy to sleep, but there is so much soul here I do not need a book. When I come to yourself, I cannot receive you, and you cannot give yourself; it does not profit. But when I cannot find you the the beauty and permanence of your life come to me.

"She (Poesie) has ascended from the depths of a nature, and only by a similar depth, shall she be apprehended!"— I want to say while I am feeling it, what I have often (not always) great pleasure in feeling— how long it must be, before I am able to meet you.— I see you—and fancied it nearer than it was, you were right in knowing the contrary.

How much, much more I would fain say and cannot. I am too powerfully drawn while with you, and cannot advance a step, but when away I have learned something. Not yet to be patient and faithful and holy however, but only have taken off the shoes, to tread the holy ground. I shall often depart through the ranges of manifold being, but as often return to where I am tonight

AL (MH: bMS Am 1280 [2357]); MsC (MB: Ms. Am. 1450 [75]). Published in *Publications of the Modern Language Association* 50 (June 1935):590; Rusk, *Letters of RWE*, 2:455; Chevigny, pp. 126–27. *Endorsed:* Margaret F. / Oct 1841. Letter written at Concord / from room to room.

This letter and the one following may have been written on 3 October, the same day Fuller wrote letter 326, to Ellery Channing.

1. On 25 September 1840, when Fuller and Emerson were defining the nature of their friendship, he told her that changes in life constantly caused him to reformulate his opinions: "Whoever lives must rise & grow. Life like the nimble Tartar still overleaps the Chinese wall of distinctions that had made an eternal boundary in our geography— and I who have taxed your exclusion in friendship, find you—last Wednesday, the meekest & most loving of the lovers of mankind" (Rusk, *Letters of RWE*, 2:337).

324. To Ralph Waldo Emerson

[October, 1841?]

My dear friend, We shall never meet on these subjects while one atom of our proper indididividualities remains. Yet let me say a few words more on my side. The true love has no need of illusion: it is too deeply prophetic in its nature to be baffled or chilled, much less changed by the accidents of time. We are sure that what we love is living, though the ruins of old age have fallen upon the shrine. The "blank gray" upon the hallowed locks, the dimmed eye, the wasted cheek cannot deceive us. Neither can the dimunition of vital fire and force, the scantiness of thought, the loss of grace, wit, fancy and springing enthusiasm, for it was none of these we loved, but the true self, that particular emanation from God which was made to correspond with that which we are, to teach it, to learn from it, to torture it, to enchant it, to deepen and at last to satisfy our wants. You go upon the idea that we must love most the most beauteous, but this is not so. We love most that which by working most powerfully on our peculiar nature awakens most deeply and constantly in us the idea of beauty. Where we have once seen clearly what is fit for us, if only in a glance of the eye we cannot forget it, nor can any change in the form where we have seen it deceive us. We know that it will appear again and clothe the scene with new and greater beauty.

For the past year or two I begin to see a change in the forms of these my contemporaries who have filled my eye. It is a sight that makes me pensive, but awakens, I think, a deeper tenderness and even a higher hope than did these forms in the greatest perfection they ever attained. For they still only promised beauty not gave it, and now seeing the swift changes of time I feel what an illusion all ill, all imperfection is. As they fail to justify my expectation, it only rises the higher and they become dearer as the heralds of a great fulfilment. The princely crest is lowered, the proud glow of youth, its haughty smile and gleaming sweetness are fled, every languid motion assures me that this life will not complete the picture I had sketched, but I only postpone it for ages, and expect it on the same canvass yet."

The fact you repel of the mother and the child as seen in other nature does not repel, why should it in human Nature? It is beautiful to see the red berry, the just blown rose and the rose bud on the same stalk as we sometimes do; nor are we displeased with the young blossoming scion that it grows up beside the aged tree; it borrows rather a charm from the" neighborhood of that which it must sometimes resemble. But" I might write a volume, and then should not have done. I seem to myself to say all when I say that the chivalric idea of love through disease, dungeons and death, mutilation on the battle field, and the odious changes effected by the enchanter's hate answers my idea far better than the stoical appreciation of the object beloved for what it positively presents. I would love in faith that could not change and face the inevitable shadows of old age happy in some occasion for fidelity.

Nevertheless I will not send the letter to Ellery, for he may feel more like you than me about it though I think not, for what I have known of him is that he is tender and ever fond, and takes peculiar pleasure in the natural relations. He admired my mother just as William C. does, and I felt as if his feelings would be the same. But since I have been led to question I will keep this and write another letter.

Waldo has brought me your[n] page, and he looked so lovely as if he were the living word which should yet reveal to the world all that you do not feel ready to say.— I really did not mean to show you the letter to Cary but merely to gratify my fancy by having all the letters to these interesting persons under your seal. Do not regret having read it, for I do not care, since I can tell you I did not intend it; the only feeling was that what I had to say to you I should wish to say to yourself direct, and not to another, letting you see it. But just as I should not care for C. to show you the letter, so I do not now, for your having seen it[n] Do not fancy that I complain or grieve. I understand matters now, and always want you to withdraw when you feel like it; indeed, there is nothing I wish more than to be able to live with you, without disturbing you. This is the main stream of my feeling. I am satisfied and also feel that our friendship will grow But I am of a more lively and affectionate temper[n] or rather more household and daily in my affection than you and have a thousand evanescent feelings and ebullitions like that in the letter. Cary has made a picture of the rock and the wave; if she had made the rock a noble enough figure it might stand for frontispiece to the chapter of my deepest life. For the moment the rock dashes back with a murmur, but it always returns. It is not now a murmur of sorrow but only the voice of a more flexible life. *I would not have it otherwise.* The genial flow of my desire may be checked for the moment, but it cannot long. I shall always burst out soon and burn up all the rubbish between you and me, and I shall always find you there true to yourself and deeply rooted as ever.

My impatience is but the bubble on the stream; you know I want to be alone myself.— It is all right. As to the shadow I do not know myself what it is, but it rests on your aspect, and brings me near the second-sight as I look on you. Perhaps if we have Scotch trists enough I shall really see the tapestry of the coming time start into life, but, if I do, I shall not tell you, but with wise economy keep it for a poem which shall make ever sacred and illustrious the name of yours

MARGARET.

ALS (MH: bMS Am 1280 [2358]). Published in Rusk, *Letters of RWE,* 2:455–57, and Miller, pp. 109–11. *Endorsed:* Margaret Fuller / Oct. 1841.

yet.] *In the margin Fuller added a commentary to this paragraph:* This only applies to
what lies beyond their power. A *low choice* on their part we cannot forgive.
charm from the] charm from ⟨that⟩ the
must sometime resemble. But] must sometime ↑ resemble. ↓ ⟨?⟩ But
brought me your] brought me ⟨ano⟩ your
not now, for your having seen it] not now, ↑ for your having seen it ↓
affectionate temper] affectionate ↑ temper ↓

325. To Charles K. Newcomb

Private.—
Concord
2d Octr 1841.

My dear Charles,

I wish indeed I could see you, or else had seen you fitly, while at
Spring St. I fully intended, thinking you would remain at Spring St,
to have given a day to uninterrupted" converse with you. But, *between
ourselves alone*, for I do not wish the annoyance of being misunder-
stood by those kindly intentioned towards me, I cannot as yet bear the
idea of going to Providence. My associations with that place are painful, and peculiarly uncongenial with the present state of my mind. I
feel, not sad, but deeply grave, deeply lonely. I can with difficulty
rouse myself to live on the footing kindness demands with those who
are unobtrusive, and unasking, and I cannot offer myself to the busy,
prying intellect of P. circles. Should the hour come when I can meet
them" without pain, without finding myself in false relations, I will
come, for I do not like to seem ungrateful to the kindness which desires my presence. But it seems, sometimes, as if the courageous lightness with which I used to encounter the world of every-day would
never return. I long to depart from a scene where most men seem
only, ape-like, to grimace their parts, to some verdant solitude of
"truthful earnestness" I long to draw thought pure from its source
and wash from my life the soil of the world. I long, in short, "to die to
earth and live forever."

My faith never changes, and I do not, however I may feel, consent
for a moment to these fugitive or anchorite measures. I will stay in
the wilderness, and work and wander with the rest. But it must be to
work, not play. In my present mood the idea of a visit, which shall
throw me into the society of persons with whom I have no natural
connexion of work, fills me with loathing. This mood may pass. I may

feel able to come, without wounding myself, and, if I do in the course of the winter, I will.

It is best, I believe, that I should give no critical opinion of the little poems, because it will chill you, and interfere with the natural work- ing of your mind. They pleased me much, as genuine, poetical rev- eries, and fragrant with the breath of the fields. Continue to write, and with a view to finish your pieces. I think you are now so far ad- vanced that you will find that you search and deepen in proportion as you mould and harmonize. Do not fail to send me the Cave, and the ballad. Let me be your audience, but not your judge. I shall be of use to you, if faith that I shall read and appreciate induces you to finish your pieces, but dissection would hurt you now; The time has not come. Your own delicate taste will teach you through repeated experiments to simplify, refine and condense better than any friend could. But send me from time to time what you write. It is my impres- sion that you are capable of doing yourself justice with the pen, and if so you would fairly take root on this diurnal sphere, and could lift the head to the stars in calm security.

Cary, perhaps, has written to you again. She is alone at Newbury. I have not, hadⁿ a letter for some time back, because, I suppose she is expecting me there, but I think I shall not go.

Lately I went to Spring St with Mr Emerson.¹ I wished you had been there. George Bradford spoke of you with warm regard, and Mr Haw- thorne not only with that, but with more discrimination than I have ever heard any person.

Take good care of yourself this winter. Remember how useful exer- cise has been, and let not the mind lose its tone and healthful fresh- ness from inattention to its helpmeet, the body.

Could I transport myself on some Aladdin carpet and return in a few hours, unseen by any one but you, we would take a walk together today. Tis one of the brilliant autumn mornings, and the first frost has flushed the woods with the hectic beauty of October. It suits my humor well.— Will you not write to me at once and address to the care of Mr Emerson. I shall remain here till Friday or Saturday of next week. Your friend always

MARGARET F.

ALS (MH: fMS Am 1086 [10:137]). *Addressed:* Charles King Newcomb. / Providence / R.I. *Postmark:* Concord Mas. Oct 4
a day to uninterrupted] a day to ↑un↓interrupted
can meet them] can meet ⟨such relations⟩ ↑them↓
have not, had] have not, ↑had↓
1. In an undated journal note Emerson recorded their visit to Brook Farm (*JMN*, 8:92).

326. To Ellery Channing

[3 October 1841]

Dear Ellery,

I had fixed today as the one on which I would write to you for this third of October has been a saint's day in my calendar, as the birthday of our friend Ward, who for many years seemed born for cheer and companionship to me, the fair child of my hopes. Last year it was his marriage day also. I must always think of him in connexion with you, for almost as early as we were intimate he wished to have me prize you also, and you were the only living man about whom he desired my sympathy, indeed the only one whom he had worthily met.[1] And all along these years, he has copied your verses and quoted your words whenever his own seemed inadequate, esteeming you of clearer insight, and in some respects, of finer temper than himself. Thus have you been so far made known to me that I feel little doubt how I shall feel towards you. You say you cannot promise me any thing nor tell how my character shall affect you. I had not thought of this for, of a nature which the observer may call vain and presumptuous or affectionate and trustful at[n] his pleasure, it never occurs to me that those I am inclined to love may not receive me till they themselves suggest it. But now I do think of it, there may be much you cannot meet. My character and life have been of various strain and mine is now in a sense a worldly character and one of many sides. You may not like or enjoy meeting me, and I shall not set my heart upon it. It will, however, be easy for me to bear it, if you do not, as I have been long trained to all the forms of separation, and I shall not prize you the less. Should you prove the wise and faithful guardian of my sister's happiness; should you be the means of unfolding what is beautiful in her character, and leading her tenderly to her true aim, you will have conferred on me a benefit, beyond requital, and only to be answered in prayer.

I think still more of Mother than myself in reference to Ellen. Eugene and Ellen are truly Mother's children in all that can adorn and enliven domestic life. Mother's eyes were of the same glistening blue, and she gave herself with[n] the same full heart up to a feeling that Ellen does. Those bright tints are faded now, and Mother's sweetness is more saintly since she is less a wife and Mother and more of the lay nun. Yet I could not wish more for Ellen than that she should be as lovely, as happy, and as good as her Mother has been while the springs of life were yet unbroken. I feel sure you will be able to love Mother, and that the bond between her and Ellen will not be weakened by her marriage.

This has been a great shock to Mother for it was an event so important in time and eternity that those at a distance felt as if all was done too hastily, and the thoughts of all that it might lead to thronged too fast upon a Mother's heart. Yet we all feel a greater degree of clearness that you have taken your mutual destiny so decidedly in your own hands; we wish to trust your inward leading which has spoken in tones so determined.— Yet, as to the future I hope you will advise with your cousin William as to whether it will be for your good to come here. He knows you, and knows Ellen; he has surveyed the ground with reference to himself, and can give you a wise judgment. Of all the plans of which Ellen wrote to me the only one which strikes me favorably is that which projects your connexion with him. In the Ripley's community you would find a little city, and, *at present*, with less freedom of walk and feeling than elsewhere. It will not be so always if they carry out their original intention, but at present you would hardly find quiet and an atmosphere pure and genial for young affections. By and by if you could have a little cottage of your own, and only labor not live with the rest, it might be well for you.— I have written as to my brother, yet I do not know whether the vow has been pronounced in the sight of Man. Tomorrow I trust will bring us a letter In hope and affectionate goodwill yours

Margaret F.

ALS (MH: fMS Am 1086 [9:82]). Published, incorrectly dated, in Wade, pp. 562–63. *Addressed:* W. E. Channing Jr / Cincinnati / Ohio.

and trustful at] and trustful ⟨of⟩ at
gave herself with] gave herself ⟨by⟩ with

1. Ward sent Emerson some Channing poems in October 1839, thus introducing the young poet to the man who became his mentor and idol. Ward later financed the publication of Channing's first volume of poems and steadfastly encouraged his eccentric friend through their long lives (Rusk, *Letters of RWE*, 2:226–28; Hudspeth, *Ellery Channing*, pp. 30–32).

327. To Margarett C. Fuller

Concord.
5th Octr, 1841.

My beloved Mother,

I do not know but suppose the enclosed will bring you the earliest intelligence of our dear Ellen's marriage. Since all is now decided we will look upon the future with hope and trust that the tears with which it is stained are but dew drops in the morning of a golden day.

I trust you will be able to send some news of Eugene by Mr Emerson. The accounts of fever are certainly appalling, yet let us not poison life by apprehensions of an ill that may never come. I am sorry William still intends to go this week; he will get there dangerously early.

I think of you day by day, fearing you are much depressed, alone in these gloomy hours. E and B. were here on Saturday, and expected to return yesterday to Boston, but I suppose the rain prevented, and will today.[1] B. expressed great regret at losing so much of your visit, and I hope you will be able to stay sometime after their return. I am sure it will be no inconvenience but a great pleasure to all concerned.

I hope you take books from Miss Peabody's and read a good deal for continual application to sewing is bad for your spirits.

Is there any letter from M. D.' Wolf.? Has not W. H. Channing returned, and have not you seen him? I want very much to know what he says.— Write me a note by Mr E. he will leave word when he will return.

I expect to be in town on Saty and remain till Tuesday, if so shall see Uncle A. on Monday, but you need say nothing to him of it till I come lest there should be some new change Most afftely your daughter

M.

Mr E. will leave word when you must send your answer to Mr Adams's Winthrop place. He thinks he shall stay all night, but may return at three, p. m.

ALS (MH: fMS Am 1086 [9:76]); MsC (MH: fMS Am 1086 [Works, 2:551–55]). *Addressed:* Mrs Fuller / 20 Winter St / Boston.

1. Probably Elizabeth Randall Cumming and her sister Belinda.

328.   To Caroline Sturgis

10 Oct 1841.

O Carrie! What a poor first sketch this life is,—all torn and thrown aside too. Were it not for the muse who peeps in, now and then, at the window, how lonely here at home! I wish she would come and light my candles, it is dark here, except one little rush-candle in the corner, that only serves to show how many silver branches there are that might be lit up.

MsCfr (MH: bMS Am 1280 [111, pp. 59–60]). Published in *JMN*, 11:469.
This may be part of the letter Fuller mentions in letter 324, to Emerson.

329. To Henry D. Thoreau

18th Octr 1841.

I do not find the poem on the mountains improved by mere compression, though it might be by fusion and glow.[1]

Its merits to me are a noble recognition of nature, two or three manly thoughts, and, in one place, a plaintive music. The image of the ships does not please me originally. It illustrates the greater by the less and affects me as when Byron compares the light on Jura to that of the dark eye of woman.[2] I cannot define my position here, and a large class of readers would differ from me. As the poet goes on to

> Unhewn, primeval timber
> For knees so stiff, for masts so limber"

he seems to chase an image, already rather forced, into conceits.

Yet now that I have some knowledge of the man, it seems there is no objection I could make to his lines, (with the exception of such offenses against taste as the lines about the humors of the eye &c as to which" we are already agreed) which I could not make to himself.[3] He is healthful, sane, of open eye, ready hand, and noble scope. He sets no limits to his life, nor to the invasions of nature; he is not wilfully pragmatical, cautious, ascetic or fantastical. But he is as yet a somewhat bare hill which the warm gales of spring have not visited. Thought lies too detached," truth is seen too much in detail, we can number and mark the substances embedded in the rock. Thus his verses are startling, as much as stern; the thought does not excuse its conscious existence by letting us see its relation with life; there is a want of fluent music.

Yet what could a companion do at present unless to tame the guardian of the Alps too early? Leave him at peace amid his native snows.

He is friendly; he will find the generous office that shall educate him. It is not a soil for the citron and the rose, but for the whortleberry, the pine or the heather. The unfolding of affections, a wider and deeper human experience, the harmonizing influences of other natures, will mould the man, and melt his verse. He will seek thought less and find knowledge the more. I can have no advice or criticism for a person so sincere, but if I give my impression of him I will say He says too constantly of nature She is mine; She is not yours till you have been more hers. Seek the lotus, and take a draught of rapture. Say not so confidently All places, all occasions are alike. This will never come true till you have found it false.

I do not know that I have more to say now, perhaps these words will say nothing to you; If intercourse should continue, perhaps a bridge may be made between the minds so widely apart, for I apprehended you in spirit, and you did not seem to mistake me as widely as most of your kind do. If you should find yourself inclined to write to me, as you thought you might, I dare say many thoughts would be suggested to me! many have already by seeing you day by day. Will you finish the poem in your own way and send it for[n] the Dial. Leave out "And seems to *milk* the sky"[4]

The image is too low. Mr Emerson thought so too. Farewell. May Truth be irradiated by Beauty!— Let me know whether you go to the lonely hut, and write to me about Shakespeare, if you read him there.[5] I have many thoughts about him which I have never yet been led to express.

MARGARET F.

The pencilled paper Mr E. put into my hands. I have taken the liberty to copy it You expressed one day my own opinion that the moment such a crisis is passed we may speak of it. There is no need of artificial delicacy, of secrecy, it keeps its own secret; it cannot be made false. Thus you will not be sorry that I have seen the paper. Will you not send me some other records of the *good week*.[6]

ALS (TxU). Published in Sanborn, *Thoreau*, pp. 169–72, and *Thoreau Correspondence*, pp. 56–57; published in part in Hanscom, *Friendly Craft*, pp. 194–95. *Addressed:* Henry Thoreau. *Endorsed:* S. M. Fuller.

eye &c as to which] eye &c ⟨with regard⟩ ↑ as ↓ to which
lies too detached,] lies too ⟨obvious⟩ ↑ detached, ↓
send it for] send it ⟨me⟩ for

1. On 19 August Emerson sent Thoreau's poem "With frontier strength ye stand your ground" to Fuller, then wrote again on 8 September: "if you will send him [Thoreau] his 'Mountains' he will try to scrape or pare them down or cover the peaks with a more presentable greensward." The poem, however, was never published in the

Ellen Kilshaw Fuller. Courtesy of Willard P. Fuller, Jr.

Ellery Channing. Painting by John Cranch. Courtesy of Judith C. Marriner.

Dial. Thoreau included a version in "A Walk to Wachusett," *Boston Miscellany of Literature and Fashion* 3 (January 1843):31–36 (*Collected Poems of Thoreau*, pp. 292–93; Rusk, *Letters of RWE*, 2:442–43, 445).

2. *Childe Harold's Pilgrimage*, canto 3, stanza 92:

> The sky is changed!—and such a change! Oh Night,
> And Storm, and Darkness, ye are wondrous strong,
> Yet lovely in your strength, as is the light
> Of a dark eye in Woman!

3. The draft of the poem now in the Huntington Library has these additional lines:

> The in's of the sky, ye run
> Round the horizon of its eye
> Whose pupil is the sun.

(*Collected Poems of Thoreau*, p. 293).

4. Apparently Thoreau took this advice, for none of the versions contains the image.

5. Since September, Thoreau had been planning a cabin at Flint's Pond in Lincoln (Thoreau, *Week*, p. 441).

6. Emerson had given Fuller either Thoreau's autobiographical sketch or a journal fragment, for the reference clearly is to Thoreau's first book, one he was then planning (Thoreau, *Week*, p. 442).

330. To Elizabeth Hoar

Newbury, [ca. 20?] Oct 1841

Your Aunt Mary too has been to see us, but the best I have got from her is to understand as I suppose W[aldo] better.[1] Knowing such a person who so perpetually defaces the high by such strange mingling of the low, I can better conceive how the daily bread of life should seem to him gossip, and the natural relations sheaths from which the flower must burst and never remember them. It certainly is not pleasant to hear of God and Miss Biddeford in a breath Still some sparkles show where the gems might in better days be more easily disengaged from the rubbish. She is still valuable as a disturbing force to the lazy. But, to me, this hasty attempt at skimming from the deeps of theosophy, is as unpleasant as the rude vanity of reformers. Dear Beauty where where amid these morasses and pine barrens shall we make thee a temple[?] Where find a Greek to guard it! Clear-eyed, deep-thoughted, and delicate to appreciate the relations gradations which nature always observes.

MsCfr (MH: bMS Am 1280 [111, pp. 222–23]). Published in part in *Memoirs*, 1:315; published entire in *JMN*, 11:493–94.

1. Almost without peer in energy, wit, learning, and eccentricity, Emerson's aunt Mary Moody Emerson (1774–1863), daughter of the Reverend William and Phebe Bliss Emerson, was a powerful force in the poet's life. At her death he said of her, "It is a representative life, such as could hardly have appeared out of New England; of an age now past, and of which I think no types survive" (*Ipswich Emersons*, p. 129; *Complete Works of Emerson*, 10:399).

331. To Richard F. Fuller

Newbury,
25th Octr, 1841.

My dear Richard,

On seeing Mr Emerson tonight, I hoped to get a particular account of you, but he had not seen you for some time. I will hope for a letter from you soon, to tell how Horace and Xenophon and *Goodenow* go on,[1] and whether you still like the lonely life, and think the woods bring pleasure enough for a sober man:—" My life here is very pleasant. We rise, I fear some hour or two later than you would approve, breakfast, then Miss Sturgis rows me in a little boat she has here, green with an orange rim, to some pleasant place on the river; there we sit and study or think till noon. In the afternoon, we walk, and spend our evegs in a little room over the mill, beside a bright wood fire, from which I do not yet experience the soporific influences of which you complain. The ten days have been most welcome as was the stay at Concord, bringing tranquillity and rest, remote from care and excitement, but I should not like such a life constantly. There are few characters so vigorous and of such sustained self-impulse that they do not need frequent and unexpected difficulties to awaken and keep in exercise their powers.

There is a young man here of the name of Curson who has interested me much by his spirited sketches of the scenes he has been through, especially of the hunter's life in the West of this country.[2] When we are tired at night he tells one of these stories, and we lazily enjoy the chase of a buck of ten tynes. He is adroit, ready, courageous, clear-sighted, and of fine feelings, but has been repeatedly unsuccessful in business, because he cannot cope with men in their own sharp way, and now, at four and twenty, sees no clear path in life before him. Our conversations have suggested many thoughts with which you will sometime be favored.

This is a sweet place, beautiful enough to live in, but this family are going to part with it soon, for they cannot afford to keep it, though they keep no servant but one laboring man, and the daughters of the family do all the indoor work. There is some mystery about the economics of a farmer's life which I cant get at.

I have not heard any thing from Boston since I came away. I hope you have and from Arthur *in propria*. The best thing I heard while there was Eugene's recovery; that was indeed a wondrous boon, under the circumstances and leaves him free to do what he will at N. O. if he only makes use of it. One thing our anxiety has surely taught, that he is indeed dear to us. His letter to mother was very sweet, but characteristically light in its tone.

I think of you, dear Richard, with great satisfaction as having chosen your own path, and being at liberty, at least for the present to walk in it quite unfettered. When we are separate, I think of you as passing the hours in a way I can approve and as on the way to a broader and higher course. Write to me soon and often, of your studies, and also what you see of my friends. Do not be superstitious, in devoting *all* the time to study; the mind works better when quickened by really good society and easily makes up for the loss of an hour or two. Besides, you may not again have an oppory of cultivating such persons as Miss Hoar and Mr Thoreau. Again, let me charge you take good care of your eyes, with which sisterly admonition I conclude,
Affectionately yours

Margaret F.

ALS (MH: fMS Am 1086 [9:72]); MsC (MH: fMS Am 1086 [Works, 2:643–49]). Published in part in Higginson, *MFO*, p. 111. *Addressed:* R. F. Fuller / Concord / Mass.

sober man:—] sober man: ⟨a life⟩ —

1. Smith Bartlett Goodenow, *A Systematic Text-book of English Grammar* (Portland, 1839).

2. George Curzon (b. 1818), son of Samuel and Margaret Searle Curzon of Newbury. In the mid-1830s the younger Curzon had gone broke as a sheep rancher in Cairo, Illinois (Newburyport VR; Briggs, *Cabot Family*, p. 686). On 1 April 1849 (MH), William Clarke wrote Fuller: "George I am very sorry to say is partially insane, owing to his intemperance."

332. To Ralph Waldo Emerson

Nov 1841

The papers we spoke of I have again looked over, and they, I believe finally, refuse to be shown. Let all that lie apart. If you enter into an intimate relation with him my sometime son it will be of quite another character, let it bear its proper fruit. The scrolls of the past burn my fingers. They have not yet passed into literature. The dry leaves clog the stream and the wind sighs amid the despoiled groves. Gladly would I wash off the whole past for a little space; the sympathetic hues would show again before the fire, renovated and lively.

MsCfr (MH: bMS Am 1280 [111, pp. 139–40]). Published in *JMN*, 11:483–84.

333.   To Richard F. Fuller

Boston,
5th Novr [1841]

My dear Richard,

Are you willing that *all* the money for Eugene be advanced out of your portion for the present, if I give my note to repay you one half. The security is no doubt more than sufficient for the whole. Uncle values it at $400—at lowest. If we pay Earle's bill too, the sum^n to be paid will not be $300— My reason is that I have only 500$ in the world, and to part with that now may cause me much more trouble than by and by. Can you trust me about it? Answer by Arthur.[1]

I am snugly established in my little room and hope to have peace enough if not pleasure, this winter. I have begun with a smaller class than ever before, and the Dial is likely to fall through entirely. But we will wait and let things come to us. If one cannot have gay hopes, yet at least one may dispense with dark fears.

I have heard from Ellen only once. Mr Channing has not got the place he hoped and I do not know what they will do; but they were very happy at the time of writing.

I trust all goes well with you and am your always affectionate sister

MARGARET.

Mr Emerson will tell you when he is going to send—

ALS (MH: fMS Am 1086 [9:77]). *Addressed:* R. F. Fuller / Concord / Mass.

the sum] the ⟨money⟩ sum

1. On the fourteenth Richard replied that he would buy Eugene's share of the estate and that he wanted Margaret to keep her $500 (MH). Mr. Earle may be John

Earle (1806–92), a Boston merchant. Richard's reply makes it clear that Earle held a note against the Fuller legacy (Pliny Earle, *The Earle Family* [Worcester, Mass., 1888], p. 319; *Boston Evening Transcript*, 14 July 1892).

334. To Ralph Waldo Emerson

[9?] Nov 1841

My little eyrie promises well and is at this moment made beautiful by the presence of a bouquet of roses geraniums and heliotrope The neighborhood of Sarah Clarke casts the mildness and purity, too, of the moonbeam on the else particoloured scene. I have three pupils for my afternoons,—Carrie, Marianne Jackson, and Anna Shaw.

MsCfr (MH: bMS Am 1280 [111, p. 280]). Published in part in *Memoirs*, 1:207; published entire in *JMN*, 11:503.

335. To Ralph Waldo Emerson

Boston—Nov 9th 1841

Dear Friend

A four hours seige this morning about that horrible Dial business has given me a headache this evening so I have begged the pen of our friend Sarah— Mr Hillard said such a small child was never before made such a fuss about before so large a public; counting up the persons now engaged in settling the affair we could reckon by dozens which gives us quite a parliamentary dignity. I went out with the advertisement in my hand but believe it will not now be necessary to use it.[1] Jordan has given up his claim to the subscription list and Weeks declares himself willing to make the transfer on such terms as I propose. Still, the covenant is not yet in black and white and I cannot tell but they may yet raise some cloud of dust that I dont dream of— Yet I think one thing is certain; we shall have our subscription list and be free to retain the name of Dial. I propose to begin printing on Monday as things stand now and should like to have what you propose to send me at your earliest convenience. I do not go into particulars lest I should have to restate them but will give you a precise account of the new agreement as soon as it is made—

I saw your cards today, both little and large and thought they wore an air of talismanic promise— Write me a letter quick before your pen gets so ethical and dignified that it will turn off nothing but lectures.[2]

I enclose a letter which I wrote you and forgot to send. I enclose the extract from the letter which you are to insert in the little paper you promised— Perhaps you will not wish to use the whole but only the part about the Quakers I have had today a very sweet lover's letter (not love letter) from Ellery which I will show you when you come— Tell Henry Thoreau to write to me when you send me Herodotus— How did you like the military-spiritual-heroico-vivacious phoenix of the day—[3] The chronicler said you were delighted but as I never knew that word made use of in your vocabulary I await your due expression— Always yours

MARGARET

L (MH: bMS Am 1280 [2359]). Published in Rusk, *Letters of RWE*, 2:461–62. *Endorsed:* Margaret Fuller / Nov. 1841.

The letter was dictated to Sarah Clarke.

1. George Stillman Hillard was representing Fuller and Emerson in the *Dial* negotiations with Jordan and Weeks, the previous publishers. Fuller is here answering an earlier note from Emerson, who had advised her to end the journal "by Proclamation, as Victoria does her Parliament. . . . Write an advertisement & let Mr Hillard show it to these men on its way to the newspaper" (Rusk, *Letters of RWE*, 2:462; Myerson, *New England Transcendentalists*, pp. 71–72).

2. On 9 November the *Boston Daily Advertiser* announced that "R. W. Emerson proposes to deliver at the Masonic Temple a course of lectures on the Times." The series began on 2 December (*Emerson Lectures*, 3:335–82).

3. Probably Fuller refers to Fanny Elssler (1810–84), the Austrian dancer who began a series of performances in Boston on 13 October, the night Emerson saw her. To his brother he wrote: "Where do you think I went on Wednesday eve last? Where but to see the dancing Fanny? I killed that lion well: Had a good sight, was much refreshed, and shall know better what people mean when they talk of her. She is not wonderful but she is very good in her art" (Ivor Guest, *Fanny Elssler* [Middletown, Conn., 1970], pp. 18, 177, 261; Rusk, *Letters of RWE*, 2:460).

336. To Richard F. Fuller

Boston, 17th Novr 1841

My dear Richard,

I was very glad of your letter and to see how you are now really thinking, and your mind getting into flow. It is no wonder you complain of me and my *cash letters*. Indeed I wish it might be otherwise.

251

But the tax on my mind is such from my employments that I dont take pleasure in writing to any one. I give eight or nine lessons a week, beside the Dial and my class. I really ought to be out in the open air all the time I am not doing these things, if I would keep up the spring of my spirits. When you are here and we can walk together I shall have things to say, meanwhile excuse my dull business letters, and write good ones yourself.

I am much pleased to see that you are becoming acquainted with Mr E. and that he entertains a growing regard for you. I doubt not the knowledge of his pure and steadfast life will be the solace and incitement to you that it has to me.

My confidence in your aspiration and justness of feeling increases. I need say no more.

Our dear Mother has been dangerously ill. On Monday Aunt Abba wrote that she feared she would not recover, but I did not feel seriously alarmed, as Aunt is not, like me, accustomed to see her in these violent attacks. As she was materially better on Tuesday, and it is extremely inconvenient for me to leave Boston, I did not go to her yesterday as I thought of doing. If I do not hear good news, I shall tomorrow, you need not be alarmed about her now; as, after once beginning to improve, she has never yet shown a tendency to relapse. But as I understand she says[n] this is the severest attack she has ever had, and it is also the fourth within as many months. There is great reason for anxiety about the recurrence of them, unless she can be preserved from sorrow[n] and fatigue.

I had a most cheery letter from Arthur, but he said he should write you the same day— A sweet one from Eugene. He has plans, but does not wish me to speak of them, as there is a circumstance that may make all fall through. He and Wm are living together in the store, setting up W's affairs.

I have also a quite lovely letter from Ellen, full of happiness, though she is not very well. Mr C. has got the sub-editorship of a newspaper which will yield 900 a year, thus, if he likes it, and suits others, their support is in part provided for at present.[1]

Of other things anon, meanwhile dear Richard your sister and friend

M. F.

Are you in want of money or aught else, if so Mother has commissioned me to supply you.

ALS (MH: fMS Am 1086 [9:78]); MsC (MH: fMS Am 1086 [Works, 2:655–61]). *Addressed:* R. F. Fuller / Concord / Mass. / Mr Emerson.

she says] she ⟨l⟩ says
from sorrow] from ⟨anxiety⟩ sorrow
    1. Ellery Channing was working for the *Cincinnati Daily Gazette* under J. C. Wright, the editor (Margarett C. Fuller to Margaret Fuller, 15 May 1842, MH).

337. To Samuel G. Ward

25th Nov 1841
Thursday eveg.

My dear Sam,

I hope the storm this evening has pleaded my excuse, (as I had no one by whom to send a note,) and prevented your waiting in any way for me. I know the absence of no one can spoil your Thanksgiving evening.

I find Mother is desirous of receiving the money of which we spoke on Saturday next,[n] if possible. Can you, with convenience, call on me in the course of that day? I will be at home any hour you please, but should rather prefer the afternoon. If this is not convenient, please let me know by note, how I ought to send the paper to you.

My love to Anna, and the little fair one.[1] Say to Anna that I hear often of her health. As to seeing me, she will find more pleasure in it, when my mind is more free and animated than at present, therefore should my visits be deferred she will not be the loser.

With affection

MARGARET F.

ALS (MH: bMS Am 1465 [919]). *Addressed:* S. G. Ward Esq / Boston. *Endorsed:* 1841 / S. M. Fuller / Nov. 25.

on Saturday next,] on Saturday ↑next↓,
    1. The Wards' first child, Anna Barker Ward (1841–75), who later married Ward Thoron of New York, was born on 23 September (*CVR*; Suffolk Probate, no. 58335).

338. To Richard F. Fuller

Boston,
1st Decr 1841.

My dear Richard,

I had no time to write to you the other day when Mr Emerson was here, but sent you five dollars. Mother wishes you from now to begin bills with the people who supply you, and pay them at the end of the time, as it is troublesome to keep getting these little sums. If there is, however, any thing that you cannot manage in this way, let me know, and during these two months that Mr E will lecture here I can always send by him.

I wish you would always write when he comes, if not a letter, at least a short note to tell me how you fare. A letter from Arthur bespoke him in high spirits, but he had just been writing to you.

(By an unwary jerk of my pen I have spattered the ink all over the page. You must excuse me, if I dont take a new sheet; time permits not what courtesy would prompt.) Lloyd came to see me last week. He seemed very gentle and rather sad. He wanted to go see you especially at Thanksgiving, when he was all alone, but thought the walk too long, at this severe season, and did not know the way. At Xmas, he will go to see Mother at Canton.— No news from Ellen for about a fortnight—

I suppose you know Wm has failed. He has given over every thing to his creditors, and seems to hope he may get his affairs arranged so as to take a new start in the world. But even if this can be, of course his path will be encumbered for a good-while and his reputation lowered for prudence if for nothing else. Fanny is going to Canton for the winter. She, with her baby, will board at Aunt Betsey's.[1] The baby is a very pretty one. I am sorry it must go away. Have you seen Mr Emerson's new little daughter?[2] I heard you were there Thanksgiving day.

Eugene writes in good spirits, though with no great cause to be sure.

After looking into your affairs, Mother who has already advanced the money to pay Mr Farley, thinks this portion of the estates had better be mortgaged to you at the sum you name, and the money be paid out of your portion.[3] If Eugene is not able to redeem it by the time you want the money, and if it cannot then be raised on the property, Mother or I will pay it you.

I have got pretty well settled now. My class is larger than at first and I give some private lesson[s] beside writing. I am very busy [for] one[n] of my strengths, but it does give me bad headachs. I am far better than for six years back and hope to keep so. It delights me to hear of you so happy and doing so well. Continue to write often and as fully as in your last. In about two months you come to Cambridge to be examined do you not. Mrs Clarke lent me a bedstead, so I can now think of *you* in *mine[n] with sweet composure.*[4] Very afftly your sister

MARGARET.

Is there anything you want that I can get for you?

ALS (MH: fMS Am 1086 [9:85]); MsC (MH: fMS Am 1086 [Works, 2:663–67]). *Addressed:* Richard F. Fuller / Concord / Mass.

[for] one] *added from the manuscript copy.*

you in *mine* [*you* in ⟨yo⟩ *mine*

1. Cornelia Fuller (1841–1901) was born on 23 October. She married Henry Devens, a merchant and shipbuilder (William Dawson Bridge, *Genealogy of the John Bridge Family in America, 1632–1924* [Cambridge, Mass., 1924], p. 441; *Boston Evening Transcript*, 28 August 1901).

2. Edith Emerson (1841–1929) was born on 22 November. In 1865 she married William Hathaway Forbes (*Ipswich Emersons*, p. 267; MVR 1929, 49:495).

3. Probably the Groton lawyer George Frederick Farley (1793–1855), a Harvard graduate of 1816 (Samuel Abbott Green, *An Account of the Lawyers of Groton* [Groton, Mass., 1892], pp. 49–50).

4. Mrs. Fuller's good friend Marianne Mackintosh Clarke (1815–82), wife of Thomas Clarke (1809–48) and daughter of Peter and Dorcas Burditt Mackintosh of Boston (*CVR*; MVR 339:126; *CC*, 4 November 1837; Newton VR; Mt. Auburn).

339.   To Richard F. Fuller

[2 December 1841]

My dear Richard

Mr Kuhn and Mother have looked over your account.[1] They find you have recd as yet from your inheritance only $546.[n] You have therefore a claim for a thousand or twelve hundred dollars more, according as the property may turn out, beside your claim on the Easton and Cambridge Port property.

This, if you conduct with the same economy as heretofore, will be sufficient to give you two years at College, and leave something to begin the world with. You will, also, be able to devote yourself, while at College, exclusively to your studies, and not be obliged to break up your time by keeping school like Arthur, for whom more than eleven hundred dollars has now been paid out. At the end of the two years you will be about even with him.

Under these circumstances I have decided to mortgage Eugene's claims to you for the sum you mentioned $297 I have written to him that you would consent to his redeeming it if he can before you want the money at the price for which it is mortgaged on paying interest, even if the land should rise in value.

I have heard from Ellen that she is well again, but nothing decisive of her plans. We hear frequently from Wm; he is still the same man!— Dear Mother went away much fatigued, and not, I fear to find peace and rest. If you write to her and send your letters by Mr E. I can send them always the following Saturday.

I am well myself, but very busy, giving ten[n] lessons a week beside class. I hope Mr E. will bring a note from you. In haste, but always afftely your sister

M.

ALS (MH: fMS Am 1086 [9:85]); MsC (MH: fMS Am 1086 [Works, 2:669–71]). *Addressed:* R. F. Fuller / Concord. *Endorsed:* 2 Dec / 41.

only $546] only ⟨526⟩ ⟨$550⟩ ⟨?cts⟩ $546
giving ten] giving ⟨nine⟩ ⟨eight⟩ ten

1. George Kuhn of Cambridge was the husband of Mrs. Fuller's half sister Nancy Weiser Kuhn.

340. To Samuel G. Ward

Tuesday morning.
[6 December 1841]

My dear Sam,

I wish to say a few words that have occurred to me previous to your seeing Dr Walter Channing.[1]

—If you call to mind what your feelings have been during the first year of your wedded life I think you cannot lend yourself at all to any plan that proposes separation from Ellen to Ellery. Any such forgetfulness of the common feelings of human nature, and which are as strong in this case as any, will only make well meant efforts to aid quite useless.

For myself, I see no reason whatever, if Ellery could have a small farm of his own against his serving[n] his apprenticeship by himself with the instruction of a hired farm servant.[2] If he found on trial that he[n] could not succeed in maintaining a separate home, which is so desirable to young married people, *then* he might join himself to others and work at better[n] advantage. If they were in a situation which I should not think too difficult and fatiguing for my mother, she might live with them, join her means to theirs, and give Ellen the benefit of her experience which is considerable as to the economics of a farming life, as well as her tender care.

If they lived in a place that suited me, I might make it a frequent home, and aid them by the money I must pay somewhere. But this is only a possibility, for I do not now see into the future, or know that I may not be obliged to leave N. England.—

Please let me know if you find anything more on this subject.

If you and Anna go to Mr Emerson's lecture, will you not come home with me?[3] Mr E. will be here and a few persons whom I shall[n] ask to meet him.

MARGARET.

ALS (MH: bMS Am 1465 [921]). *Addressed:* Mr S. G. Ward / 4. Louisburg Square. *Endorsed:* 1841 / S. M. Fuller / Decr 6th.

against his serving] against his ⟨tre⟩ serving
If he found on trial that he] ↑ If he found on trial that he ↓
work at better] work at ↑ better ↓
I shall] I ⟨have⟩ ↑ shall ↓

1. Walter Channing (1786–1876), Ellery's father, graduated from Harvard in 1808 and from the University of Pennsylvania Medical School in 1809. He was a reformer, a pacifist, and a temperance man known for his wit and energy. The first professor of obstetrics at Harvard, he introduced the use of ether in childbirth. He was dean of the Medical School from 1819 to 1847. His first wife—Ellery's mother—was Barbara Higginson Perkins (1795–1822). His second was Elizabeth Wainwright (*DAB*; Harvard archives; Higginson, *Reverend Francis Higginson*).

2. According to Mrs. Fuller's letter to Margaret of 16 December (MH), Ellery had written asking his sister-in-law to investigate the "Curson farm," which he was thinking of buying. Presumably the farm was owned by the Curzons in Newburyport.

3. On 9 December Emerson read "The Conservative," the second of his series "The Times" (*Emerson Lectures*, 3:341).

341. To Margarett C. Fuller

Boston Dec 13th. [1841]

My dear Mother,

Mr Cleverly preached in town last Sunday,[n] so I could not send.[1] I think I will write this time by post, as the delay till Saturday may seem to you long.

I have, however, no family news for you, not having heard from any of the children, except Richard and Lloyd, both of whom were well, since Fanny went away.

Tell me in your next, if you had not rather Lloyd should make you his visit, while Aunt Abba is away, (on account of accommodations) and fix the time finally for his coming that I may let him know.

I want much to hear how Fanny and the baby find themselves. Tell F. I have her bracelet, and will send it by the first safe oppory.

Mr Cumming arrived the aftn you went away and staid till Wednesday p. m. He thought best to leave Lizzy in the care of Dr Channing who has begun his course of treatment which will reduce her very much. She feels somewhat dispirited at the prospect of the long, dull months of confinement and separation from her husband which seem in store for her. Belinda is quite unwell with cold and fever. Maria has got out and is very "chipper."[2]

Mine hostess has been very ill with this terrible influenza, as has Mrs Farrar.[3] I hope you will take care of yourself in your present exposed situation, so bad in itself and such a change from the city. Do remember how sad it would be for you to be sick there and what a trial to your constitution, and dont yield to the impulse of the moment, however sweet may be its character!

Did you ever send Arthur my letter? Because, if he got it, I am surprized that I do not hear again.[4]

Mrs Barker has arrived safe at N. Orleans. Mary Tilden was here today and laments much that she cannot see you.[5] I believe she intends to write. When you meet she can amuse you with the account of her reception at the south. The room they gave her to sleep in was not plastered, nor the windows glazed. She seems now in a wise and tranquil state of mind, and sees the way open before her to an honorable and independent, if not a pleasurable existence.

I have three new scholars this week. M. Channing, M. Ward, and Miss Burley's niece, E. Howes.[6] But Marianne Jackson has been too unwell to take her lessons. Perhaps, however, she will revive again, as she has repeatedly before.

Mr Emerson's last lecture was brilliant, but not as complete as the one before. I went last night to hear Braham in the Creation, which gave me great pleasure. Though I know many of hi[s] airs, I have never before heard them connectedly. He was grand in parts, but disappointed in the one "In native worth &c from which I expected great delight. I would give much that Eugene could hear him in "Rocked in the cradle of the Deep" I shall go again next Sunday to hear the Messiah.[7] Sorry you are not here to go. Yet I should be resigned, if I thought you were in peace and comfort but alas!

Remember me affectionately to Grandmother and Aunt. Say to Fanny that if Mr C. goes on Saty I shall try and write to her. Let me know, dearest Mother, if I can do any thing for you.

S. M. F.

ALS (MH: fMS Am 1086 [9:106]); MsC (MH: fMS Am 1086 [Works, 2:257–63]). *Addressed:* Mrs Margaret Fuller / Canton / Mass. *Postmark:* Boston Ms Dec 14.

town last Sunday] town last ⟨Satur⟩ Sunday

1. Asa P. Cleverly (1807–71), a native of Weymouth, was a Universalist minister. In addition to his duties in Boston, he had in June undertaken the charge of preaching

to the Universalist congregation in Canton. In 1831 he married his distant kinswoman Rebecca Whiton Cleverly (1807–95) (Weymouth VR; George W. Chamberlain, *History of Weymouth, Massachusetts* [Weymouth, Mass., 1923], 3:163–64; MVR 455:559; Daniel T. Huntoon, *History of the Town of Canton* [Cambridge, Mass., 1893], p. 553).

2. Fuller mentions Elizabeth Randall Cumming and her husband, Alfred. Belinda is Belinda Randall; Maria is Maria Howard Randall (1820–42), who died on 25 May the following year (John W. Randall, *Poems of Nature and Life* [Boston, 1899], p. 42).

3. Fuller was staying with her uncle Henry Holton Fuller and his wife, Mary Buckminster Stone.

4. In her reply, Mrs. Fuller said she mailed the letter (now lost) (Margarett C. Fuller to Margaret Fuller, 16 December 1841, MH).

5. Mary Parker Tilden, daughter of Joseph Tilden of Boston, was a good friend of Mrs. Fuller's.

6. M. Channing is probably Mary Channing, Dr. William Ellery Channing's daughter (though it might by Mary Elizabeth Channing [1820–77], Ellery's sister, who married Thomas Wentworth Higginson in 1847) (*Cleveland and Cleaveland*, p. 1061). M. Ward is Mary Ward (1820–1901), Sam's sister, who married Charles H. Dorr (1821–93) in 1850 (MVR, marriages, 47:52, deaths, 438:42, 519:612). Elizabeth Howes (1826–93) was the daughter of Frederick and Elizabeth Burley Howes (b. 1787) of Salem (Salem VR; MVR 483:140). Susan Burley (1791–1850), Elizabeth Howes's aunt, was known for her literary salon in Salem (MVR 48:143).

7. John Braham (1774–1856), whose real name was Abraham, was a ballad writer and a tenor with a three-octave voice. From 1840 to 1842 he conducted a successful American tour. Both "Creation" and "Messiah" were popular works in Boston: the Handel and Hayden Society performed the former some sixty times from 1818 to 1870 and the latter more than seventy times (Dwight, "History of Music," pp. 418–19; *Baker's Biographical Dictionary*).

342.   To Margarett C. Fuller

Boston
Friday eveg.
[17? December 1841]

My dear Mother,

It is indeed very soothing to me to have news that you are better. *Pray* now avoid exposure *as much as possible.* Do not go out of a warm room prematurely and take great care what you eat. I will ask Dr Randall tomorrow about the wine, and get the bombazine and velvet too, if the weather permits me to go out.

The accompanying letters will, I think, give you pleasure. It is cheering that Ellery has begun an employment, and Ellen writes sweetly. The Channings also had a letter from her today. They were to have spent this eveg here, but the snowstorm prevents. I have not had any talk with them since you went away.

I am very, very sorry Fanny went to C. but it cannot, and could not be helped.¹ Let those around her try to look on her discontent with indulgence, for the reverse can do no good. If the care of her child do not soothe and sustain her, probably nothing would. If it could be made good to Aunt B. or she could get another lodger, I should wish very much she might, in a few weeks return to her uncle Stacy's. In April she can probably go to Cincinnati, and *to me* it seems that month is coming lightning swift.

Mrs Farrar is getting better. Tonight Deborah came in with a face of joy, bringing me from Mrs F. a little new tin kettle, teapot, sugar-box, and from Mr F. the nice tea and sugar. It was so like them and gave me real pleasure. Belinda is still sick. Dear Lizzy is very nervous and depressed under Dr C's treatment. Loss of blood acts very unfavorably on her brain. But more of her when I see more. I have had time to go only once.

I will write about William Channing when there is any thing decisive to tell. He is in better spirits.

Mrs Ripley was here last night, says Lloyd is in a gay mood at present, also studies well.

I am very well, but this mode of life tires my spirits. Giving so many lessons makes more serious work impossible, so that I do not feel that ardor without which I can scarcely be said to live. After next week I shall not be so busy, as the Dial will be all in print.

Please be very careful, not to [   ] "Monaldi" soiled, as it is Sarah's book, and to return it by Mr C. at the end of a fortnight.²

Now, farewell, dearest Mother. If I had not heard the good news, I meant to go and see you tomorrow, but am glad not to, as the fatigue, and break of time are undesirable at present. If you are tolerably well, I shall not come for three or four weeks. With much love to my Grandmother and Aunts your affectionate

MARGARET.

but if you should be ill I *depend* on knowing directly. Will you send back Ellen and Eugene's letters by Mr C and write me a short note. Eugene's, of course, is private.

ALS (MH: fMS Am 1086 [9:105]); MsC (MH: fMS Am 1086 [Works, 2:271–75]). *Addressed:* Mrs Margaret Fuller / Canton.

1. Frances Fuller was going to Cincinnati to join her husband, despite the objections of Margaret and her mother (Margarett C. Fuller to Margaret Fuller, 6 February 1842, MH).

2. Washington Allston's novel, *Monaldi: A Tale*, was published in 1841 by Charles C. Little and James Brown.

343. To Margarett C. Fuller

[I] Christmas eve.
[24 December 1841]

Dearest Mother,

I want very much now to hear from you again, whether you continue to improve, and how you bear this cold weather. I hope you will have a full letter for me ready to send back by Mr Cleverly.

Will you also let me see this letter from Eugene, if you can, and send me back this letter of dear Richard's without letting any see it. Can you not write a few lines to R. I talked with Mr E. of your anxiety about him; Mr E says he looks blooming, but fears he does not take exercise enough. H. Thoreau reports him to have done a great deal in his studies.

Lloyd I suppose will be with you this week.

I am in a state of extreme fatigue; this is the last week of the Dial and as often happens, the "*copy*" did not hold out, and I have had to write in every gap of time. Marianne J. and Jane have been writing for me extracts and &c, but I have barely scrambled through, and am now quite unfit to hold a pen. Tomorrow I mean to spend all the morning at the bath and in the open air, and see if I cannot get revived.

I have had some great pleasures lately. I believe I wrote you of my happiness in hearing the Creation. Last Sunday night I heard the Messiah, and then for the first time truly recognized the might of Braham. On Tuesday I heard him again at his concert. Of all these I shall write a particular account to Eugene and will send you the letter before I send it him that you may see in detail what I think of this truly great singer.

I very much regret you should not have heard him; there is hope of his return in the spring, if so, you must not forego it on any account.

I also have heard at the Odeon one of Beethoven's grand symphonies of itself worth living for.[1]

Every body is running to the Anti-Slavery fair, said to be full of beautiful things from England.[2] I wish I could go and buy pretty new years gifts for you and those I love, but I must not so avoid temptation. I had myself a beautiful present from there yesterday.

Mrs Farrar desires much love to you. She has not got out yet. Have not seen the Randalls for several days but both E. and B. heard Braham on Tuesday. The Channings spent an eveg here, are much delighted to hear of Ellery's getting the place, send much love to you.

W.H.C. asks much of you; he was here on Sunday and went with us to hear the Messiah. You can think of him now as in better health and spirits.

Mrs Clarke is taken suddenly very ill, but the medicines seem to relieve her.

I send you a book which must have back by a week from next Monday. Say whether you like it, and want the rest; whether you can get books there; how much time you have for reading &c &c &c

Best love to F. and kiss to pretty baby. Is there any thing else I can do for you, dearest Mother your much fatigued but cheerful daughter

MARGARET.

[II] Saturday morng
Half past one.

I feel much better this morng for exercise, and will scribble a few words more. This morning I recd from Anna Ward a Xmas box of a sweet pretty collar, a sweet pretty note and a cake^n frosted by her own hands with Christmas on it in blue letters. This was a kind little attention.

How I wish I had twenty dollars to lay out in presents for my friends! One is sorry to be poor these festal days, as well as in those of famine.

I gave two dollars a yard for your bombazine; that at nine shillings or ten and six was a great deal too coarse and would just have spoiled the garment. I suppose you would have done differently, but dont believe you will be sorry in the end. Velvet was two dollars and a half a yard, this is the same as I got for my bonnet and cheap I believe as any that is good.— The black gloves are my Xmas present to you. The other pair please give to Aunt Abba with my love. I thought they would be nice to slip on when she is doing the "cold things" she spoke of in her letter to N. Kuhn.

Elizabeth and Maria have just been here. E. said she was feeling pretty well. Before I got talking with them Mr Eustis and M Channing came in so I cant tell you much about them.

Mrs Clarke continues very ill; they fear she will have a lung fever. I shant feel easy till I hear from you

MARGARET.

I send also a pair of my woolen hose. I do not wear them in town and they will be of use to you in that cold pl[ace.] I have kept a pair to wear when I ride

I: ALS (MH: fMS Am 1086 [9:79]). II: ALS (MH: bMS Am 1610 [51]); MsCfr (MH: fMS Am 1086 [Works, 2:285–93]). Published in part in Higginson, *MFO*, p. 165. *Addressed:* Mrs M. Fuller / Canton / Mass.

and a cake] and a ⟨Xmas⟩ cake

1. On Saturday, 18 December, the Boston Academy of Music performed Beethoven's Fifth Symphony (*Boston Daily Advertiser*, 17 December 1841).

2. The eighth annual Anti-Slavery Fair had opened in Boston on 22 December, with an emphasis on imported goods (*Boston Daily Advertiser*, 24 December 1841).

344. To Richard F. Fuller

Thursday morng
[30? December 1841]

My dear Richard,

I take great pleasure in that feeling of the living presence of beauty in nature which your letters show— But you, who have now lived long enough to see some of my prophecies fulfilled, will not deny though you may not yet believe the truth of my words when I say you go^n to an extreme in your denunciation of cities and the social institutions.[1] *These* are a growth also, and as well^n as the diseases which come upon them, under the control of the One spirit as much as the great tree on which the insects prey and in whose bark the busy bird has made many a wound. When we get the proper perspective of these things we shall find man however artificial still a part of Nature. Meanwhile let us trust, and while it is the soul's duty ever to bear witness to the best it knows, let us not be hasty to conclude that in what suits us not there can be no good, nay let us be sure there *must* be eventual good could we but see far enough to discern it. In maintaining perfect truth to ourselves and choosing that mode of being that suits us we had best leave others alone as much as may be. You, dear R. prefer the country, and I doubt not it is on the whole a better condition of life to live there, but at Mr Frost's Sociable you saw that no circumstances will keep people from being frivolous.[2] One may be gossiping and vulgar and idle in the country,— earnest, wise and noble in the city. Nature cannot be kept from us while there is a sky above with^n so much as one star to remind us of prayer in the silent night. As I come back into town over the Milldam at sunset, I see very distinctly that the city also is a bed in God's garden. More of this some other year.

I am very glad to hear so good an account of your studies. As you desire I will make no plan about your entering College as yet; you know the great thing with me is that you should grow and learn, if this be so I can wait for outward signs.

Dear Mother is almost well now. She had a very pleasing letter this week from Ellen and Ellery. They are pretty well and Ellery now very busy. I feel sure that Ellery would like to receive a letter from you. He may not answer it, for he is of an uncertain temper about such things, and disappoints his family and S. Ward very much by neglecting to answer them. Still, if you have any thing to say to him I would write, for if he receive aught good and true, he knows how to value it and will answer in spirit, if not by words.

I dont know whether I've given you Ellen's various messages and think I will send you her last letter to me, send it back next week. She said in that to Mother she should write to you next. I send you ten dollars and a little bit of New Year's gift which you will value because it is from me. The doorbell rings and I suppose it to be a scholar for me. Give my love particy to E Hoar when you see her

Always affectionately your sister

M.

I wish very much you were here to walk with me these soft misty moonlights. The trees round the common look very beautiful then, and the distance is fairy land.

ALS (MH: fMS Am 1086 [9:86]); MsC (MH: fMS Am 1086 [Works, 2:649–55]). Published in part in *WNC*, pp. 349–50, and Miller, pp. 76–77. *Addressed:* R. F. Fuller. / Concord / Mass.

you go] you ⟨are⟩ go
and as well] and ⟨may with⟩ as well
sky above with] sky above ⟨us⟩ with

1. In his letter to her of 12 December (MH), Richard had originally said that he did not "care whether the institutions of man be worthy to stand, or not," but went back to alter slightly his strident remark.

2. Barzali Frost (1804–58) graduated from Harvard in 1830 and from the Divinity School in 1835. From 1837 to 1858 he was minister of the Unitarian church in Concord. In 1837 Frost married Elmira Stone, sister of Henry Holton Fuller's wife (Harvard archives).

INDEX

Abraham, John. *See* Braham, John.

Ackermann, Georg Christian, 37

Adam, William, 194, 195n

Adams, Abel, 83, 86n, 231, 241

Adams, Abigail Larkin, 32

"Adelaida" (Beethoven), 149n

Adventures of Caleb Williams, The
(Godwin), 176n

Alcott, A. Bronson, 33n, 84, 92n, 98, 99,
100n, 130n, 164n, 194, 195n,
209n; and *Dial*, 95n, 135, 137n–38n,
146, 181, 182n, 189, 190n; Fuller on,
32, 129, 135, 136–37, 176; philosophy
of, 143n

—letters to, 94, 143

—works of: "Interpretations of Christianity," 98, 100n; "Orphic Sayings,"
135, 137n–38n, 146, 189, 190n

Allston, Washington, 32, 33n, 66, 68, 72,
75, 145, 260n

Alnwick Castle (Halleck), 51n

"American Philosophy" (Milnes), 136,
138n

Anaxagoras, 128, 129n

André (Sand), 99, 100n, 137

Anti-Slavery Fair, 197, 198n, 261, 263n

Appleton, Samuel Appleton, 51

Archaeus. *See* Sterling, John.

Arnim, Bettina Brentano von, 83, 86n,
92n, 172, 176n, 181–82, 202–3,
220; *Goethes Briefwechsel mit einem Kinde*,
83, 86n, 202; *Die Günderode*, 86n,
92n, 172, 176n, 182n, 201, 202–3, 220,
221n

Arnim, Joachim von, 86n

"Art" (Emerson), 188n

"Art of Life,—The Scholar's Calling,
The" (Hedge), 114n

Aspasia, 41, 44n

"Atheneum Exhibition of Painting and
Sculpture, The" (Fuller), 152, 153n

Atkinson, James, 122n

"Aulus Persius Flaccus" (Thoreau), 133,
134n

Aus meinem Leben: Dichtung und Warheit
(Goethe), 145

Austin, Sarah, 60, 61n

Bacon, Francis, 54, 55n

Bailey, Philip, 201n–2n

Balch, Caroline Williams, 73n

Balch, Joseph, Sr., 73n

Balch, Joseph Williams, 71, 73n

"Ballad" (Hood), 162, 163n

Ballou, Abigail Sayles, 178n

Ballou, Adin, 174, 178n

Ballou, Lucy Hunt, 178n

Balzac, Honoré, 150

Bancroft, Elizabeth Davis, 101, 102n

Bancroft, George, 102n

Bancroft, Sarah Dwight, 102n

"Banquet" (Plato), 39, 44n

Barker, Mrs. (at Brook Farm), 212

Barker, Anna Hazard. *See* Ward, Anna
Hazard Barker.

Barker, Eliza Hazard, 151n, 258

Barker, Jacob, 151n

Barker, Thomas Hazard, 150, 151n

Barlow, Almira Penniman, 145n
—letter to, 145
Barlow, David Hatch, 145n
Baron Munchhausen's Narrative (Raspe),
   182
Bartlett, Lucretia Archbald, 137n
Beethoven, Ludwig, 7, 98, 147, 149n,
   205, 206, 223, 225n, 261, 263n
Behr, Charles de, 118, 120n
Bellini, Vincenzo, 190–91
Bellows, Henry, 72, 74n
Bible, 31, 54, 109, 119, 169, 172, 176, 215
"Bible Is a Book Worthy to Read, The"
   (E. Channing), 103–4
Biographie universelle des musiciens (Fétis),
   150, 151n
Bird, Robert, 129n
Blackwood's Edinburgh Magazine, 54, 55n,
   59, 69, 70n
Bliss, Daniel, 102n
"Blonde Eckbert, Die" (Tieck), 215, 216n
Boston Athenaeum, 32, 33n, 43, 50,
   75, 148, 152, 153n, 175, 178n, 189,
   190n
Boston Female Anti-Slavery Society, 198n
Boston Quarterly Review, 95n, 118, 150
Bradford, George Partridge, 137n, 182,
   228, 238
Bradley, Charles Smith, 65
Braham (Abraham), John, 258, 259n, 261
Briggs, George Ware, 137
Brimmer, George Watson, 32, 33n
Brisbane, Albert, 179, 180n
Brodhead, Mr., 210
Brook Farm, 57n, 174, 206, 210, 240;
   Emerson on, 164n, 195n; Fuller
   on, 163, 180, 194, 205; visits to, 209,
   211, 212, 217, 237, 238. *See also*
   Ripley, George, and Brook Farm.
Brough, Mr., 190
Brown, Mrs., 227
Brownson, Orestes Augustus, 95n, 118,
   120n, 150
Buchanan, Joseph Roades, 63, 64n
Buke of the Howlat (Holland), 171, 176n
Burditt, James W., 118, 120n
Burges, Eleanor Burrill, 135, 137n
Burges, Mary Arnold, 135, 137n
Burges, Tristam, 137n
Burges, Walter Snow, 137n
Burley, Susan, 258, 259n
Burling, William, 180n
Burns, Robert, 119

Burrill, James, 137n
Bussey, Benjamin, 151n
Bussey Institute, 151n
Butler, Caleb, 39
Byron, George Gordon, Lord, 33, 49–50,
   51n, 81, 242; "Childe Harold's
   Pilgrimage," 242, 246n; "She Walks in
   Beauty," 49–50, 51n; "Stanzas to
   Augusta," 81

Carlyle, Thomas, 57, 136, 137n, 147, 148,
   149n, 153
Cervantes, Miguel de, 42
Channing, Ann, 33n
Channing, Ellen Fuller. *See* Fuller, Ellen
   Kilshaw.
Channing, Ellery, 104n, 235–36, 251;
   in Cincinnati, 249, 252, 253n, 259, 261,
   264; and *Dial*, 147, 149n, 181, 182n,
   189, 190n; in Illinois, 150, 151n, 154;
   marriage of, 7, 39n, 230, 231n, 232,
   233n, 239–41, 256; poetry of, 51, 107
—letter to, 239–40
—works of: "The Bible Is a Book Worthy
   to Read," 103–4; "Theme for a
   World-Drama," 182n
Channing, Frances Maria, 50, 51n, 180n,
   224
Channing, Lucy Ellery, 127
Channing, Mary, 50, 51, 218, 219n, 223,
   258, 259n, 262
Channing, Mary Elizabeth, 258, 259n
Channing, Ruth Gibbs, 124
Channing, Susan Higginson, 131, 183,
   226
Channing, Walter, 51n, 256, 257, 259,
   260, 261
Channing, William Ellery, 31n, 33n, 51n,
   64, 92n, 121, 124n, 176n, 195n,
   219n, 222–23, 226
Channing, William Ellery (the younger).
   See Channing, Ellery.
Channing, William Henry, 31n, 50,
   226, 236, 240, 241, 260, 262; in Cincinnati, 158, 184n, 217, 218n; Fuller
   on, 31, 173, 203, 214–15
—letters to, 31, 108–10, 111, 125–27,
   130–32, 162–63, 164–66, 170–80, 183–
   84, 187, 190–94, 201–3, 204, 205–6,
   213–15, 220–21, 223–25, 227–28
—works of: "The Child Asleep," 50, 51n;
   "Ernest the Seeker," 113n, 125, 126,

Channing, William Henry (*cont.*)
127n, 130, 184, 185n, 201; "Moral
Evil," 203
Chapman, George, 124
Chapman, Henry Grafton, 198n
Chapman, Maria Weston, 49n, 195n,
198n
—letter to, 197–98
Chardon Street Convention, 194, 195n,
197–98
Chartism (Carlyle), 136, 138n
"Chartists, The" (Vaughan), 111, 113n
"Child Asleep, The" (W. H. Channing),
50, 51n
"Childe Harold's Pilgrimage" (Byron),
242, 246n
Christian Examiner, 6, 37
Christliche im Plato, Das (Ackermann), 37
"Church-Porch, The" (Herbert), 60, 61n
Church, the Pulpit, and the Gospel, The
(Young), 128–29, 130n
Clark, Ellen, 61n
Clark, Gardiner H., 162n
Clark, L. B., 61n
Clarke, Herman Huidekoper, 175, 178n
Clarke, James Freeman, 34n, 47, 48n,
50, 125, 131, 175; and *Dial*, 126, 127n,
136, 146; love affairs, 35, 36n, 43
—letters to, 33–34, 144–45
Clarke, Marianne Mackintosh, 254, 255n,
262
Clarke, Sarah Ann, 35, 36n, 43, 47, 50,
63, 89n, 148, 153, 250, 260
Clarke, Thomas, 255n
Clarkson, Thomas, 48, 49n
Clevenger, Shobal, 178n
Cleverly, Asa P., 257, 258n–59n, 261
Cleverly, Rebecca Cleverly, 259n
Cogswell, Joseph G., 72, 74n
Coleridge, Samuel Taylor, 59, 65n, 119,
120n; "Dejection: An Ode," 183,
184n; "On Poesy or Art," 120n
"Conservatism and Reform" (Hedge),
227–28
"Conservative, The" (Emerson), 257n,
258
Conversations (Fuller): in 1839, 5, 86–89,
92, 97–98, 101–2, 106, 114, 118–19,
145; in 1840, 164, 182, 183, 189;
in 1841, 203–4, 249, 252, 254, 255–56;
include men, 189, 203–4; plans
for, 86–89
Cooper, James Fenimore, 128

Corinne (Staël), 97
Coriolanus (Shakespeare), 110
Correggio, Antonio Allegrida, 172
Cranch, Christopher Pearse, 146, 148n
Crane, Abigail, 252, 262
Crane, Elizabeth Crane, 229
Crane, Elizabeth Jones Weiser, 217, 222
Creation (Handel), 258, 259n, 261
"Crystals from a Cavern" (Sterling), 70n,
75
Cumming, Alfred, 257
Cumming, Elizabeth Randall. *See*
Randall, Elizabeth Wells.
"Cupid's Conflict" (More), 181, 182n
Curtis, George William, 137n
Curtis, George William Scarbrough, 206,
208n
Curtis, Joseph Herman, 206, 208n
Curzon, Elizabeth Burling, 180n
Curzon, George, 247, 248n
Curzon, Margaret Searle, 179, 180n,
248n
Curzon, Samuel, Jr., 180n, 248n, 257n
Curzon, Samuel, Sr., 180n

Dana, Elizabeth Ellery, 33n
Dana, Francis, 33n, 89n
Dana, Martha R., 33n
Dana, Richard Henry, Sr., 32, 33n, 53,
55n, 72, 74n
Dana, Ruth Charlotte, 72, 74n
Dante, 198–99
Da Ponte, Lorenzo L., 119, 120n
Davis, Ellen Watson, 38n
Davis, John, 38n
Deacon, W. F., 55n
"Defence of Poetry" (Shelley), 133, 134n,
136, 138n
"Dejection: An Ode" (Coleridge), 183,
184n
"Demonology" (Emerson), 69, 70n
Devens, Henry, 255n
Dewey, Orville, 172, 173, 176n
DeWolfe, Mary Soley, 216–17, 218n, 227,
229, 241
DeWolfe, William Bradford, Jr., 217,
218n
DeWolfe, William Bradford, Sr., 217,
218n
Dial, 5, 92, 145, 155, 182, 231, 233n, 249,
251n, 252; appeal for contributions
to, 111, 113, 114n, 124–26, 130, 151–

Dial (*cont.*)
52, 153, 161, 181, 225; business
affairs of, 132, 146, 148n, 231, 233n,
250–51; creation of, 95n, 111, 115–
16, 126, 130–31, 132; criticism of
manuscripts for, 151, 185, 188–89,
242–43; editing of, 7, 130–31, 133,
134n, 147, 148n, 149, 151, 153, 181,
182, 212–13, 217, 229, 230, 232,
248–49, 260, 261; Fuller on, 126, 131,
145, 146–47, 181, 201, 230. *See also*
Alcott, A. Bronson, and *Dial*; Channing,
Ellery, and *Dial*; Clarke, James
Freeman, and *Dial*; Emerson, Ralph
Waldo, and *Dial*; Ripley, George,
and *Dial*; Sturgis, Caroline, and *Dial*;
Thoreau, Henry David, and *Dial*.
Discourse on the Latest Form of Infidelity, A
(Norton), 115n
Disraeli, Benjamin, 59, 61n
Dix, Dorothea, 149, 151n
Döring, Heinrich, 69, 70n
Dorr, Charles H., 259n
"Drachenfels" (Fuller), 40, 44n, 98
"'Dream, The'" (Sturgis), 149, 151n
Dughet, Gaspard (Gaspard-Poussin), 35,
36n, 37, 75, 76n, 195n
Duncan, Samuel W., 162n
Dwight, John Sullivan, 37, 111, 182;
review of *Wilhelm Tell*, 37

Earle, John, 249, 250n
Eastman, Samuel C., 162n
Eckermann, Johann Peter, 5, 52, 53n
Eckermann's Conversations with Goethe
(trans. Fuller), 5, 37, 51–52, 53n, 59,
67, 73, 75; Whitman's review of,
118, 120n
"Elegiacs" (Tennyson), 190, 191n
Elssler, Fanny, 251
Emerson, Charles Chauncy, 51n, 116n,
129n, 131, 132n, 214, 215n
Emerson, Edith, 151n, 254, 255n
Emerson, Edward Bliss, 134n
Emerson, Edward Waldo, 63n
Emerson, Ellen, 182n
Emerson, Lydia Jackson (Lidian), 32,
70n, 160
Emerson, Mary Moody, 246, 247n
Emerson, Phebe Bliss, 247n
Emerson, Ralph Waldo, 5, 6, 31, 43, 51n,
75, 83, 94, 100n, 115, 131, 192, 203,
204n, 214, 215, 227, 228, 238, 240n,
241, 243, 246, 247, 252, 254–54, 255,
257, 261; and Brook Farm, 164n,
194, 195n; Fuller on, 161n, 170, 192,
194, 213, 233–34; lectures of, 32,
33n, 37, 69, 70n, 92, 99, 111, 114, 119,
135, 137n, 198, 201, 251, 257, 258;
letters of, 35, 36, 73, 74n, 124,
150, 183; visits to, 62, 63, 84, 94, 157,
210
—and *Dial*: contributor to, 116, 126,
132–33, 134n, 136, 138n, 145, 146–47,
151–52, 153, 181, 182n, 187–89,
201, 212–13, 230, 232, 233n, 250–51;
founder of, 95n, 111, 113, 125;
opinion of, 148n, 185
—letters to, 32, 53–54, 68–70, 97–99,
104–5, 110–11, 115–16, 121–22, 127–
29, 132–37, 145–48, 151–53, 159–
60, 181–82, 187–89, 208–9, 212–13,
230–36, 248–49, 250–51
—works of: "Art," 188n; "The Conservative," 257n, 258; "Demonology,"
69, 70n; *Essays: First Series*, 201, 232,
233n; "Genius," 32, 33n; "Human
Life," 33n, 37n, 70n, 137n; "Man the
Reformer," 198, 201; *Nature*, 128,
182; "New Poetry," 149n; "Politics,"
111, 113n; "The Present Age," 113n,
124n, 137n; "The Protest," 37;
"The Sphinx," 214, 216n; "Thoughts
on Art," 187–88, 189; "Thoughts
on Modern Literature," 137n, 146–47,
148n, 152; "The Times," 251, 257n;
"Walter Savage Landor," 230, 231n,
232, 233n; "Woodnotes," 147, 149n,
181, 213n
Emerson, Ruth Haskins, 63n, 70n
Emerson, Waldo, 70n, 84, 236
Emerson, William (brother of Ralph
Waldo), 62–63
Emerson, William (father of Ralph
Waldo), 63n, 247n
"Ernest the Seeker" (W. H. Channing),
113n, 125, 126, 127n, 130, 184,
185n, 201
Essays: First Series (Emerson), 201, 232,
233n
*Essays, Letters from Abroad, Translations
and Fragments* (Shelley), 133, 134n
Eugénie Grandet (Balzac), 150, 151n
Eustis, Elizabeth Gray, 166n
Eustis, Frederic Augustus, 262
Eustis, Jacob, 166n

Eustis, Dr. William, 164, 166n
Eustis, Governor William, 166n
Everett, Edward, 63
"Excursion, The" (Wordsworth), 169

Fable for Critics, A (Lowell), 44n
Faerie Queene, The (Spenser), 214,
215n–16n
Farley, George Frederick, 254, 255n
Farrar, Eliza Rotch, 6, 176n, 183–84,
185n, 192–93, 195n, 228, 229, 258,
260, 261
Farrar, John, 6, 184n, 212, 217, 228, 229
Faust (Goethe), 69, 75
Fenner, Cornelius, 162n
Festus (Bailey), 201; Fuller's review of,
201n, 218n, 230
Fétis, F. J., 150, 151n
Firdawsi, 122n
"Fisher's Son, The" (Thoreau), 232, 233n
Forbes, Margaret, 150
Forbes, Margaret Perkins, 151n
Forbes, Ralph Bennett, 151n
Forbes, William Hathaway, 151n, 255n
Forrest, Edwin, 128, 129n
Fourier, Charles, 180n
Francis, Convers, 95n
Frost, Barzali, 263, 264n
Frost, Elmira Stone, 264n
Fuller, Abraham Williams, 73, 74n, 207,
241
Fuller, Anna Eliza Rotta, 161
Fuller, Arthur Buckminster, 39n, 62,
143, 155, 197n, 207, 210, 217, 219,
222
—letters to, 38–39, 61–62, 195–96, 248,
252, 254, 255, 258
Fuller, Cornelia, 254, 255n, 260
Fuller, Edward Breck, 187
Fuller, Ellen Kilshaw, 38, 39n, 58, 59, 61,
63, 71, 72, 73, 77, 219; marriage of,
7, 230, 231n, 232, 233n, 239–41, 256;
in West, 158, 159n, 196, 217, 222,
226, 229, 249, 252, 254, 255, 259, 264
Fuller, Eugene, 37, 38, 158, 161, 174,
210, 211n, 217, 222, 226, 229,
241, 248, 249, 252, 254, 255, 258, 260,
261
—letters to, 62–63, 70–73
Fuller, Frances Hastings, 210, 219, 222,
226, 229, 254, 257, 259–60
Fuller, Henry Holton, 259n

Fuller, Hiram, 33n
—letter to, 67
Fuller, Lloyd, 38, 39n, 48, 73, 144,
158, 175, 207, 208, 210, 212, 254, 257,
260, 261
Fuller, Margaret: lyrical expressions
of, 34, 40–41, 56, 66, 75–76, 82–83,
84, 93, 95–96, 107, 123, 126, 145–46,
157–58, 159–60, 163, 166–69, 187–88,
199, 202, 206, 215, 220–21, 224–25,
236, 239, 241–42, 248; mystical
experience of, 6, 158–59, 167–69, 183,
192; private classes of, 36, 57n, 59,
61n, 72, 94, 114, 158, 250, 252,
254, 255, 258, 260; reading of, 37, 39,
47–48, 50, 54, 59, 69, 99, 102, 104,
106, 128, 150, 162–63, 204. *See also*
Conversations.
—and friendship, 60, 147, 171; with
Emerson, 6, 93, 104, 105, 150, 157n,
159–60, 161n, 163, 164n, 167, 169n,
170, 171, 178n, 214, 233–36; with
Newcomb, 56, 64, 67–68, 101, 123,
238; with Sturgis, 35, 47, 60, 79–80,
81–82, 92–93, 105–6, 107, 163, 166–
67; theory of, 214–15, 234–35
—opinions of: on abolition, 48, 197; on
beauty, 84, 97, 102, 105, 131, 246;
on genius, 33, 75, 102, 203; on German
literature, 47–48, 59, 69, 114 (*see also
entries for individual works*); on letter
writing, 48, 58–59, 60, 113, 118, 195,
228; on literary criticism, 53, 75,
87–88, 116, 118–19, 126, 127, 136; on
love, 93, 96, 166–68, 199, 202, 214–
15, 234–35; on music, 99, 102–3, 147,
190–91, 196, 205, 206, 258, 261; on
mythology, 34, 102, 118, 166, 198,
223–24; on nature, 56, 66, 68, 74,
75–77, 83–84, 100–101, 164, 178–79,
187–88, 204, 220–21, 223–25; on
painting, 42, 75; on philosophy, 39–41,
110, 205; on religion, 47, 108–10,
123, 129, 135, 172–74, 192, 214–15; on
solitude, 31, 167, 174, 191–92, 236;
on transcendentalism, 109, 129, 131,
135; on women, 86–88, 197–98;
on writing poetry, 33–34, 49, 106–7,
149, 238, 242–43. *See also* Dial,
Fuller on.
—translations of: *Eckermann's Conversations with Goethe*, 5, 37, 51–52, 53n, 59,
67, 73, 75; *Torquato Tasso*, 43, 44n, 47

Fuller, Margaret (*cont.*)
—works of: "The Atheneum Exhibition
    of Painting and Sculpture," 152, 153n;
    "Drachenfels," 40, 44n; "Festus," 201n,
    218n, 230; "Jesus the Comforter,"
    34n; "Lives of the Great Composers,"
    218n, 223, 225n; "The Magnolia
    of Lake Pontchartrain," 166n, 184;
    "A Record of Impressions," 145; "A
    Short Essay on Critics," 145;
    "Thoughts. On Sunday Morning," 34n;
    "To Allston's Picture, 'The Bride,'"
    166; "Yuca Filamentosa," 166n, 184
Fuller, Margarett Crane, 36, 37, 38, 58,
    59, 70–71, 72, 73, 144, 158, 161,
    164, 174, 196, 207, 208, 209–10, 236,
    239–40, 252, 253, 254, 255, 256, 264
—letters to, 216–18, 219, 221–23, 225–
    27, 228–29, 240–41, 257–62
Fuller, Mary Stone, 258, 259n
Fuller, Richard Frederick, 38, 39n, 58,
    63, 73, 195, 196, 218n, 226, 257,
    261; and Harvard, 217, 231–32, 255,
    263–64
—letters to, 115, 143–44, 206–8, 209–10,
    247–48, 249, 251–52, 253–56, 263–64
Fuller, Sarah, 143
Fuller, Timothy, 6, 56–57, 59, 178n
Fuller, William Henry, 73, 210, 217,
    222, 241, 252, 254, 255

Gannett, Sarah White, 210, 211n, 219,
    222
Gannett, Thomas Brattle, 211n
Garrison, William Lloyd, 49n, 195n, 198n
Gaspard-Poussin, 35, 36n, 37, 75, 76n,
    195n
"Genius" (Emerson), 32, 33n
Gifford, William, 134
Godwin, William, 171, 176n
Goethe, Johann Wolfgang, 7, 33, 42, 44n,
    53, 54, 59, 69, 70n, 75, 86n, 152, 179,
    202; public readings from, 60, 114,
    119; quoted, 48, 49, 55n, 145, 175, 178n
—works of: *Aus meinem Leben: Dichtung
    und Warheit*, 145; *Faust*, 69, 75;
    "Helena," 69, 70n, 75; *Die Leiden des
    jungen Werthers*, 75; *Die Propyläen*, 60,
    114n; *Torquato Tasso*, 43, 44n, 47;
    Über Kunst und Altertum, 70n; *Wilhelm
    Meisters Lehrjahre*, 55n, 152, 175, 178n,
    193, 195n; *Wilhelm Meisters Wander-
    jahre*, 152, 179; *Zur Farbenlehre*, 204

Goethe's Briefe in den Jahren 1768 bis 1832
    (Döring), 70n
Goethes Briefwechsel mit einem Kinde
    (Arnim), 83, 86n, 202
Goodenow, Smith Bartlett, 247, 248n
Goodwin, Ellen Davis, 37, 38n
Goodwin, Ezra Shaw, 38n
Green, Mr., 71
Greene, Albert Gorton, 135
—letter to, 161–62
Greene, Arazelia Gray, 162n
Greene, Charles, 207
Greene, Elizabeth Clifford, 162n
Greene, Mary Ann Clifford, 162n
Greene, Sarah Margaret Fuller, 162n
Greene-Street School (Providence), 33n,
    67, 155n
Greene, William Batchelder, 74n
Greenough, Horatio, 190n
Grimké, Angelina, 49n
Grinnell, Abigail Barrell, 67n, 143, 144n,
    217
Grinnell, Ellen, 103
Grinnell, William Taylor, 67, 144n
Günderode, Die (Arnim), 86n, 92n, 172,
    176n, 182n, 201, 202–3, 220, 221n
Günderode, Karoline, 202–3, 220

Hall, Ann, 72, 74n
Hall, Bathsheba, 74n
Hall, Jonathan, 74n
Halleck, Fitz-Greene, 50, 51n
Hamlet (Shakespeare), 53, 110
"Hamlet" (Very), 53, 55n
Hardenberg, Baron Friedrich von
    [pseud. Novalis], 107n, 158n
Harding's Gallery (Boston), 66, 68, 72,
    145
Harleian Miscellany, The, 99, 100n
Harley, Edward, second earl of Oxford,
    100n
Harrison, Mrs., 227
Haven, Ann Woodward, 63n
Haven, John, 63n
Haven, Susan Woodward, 63n
Hawthorne, Nathaniel, 155n, 238
Hazlitt, William, 153, 154n
Heath, John Francis, 191
Hedge, Frederic Henry, 5, 114n, 227–28
—letters to, 113–14, 124–25
Hedge, Lucy Pierce, 115n
Heinrich von Ofterdingen (Novalis), 107,
    157, 158n

"Helena" (Goethe), 69, 70n, 75
Henry, Mr., 207, 208
Henry the Fourth, pt. 1 (Shakespeare), 124, 125n
Heraud, John, 136, 138n
Herbert, George, 60, 61n
Herodotus, 251
Hickman, Louisa, 36n, 43
Higginson, Thomas Wentworth, 259n
Hildreth, Richard, 130n
Hillard, George Stillman, 250, 251n
Hinckley, Hannah Sturgis, 104n
Hinckley, Isaac, Jr., 103, 104n
Histoire de la vie et des ouvrages de Michel-Ange Bonarroti (Quatremère de Quincy), 136, 138n
Histoire de la vie et des ouvrages de Raphaël (Quatremère de Quincy), 84, 86n
Historical Sketches of the Old Painters (Lee), 37n
History of the Rise, Progress, and Accomplishment of the Abolition of the African Slave-Trade . . . (Clarkson), 49n
Hoar, Elizabeth Sherman, 50, 51n, 62, 63, 69, 83, 128, 129n, 152, 230, 248
—letters to, 66, 83–84, 203–4, 246
Holland, Richard, 176n
Holy Family, The (Raphael), 76
Hood, Thomas, 162, 163n
Hooper, Ellen Sturgis, 36, 37, 38n, 77, 145, 146, 150, 183; poetry of, 120–21, 136, 137n, 147, 148n, 153n
Hooper, Robert, 36n, 103, 104n
Hope Leslie (Sedgwick), 129n
Horace, 247
Horn, Charles Edward, 149n
Howe, Julia Ward, 72, 74n
Howes, Elizabeth, 258, 259n
Howes, Elizabeth Burley, 259n
Howes, Frederick, 259n
Hudson, Radcliff, 184n
"Human Life" (Emerson), 33n, 70n, 137n
"Hyperion" (Keats), 134

Indiana (Sand), 100n
"Interpretations of Christianity" (Alcott), 98, 100n
Introduction to Ethics (Jouffroy), 132n

Jackson, Marianne, 36, 41, 79, 80, 153, 164, 182, 250, 258, 261
Jahreszeiten, Die (La Motte–Fouqué), 44n
Jameson, Anna, 50, 60

Jarvis, Edward, 73n
Jarvis, Mary Ann, 71, 73n
Jarvis, Nabby Porter, 73n
Jesus, 47, 206
"Jesus the Comforter" (Fuller), 34n
Jonson, Ben, 54, 55n, 59, 150
Jordan, William H. S., 231, 233n, 250
Jouffroy, Théodore Simon, 131, 132n
Julius Caesar (Shakespeare), 110
J. W. von Göthes Leben (Döring), 70n

Keats, Emma, 47, 48n, 61n, 72, 74n
Keats, George, 48n, 159n, 196
Keats, John, 48n, 134
Keble, John, 65n
Kelly, Noah, 38, 39n
Keyes, Annie, 64n
Keyes, Ann Shepard, 64n
Keyes, John, 63n
Keyes, John Shepard, 63
King, Augusta, 147, 149n
King, Caroline, 147, 149n
King, John Glen, 149n
King Philip (Metacom), 128
Knight, Joseph Phillip, 147, 149n
Kuhn, Caroline, 72, 74n
Kuhn, George, 255, 256n
Kuhn, Nancy Weiser, 74n, 210, 222, 227, 256n

"Lady of Shallot, The" (Tennyson), 191
La Motte–Fouqué, Friedrich de, 44n
"Land and Sea" (Sterling), 70n
Landor, Walter Savage, 129, 130n, 136, 138n
Langtree, S. D., 92n
Laokoon (Lessing), 114n
"Last Farewell, The" (Edward Emerson), 133, 134n
Lawrence, Amos, 144
Lawrence, William, 144
Lee, Hannah Sawyer, 37n
Leicester Academy, 38
Leiden des jungen Werthers, Die (Goethe), 75
Leone Leoni (Sand), 100n
Lessing, Gotthold Ephraim, 114n
Letter to Andrews Norton, A (Hildreth), 129, 130n
Letter to Those Who Think, A (Palmer), 134n
Lettres de'Abailard et d'Héloïse, 47, 48n
Lives of Haydn and Mozart, The (Stendhal), 44n

"Lives of the Great Composers" (Fuller), 218n, 223, 225n
London and Westminster Review, 47, 48, 59, 69, 73
Loring, Ellis Gray, 147, 149n
Lorrain, Claude, 75, 76n
Lovelace, Richard, 216n
Lowell, Charles, 92n
Lowell, Harriet Spence, 92
Lowell, James Russell, 44n, 164, 190n
Luther, Martin, 64–65

McCaffery, Alexander, 209n
Mackintosh, Dorcas Burditt, 255n
Mackintosh, James, 45, 46n
Mackintosh, Peter, 255n
Mackintosh, Robert James, 46n
"Magnolia of Lake Pontchartrain, The" (Fuller), 166n, 184
Maistre, Joseph de, 184, 191, 193
"Man in the Ages" (Stone), 136, 138n
Mann, Horace, 92n
"Man the Reformer" (Emerson), 198, 201
Marryat, Frederick, 59, 61n
Martineau, Harriet, 48, 49n, 136, 138n, 232
"Martyr Age of the United States, The" (Martineau), 49n
Massachusetts Anti-Slavery Fair, 197, 198n, 261, 263n
Master Shipbuilder and His Wife of Amsterdam, The (Rembrandt), 75, 76n
Mauprat (Sand), 99, 100n
Mémoires de Luther (Michelet), 64, 65n
Memoirs of the Life of the Right Honourable Sir James Mackintosh (Mackintosh), 46n
Memorials of a Residence (Milnes), 100n
Memorials of a Tour (Milnes), 100n
Merriam, Julia, 228n
Messiah (Handel), 258, 259n, 261, 262
Messinger, Ellen Gould, 71, 73n
Messinger, Henry, 73n
Metamora (Stone), 128, 129n
Meyer, J. H., 69, 70n
Michelangelo, 90, 130, 189, 190n, 205
Michelet, Jules, 64, 65n
"Militia Musters" (Greene), 161, 162n
Milnes, Richard Monckton (Lord Houghton), 54, 55n, 99, 100n, 101, 136, 138n; "American Philosophy," 136, 138n; *Memorials of a Residence*, 100n; *Memorials of a Tour*, 100n; *Poems of Many Years*, 100n; "Shadows," 54, 55n

Milton, John, 179, 201n
Molière, 42
Monaldi (Allston), 260
Moors, Abigail, 39n
Moors, Benjamin, 39n
Moors, John, 39
"Moral Evil" (W. H. Channing), 203
Morals (Plutarch), 55n
More, Henry, 182n
Morison, Nathaniel Holmes, 41, 44n
Morton, John, 102n
Moses, 205
Motley, Eliza Davis, 151n
Motley, Thomas, 150, 151n
Mozart, Wolfgang Amadeus, 42, 75, 76n, 120n
Much Ado About Nothing (Shakespeare), 116
Munchhausen, Karl Friedrich, 182n

Nature (Emerson), 128, 182
Neal, John, 155n
—letter to, 155
Newcomb, Charles King, 57n, 72, 121, 135, 147, 176n; poetry of, 216, 238
—letters to, 55–57, 64–65, 67–68, 100–101, 122–23, 204–5, 212, 216, 237–38
Newcomb, Charlotte, 57, 71, 72, 101, 123
Newcomb, Elizabeth Wright, 57, 143
Newcomb, Rhoda Mardenbrough, 57, 65, 71–72, 73n, 111, 216, 217
Newman, John Henry, 65n
"New Poetry" (Emerson), 149n
Noblers, Mrs., 175
Norton, Andrews, 114, 115n, 129, 130n, 133
Norton, Harriet Foote, 155n
"Notes from the Journal of a Scholar" (Charles Emerson), 116n, 132n
Novalis (Baron Friedrich von Hardenberg), 107n, 158n

"Ode: Autumn" (Hood), 162, 163n
"Ode to Melancholy" (Hood), 162, 163n
Odiorne, William Henry, 212
"On Poesy or Art" (Coleridge), 120n
Onyx Ring, The (Sterling), 55n, 70n, 75
"Orphic Sayings" (Alcott), 135, 137n–38n, 146, 189, 190
O'Sullivan, John Louis, 92n
Othello (Shakespeare), 42, 44n
Oxford Movement, 65

Pabodie, William Jewett, 135, 137n
Page, William, 189, 190n

Palmer, Edward, 134n
Park, Mrs., 92
Park, John, 69, 70n
Parker, Theodore, 37, 195n, 206
Peabody, Elizabeth Palmer (daughter), 5,
 92n, 182, 197, 241
—letter to, 91–92
Peabody, Elizabeth Palmer (mother),
 155n
Peabody, Jane Todd, 137n
Peabody, Mary, 92
Peabody, Nathaniel, 155n
Peabody, Sophia, 92n, 129n, 153, 155n
Peabody, William, 137n
Pericles, 41, 44n, 128, 129n
Perkins, Barbara Higginson, 257n
Perkins, Thomas Handasyd, 190n
"Phaedrus" (Plato), 39, 44n
"Philebus" (Plato), 106
"Pianoforte, The," 69, 70n
Plato, 37, 39–40, 54, 59, 102, 104, 106,
 205; "Banquet," 39, 44n, 54; "Phae-
 drus," 39, 44n, 54; "Philebus," 106;
 "Symposium," 44n, 54; "Theatetus,"
 106
Plummer, Eliza, 63n
Plutarch, 54, 55n
Poems of Many Years (Milnes), 55n, 100n
"Poet, The" (Hooper), 147, 148n
"Politics" (Emerson), 111, 113n
Polycrates, 179, 180n
Potter, Charles, 162n
Poussin, Nicholas, 35, 36n, 37, 75, 76n,
 193, 195n
Power, Susan Anna, 76, 135, 137n
Powers, Hiram, 178n
"Present Age, The" (Emerson), 113n,
 124n, 137n
Prichard, Jane Hallett, 63n
Prichard, Moses, 63n
Prichard, William Mackay, 63
Propyläen, Die (Goethe), 60, 114n
"Protest, The" (Emerson), 37
Pückler-Muskau, Hermann, 61
"Pumpkin Pie" (Greene), 161, 162n
Pusey, Edward Bouverie, 65n

Quatremère de Quincy, Antoine, 84,
 86n, 136, 138n
Quincy, Edmund, 194, 195n
Quincy, Eliza Morton, 101, 102n, 195n
Quincy, Josiah, 102n

Rackemann, Daniel, 100n
Rackemann, Frederick William, 100n

Rackemann, Ludwig, 99, 100n, 103,
 104n, 147
*Rahel: Ein Buch des Andenkens für ihre
 Freunde* (Varnhagen von Ense),
 48n–49n
Randall, Belinda L., 73, 74n, 241, 258,
 260, 261
Randall, Elizabeth Wells, 36n, 43, 241,
 257–58, 260, 261, 262
Randall, John, 74n, 207, 218, 227, 231,
 259
Randall, Maria, 258, 259n, 262
Raphael, 42, 44n, 75, 76n, 102
Raspe, Rudolf Erich, 182n
"Record of Impressions, A" (Fuller), 145
"Red Jacket" (Halleck), 50, 51
Rembrandt, 75
*Reply to Norton's Remarks on Spinoza: A
 Second Letter* (Ripley), 114, 115n
Richter, Johann Paul Friedrich [pseud.
 Jean-Paul], 118, 120n
"Ring des Polykrates, Der" (Schiller),
 180n
Ripley, Ann Dunkin, 62n
Ripley, Christopher Gore, 45, 46n
Ripley, Elizabeth Bradford, 62n
Ripley, George, 52n, 73, 89n, 106, 113,
 184, 206, 207, 228, 240; and Brook
 Farm, 164n, 174, 180, 195n, 205; and
 Dial, 5, 95n, 111, 130, 132, 135, 138n,
 146, 152, 231; Fuller on, 135–36, 160,
 174, 194, 205; and Norton, 111,
 113n, 114, 115n
—letter to, 51–53
Ripley, Mary Emerson, 38n, 45, 46n, 62n
Ripley, Phoebe Bliss, 62n
Ripley, Samuel, 38n, 39n, 46n, 62
Ripley, Sarah Bradford, 39n, 46n, 61–62
Ripley, Sophia Bradford, 62n
Ripley, Sophia Dana, 52, 103, 164n, 174–
 75, 184, 212, 228, 260
—letter to, 86–89
Rob Roy (Scott), 131, 132n
Rogers, Maria DeWolfe, 223, 225n
Rogers, Robert, 225n
"Rosalie" (Horn), 147, 149n
Rosa, Salvator, 32, 33n, 42, 75, 76n
Rotch, Francis, Sr., 184n
Rotch, Maria, 184n
Rotch, Mary, 176n, 219n
Rousseau, Jean-Jacques, 171
Russell, Henry, 205n
Russell, John Lewis, 228
Russell, Lucia J., 137n

Russell, Mary, 211n
Ruysdael, Jacob, 75, 76n

St. Leon (Godwin), 176n
Sand, George (Aurore Lucie Dudevant),
    70n, 99, 100n, 124; André, 99, 100n,
    137; Indiana, 100n; Leone Leoni, 100n;
    Mauprat, 99, 100n; Les sept cordes de la
    lyre, 99, 100n
Schiller, Johann Christoph Friedrich,
    37n, 180n
Schlegel, August Wilhelm, 116
Schmidt, Henry, 102–3, 104n, 206
Scott, Walter, 42, 132n
Searle, George, 180n
Searle, Mary Atkins, 180n
Sedgwick, Catharine Maria, 128, 129n,
    232, 233n
Sedgwick, Charles, 100n
Sedgwick, Elizabeth Buckminster, 100n
Sedgwick, Elizabeth Dwight, 100n
Select Minor Poems, Translated from the
    German of Goethe and Schiller (Dwight),
    182
Sept cordes de la lyre, Les (Sand), 99, 100n,
    182
"Service, The" (Thoreau), 185
"Sexton's Daughter, The" (Sterling), 70n
"Shadows" (Milnes), 54, 55n
Shah Nameh (Firdawsi), 122
Shakespeare, William, 42, 53, 55n, 116,
    119, 243; Coriolanus, 110; Hamlet, 110;
    Henry the Fourth, pt. 1, 124, 125n;
    Julius Caesar, 110; Much Ado About
    Nothing, 116; Othello, 42, 44n
Shaw, Anna, 72, 74n, 150, 181, 250
Shaw, Elizabeth Parkman, 74n, 178n
Shaw, Francis George, 175, 178n, 190,
    211n
Shaw, Joseph Coolidge, 181, 182n
Shaw, Robert Gould (father of Francis),
    74n, 178n
Shaw, Robert Gould (son of Francis),
    178n
Shaw, Sarah Sturgis, 175, 178n, 190,
    211n
Shelley, Mary Wollstonecraft, 134n
Shelley, Percy Bysshe, 133, 134, 136,
    138n, 144, 145n; "Defence of Poetry,"
    133, 134n, 136, 138n; Essays, Letters
    from Abroad, Translations and Fragments,
    133, 134n

"She Walks in Beauty" (Byron), 49–50,
    51n
"Short Essay on Critics, A" (Fuller), 145
Simmons, George Frederick, 37, 148
Simmons, William, 37n
Six Etchings from Salvator-Rosa, 33n
Socrates, 40
Soirées de Saint-Petersbourg, Les (Maistre),
    184, 191, 193, 195n
Sonnambula, La (Bellini), 190, 191n, 196
Speed, Philip, 48n
Spence, Keith, 92n
Spence, Mary Traill, 92n
Spenser, Edmund, 214
"Sphinx, The" (Emerson), 214, 216n
Spinoza, Benedictus, 111
Staël, Madame de, 49, 97n
"Stanzas to Augusta" (Byron), 81
Stendhal (Marie Henri Beyle), 44n
Sterling, John [pseud. Archaeus], 54,
    55n, 59, 69, 70n, 75, 99, 100n;
    "Crystals from a Cavern," 70n, 75;
    "Land and Sea," 70n; The Onyx Ring,
    55n, 70n, 75; "The Sexton's Daughter,"
    70n; "Thoughts and Images," 70n
Stetson, Caleb, 227, 228n
Stone, John Augustus, 129n
Stone, Thomas Treadwell, 136, 138n,
    146
Story, Joseph, 44n
Story, William Wetmore, 41, 44n, 45, 46,
    47, 188–89, 190n
Stuart, Charles, 63
Sturgis, Anne, 124
Sturgis, Caroline, 36n, 53, 71, 98, 99,
    137, 146, 183, 213, 232, 233n, 236,
    238, 250; and Dial, 128, 129n, 147,
    148n, 149, 151n, 153; vacations with
    Fuller, 76, 77, 147, 178–79, 224–25,
    247. See also Fuller, Margaret: and
    friendship with Sturgis.
—letters to, 34–37, 39–51, 56–61, 79–80,
    81–82, 92–94, 102–4, 105–7, 120–21,
    124, 149–51, 153–54, 157–59, 163–64,
    166–70, 198–99, 211, 218–19, 241–42
Sturgis, Elizabeth Davis, 198
Sturgis, Ellen. See Hooper, Ellen Sturgis.
Sturgis, Nathaniel Russell, 178n
Sturgis, Susan Parkman, 178n
Sturgis, William, 52
Sumner, Charles, 136, 138n
Swain, William, 79
Swedenborg, Emanuel, 116

Symphony no. 5, in C minor (Beethoven), 205, 206, 261, 263n
"Symposium" (Plato), 44n

Tales and Sketches (Sedgwick), 129n
Talisman, The, 51n
Tappan, Caroline Sturgis. *See* Sturgis, Caroline.
Tennyson, Alfred, Lord, 99, 124, 189, 190, 191n; "Elegiacs," 190, 191n; "The Lady of Shallot," 191
"Theatetus" (Plato), 106
"Theme for a World-Drama" (E. Channing), 182n
Thoreau, Henry David, 51n, 134n, 185n, 208, 210, 231–32, 248, 251, 261; and *Dial*, 133, 134n, 146, 185, 232, 242–43
—letters to, 185, 242–43
—works of: "Aulus Persius Flaccus," 133, 134n, 146; "The Fisher's Son," 232, 233n; "The Service," 185; *A Week on the Concord and Merrimack Rivers*, 243, 246n; "With frontier strength," 242–43, 246n
Thoron, Ward, 253n
Thorvaldsen, Bertil, 178n
"Thoughts and Images" (Sterling), 70n
"Thoughts on Art" (Emerson), 187–88, 189
"Thoughts on Modern Literature" (Emerson), 137n, 146–47, 148n, 152
"Thoughts. On Sunday Morning" (Fuller), 34n
Tieck, Ludwig, 118, 120n, 215, 216n
Tilden, Bryant Parrott, 73n
Tilden, Catherine Brown, 71, 73n, 203
Tilden, Mary Parker, 258, 259n
Tilden, Zebiah Brown, 73n
Tillinghast, Rebecca, 72, 74n, 76
"Times, The" (Emerson), 251, 257n
Titan (Jean Paul), 120n
"To Allston's Picture, 'The Bride'" (Fuller), 166
"To a Poet's Niece" (Clarke), 48n
"To a Skylark" (Wordsworth), 224, 225n
Token, The, 219, 220n
"To Lucasta, Going to Warres" (Lovelace), 215, 216n
Torquato Tasso (trans. Fuller), 43, 44n, 47
Townsend, Elihu, 74n
Townsend, Eliza, 72, 74n
Tracy, Albert H., Jr., 154, 155n

Tracy, Albert H., Sr., 154, 155n
Transcendental Club, 5, 92n, 95n, 114n, 138n
Tuckerman, Gustavus A., 36, 73
Tuckerman, Jane Francis, 41, 43, 44, 45, 46, 48, 49, 73, 84, 149n, 261; letters of, 35, 36, 47, 50, 59, 147, 150–51, 158
—letters to, 76–77, 82–83
Tuckerman, John Francis, 150, 151n
Tutti-Frutti (Pückler-Muskau), 61n
Two Articles from the Princeton Review (Norton), 130n

Über Kunst und Altertum (Goethe), 70n
Underwoods (Jonson), 54, 55n
Undine (La Motte–Fouqué), 43, 44n
United States Magazine and Democratic Review, 91–92

Valle, Pietro della, 182
Vandyke, Anthony, 75, 76n
Van Zandt, Charles C., 162n
Varnhagen von Ense, Karl August, 48n
Varnhagen von Ense, Rahel Levin, 47, 48n–49n
Vaughan, John Champion, 111, 113n
Vautin, Mr., 37, 42
Very, Jones, 53, 55n, 59, 134n
Viaggi di Pietro della Valle il Pellegrino (Valle), 182n
"Violet, The" (Ellen Emerson), 181, 182n
Vivian Grey (Disraeli), 59, 61n
Vorlesungen über dramatische Kunst und Litteratur (Schlegel), 116n

Wainwright, Elizabeth, 257n
"Walter Savage Landor" (Emerson), 230, 231n, 232, 233n
Ward, Anna Barker (daughter), 253
Ward, Anna Hazard Barker, 48n, 98, 120, 147, 174, 179, 210, 211n, 218, 253, 257, 262; letters of, 47, 50, 133; marriage of, 6, 7, 158, 159n, 163, 164n, 183; visits Fuller, 93, 94n, 149–50, 153, 154, 157
Ward, Ann Eliza, 72, 74n
Ward, Francis Marion, 72, 74n
Ward, Henry Hall, 72, 74n
Ward, Julia, 72, 74n
Ward, Julia Cutler, 74n
Ward, Louisa Cutler, 72, 74n
Ward, Lydia Gray, 72, 74n
Ward, Mary, 258, 259n

Ward, Samuel (of New York), 72, 74n
Ward, Samuel Gray, 35, 36n, 49, 69, 72,
  74n, 94n, 98, 121, 146, 147, 150,
  153, 154, 179; and Ellery Channing,
  239, 240n, 264; Fuller's love for, 79,
  80–81, 90–91, 95–96; marriage of,
  6, 7, 48n, 97n, 158, 159n, 163, 164n,
  175, 176n; quoted, 46, 73, 230, 232
—letters to, 80–81, 90–91, 95–96, 253,
  256–57
Ward, Thomas Wren, 72, 73, 74n
"Washington and Franklin" (Landor),
  129, 130n
Webster, Daniel, 51n, 102n
Webster, Julia, 51
*Week on the Concord and Merrimack Rivers,
  A* (Thoreau), 243, 246n
Weeks, Jordan, and Co., 146, 233n, 250
Weld, Christopher M., 71, 73n
Weld, Ebenezer, 207, 208
Western Messenger, 34, 50, 111, 127n, 203
Weston, Anne Bates, 198n
Weston, Warren, 198n
Wheeler, Charles (father), 134n
Wheeler, Charles Stearns, 133, 134n
White, Abijah, 44n
"White Doe of Rylston, The" (Words-
  worth), 169
White, Maria, 41, 44n, 45–46, 164n
Whitman, Sarah Helen Power, 69, 70n
—letters to, 74–76, 118–19

Wilcox, Mrs., 218
Wilhelm Meisters Lehrjahre (Goethe), 55n,
  152, 175, 178n, 193, 195n
Wilhelm Meisters Wanderjahre (Goethe),
  152, 179
Wilhelm Tell (Schiller), 37n
Willing, Charles, 72, 74n
Willing, Thomas Mayne, 74n
*Winter Studies and Summer Rambles in
  Canada* (Jameson), 50, 51n
"With frontier strength" (Thoreau), 242–
  43, 246n
Wood, Joseph, 190, 191n
Wood, Mary Paton, 190, 191n
"Woodnotes" (Emerson), 147, 149n, 181,
  213n
Woods, Alice, 39n
Woods, Henry, 39
Woods, Sampson, 39n
Wordsworth, William, 65, 169, 225n;
  "The Excursion," 169; "To a Skylark,"
  224, 225n; "The White Doe of
  Rylston," 169

Xenophon, 247

Young, Alexander, 128–29, 130n
Young, Caroline James, 130n
"Yuca Filamentosa" (Fuller), 166n, 184

Zur Farbenlehre (Goethe), 204

Library of Congress Cataloging in Publication Data

FULLER, MARGARET, 1810–1850.
 The letters of Margaret Fuller.

 Bibliography: p.
 Includes indexes.
 Contents: v. 1. 1817–38 — v. 2. 1839–41.
  1. Fuller, Margaret, 1810–1850—Correspondence.
 2. Authors, American—19th century—Correspondence.
 I. Hudspeth, Robert N. II. Title.
 PS2506.A4 1983   818'.309 [B]   82-22098
 ISBN 0-8014-1575-6 (v. 2)